**50% OFF!**

TSI Online Test Prep Course

We consider it an honor and a privilege that you chose our TSI Study Guide. As a way of showing our appreciation and to help us better serve you, we have partnered with Mometrix Test Preparation to offer you 50% off their online TSI Prep Course.

Mometrix has structured their online course to perfectly complement your printed study guide. Many TSI courses are needlessly expensive and don't deliver enough value. With their course, you get access to the best TSI prep material, and you only pay half price.

WHAT'S IN THE TSI TEST PREP COURSE?

- **TSI Study Guide**: Get access to content that complements your study guide.
- **Progress Tracker**: Their customized course allows you to check off content you have studied or feel confident with.
- **1,250+ Practice Questions**: With 1,250+ practice questions and lesson reviews, you can test yourself again and again to build confidence.
- **TSI Flashcards**: Their course includes a flashcard mode consisting of over 528 content cards to help you study.

TO RECEIVE THIS DISCOUNT, VISIT THE WEBSITE AT

link.mometrix.com/tsi

USE THE DISCOUNT CODE:
STARTSTUDYING

IF YOU HAVE ANY QUESTIONS OR CONCERNS, PLEASE CONTACT MOMETRIX AT SUPPORT@MOMETRIX.COM

Free Video   Free Video

Essential Test Tips Video from Trivium Test Prep

Dear Customer,

Thank you for purchasing from Trivium Test Prep! We're honored to help you prepare for your TSI exam.

To show our appreciation, we're offering a **FREE *TSI Essential Test Tips* Video by Trivium Test Prep.*** Our video includes 35 test preparation strategies that will make you successful on the TSI. All we ask is that you email us your feedback and describe your experience with our product. Amazing, awful, or just so-so: we want to hear what you have to say!

To receive your **FREE *TSI Essential Test Tips* Video**, please email us at 5star@triviumtestprep.com. Include "Free 5 Star" in the subject line and the following information in your email:

1. The title of the product you purchased.
2. Your rating from 1 – 5 (with 5 being the best).
3. Your feedback about the product, including how our materials helped you meet your goals and ways in which we can improve our products.
4. Your full name and shipping address so we can send your **FREE *TSI Essential Test Tips* Video**.

If you have any questions or concerns please feel free to contact us directly at 5star@triviumtestprep.com.

Thank you!

– Trivium Test Prep Team

*To get access to the free video please email us at 5star@triviumtestprep.com, and please follow the instructions above.

TSI STUDY GUIDE 2024-2025:

TSI Prep Book and Practice Exams for the Texas Assessment

G. T. McDivitt

Copyright © 2024 by Accepted, Inc.

ISBN-13: 9781637987292

ALL RIGHTS RESERVED. By purchase of this book, you have been licensed one copy for personal use only. No part of this work may be reproduced, redistributed, or used in any form or by any means without prior written permission of the publisher and copyright owner. Accepted, Inc.; Trivium Test Prep; Cirrus Test Prep; and Ascencia Test Prep are all imprints of Trivium Test Prep, LLC.

The State of Texas was not involved in the creation or production of this product, is not in any way affiliated with Accepted, Inc., and does not sponsor or endorse this product. All test names (and their acronyms) are trademarks of their respective owners. This study guide is for general information only and does not claim endorsement by any third party.

Image(s) used under license from Shutterstock.com

Table of Contents

Online Resources i
Introduction iii

1: Numbers and Operations 1
Types of Numbers............................ 1
Scientific Notation 4
Positive and Negative Numbers 4
Order of Operations 6
Ratios 6
Proportions 7
Percentages 7
Exponents and Radicals 9
Answer Key 11

2: Algebra 15
Algebraic Expressions...................... 15
Operations with Expressions 16
Linear Equations 19
Linear Inequalities.......................... 23
Quadratic Equations and Inequalities 26
Absolute Value Equations and Inequalities 30
Functions.. 31

Exponential and Logarithmic Functions.................... 36
Polynomial Functions...................... 39
Rational Functions 40
Radical Functions........................... 41
Answer Key 43

3: Geometry 57
Properties of Shapes 57
Three-Dimensional Shapes............. 67
Equality, Congruence, and Similarity................................ 69
Transformations of Geometric Figures.......................... 71
Answer Key 75

4: Statistics........................ 79
Describing Sets of Data................... 79
Graphs, Charts, and Tables 81
Answer Key 90

5: Logic and Probability.. 93
Logic and Set Theory...................... 93
Probability 97
Answer Key 101

6: Reading — 105

- The Main Idea 105
- Supporting Details 109
- The Author's Purpose 110
- Organization and Text Structures 111
- The Audience 112
- Evaluating Arguments 113
- Drawing Conclusions 115
- Tone and Mood 116
- Meaning of Words and Phrases 118
- Figurative Language 126
- Graphic Sources of Information 128
- Elements of Fiction 129
- Answer Key 132

7: Language Skills — 135

- Parts of Speech 135
- Constructing Sentences 144
- Punctuation 146
- Capitalization 149
- Common Language Errors 149
- Answer Key 156

8: Writing — 159

- Writing a Thesis Statement 159
- Structuring the Essay 160
- Providing Supporting Evidence 162
- Writing Well 163

9: Practice Test — 167

- Mathematics 167
- Reading 171
- Writing 179
- The Essay 185
- Answer Key 187

Online Resources

Accepted, Inc. includes online resources with the purchase of this study guide to help you fully prepare for your TSI Assessment.

PRACTICE TESTS

In addition to the practice test included in this book, we also offer an online exam. Since many exams today are computer based, practicing your test-taking skills on the computer is a great way to prepare.

FLASH CARDS

Accepted, Inc.'s flash cards allow you to review important terms easily on your computer or smartphone.

CHEAT SHEETS

Review the core skills you need to master the exam with easy-to-read Cheat Sheets.

FROM STRESS to SUCCESS

Leave a review, send us helpful feedback, or sign up for Accepted, Inc. promotions—including free books!

REVIEWS

Leave a review, send us helpful feedback, or sign up for Accepted, Inc. promotions—including free books!

Access these materials at:
https://www.acceptedinc.com/tsi-online-resources

Introduction

Congratulations on choosing to take the Texas Success Initiative (TSI) Assessment! By purchasing this book, you've taken the first step toward preparing for your college and career goals. This guide will provide you with a detailed overview of the TSI, so you know exactly what to expect on test day. We'll take you through all the concepts covered on the test and give you the opportunity to test your knowledge with practice questions. Even if it's been a while since you last took a major test, don't worry; we'll make sure you're more than ready!

What is the TSI?

The TSI assesses students' abilities in reading, writing and mathematics, helping them prepare for college-level courses. These tests will help you and your academic advisors choose which classes are right for you as you get ready for academic work at the university level.

The TSI is made up of three different assessments—reading, writing, and mathematics. Each assessment is taken and scored separately, but all are mandatory parts of the entire test. All incoming college students in the state of Texas are required to take the TSI unless they have already met certain criteria, which include the following:

- ▶ The student has met the minimum college readiness standard on the ACT, SAT, or other statewide test.
- ▶ The student has already successfully completed college-level mathematics and English courses.
- ▶ The student is not seeking a degree.
- ▶ The student has been or is currently enlisted in the military.
- ▶ The student has enrolled in a Level-One certificate program (with fewer than forty-three semester credit hours).

How is the TSI Administered?

The TSI is a multiple-choice test administered by computer. Each assessment—reading, writing, and mathematics—is taken separately. The writing assessment also includes one essay of 300 – 600 words. None of the assessments are timed. You may stop, save your work, and complete the assessment at a later date; however, you must complete the assessment within fourteen days. You receive the assessment results immediately upon completion.

Students must directly contact their college counseling office to arrange to take the TSI. Your institution's test center will provide information about accommodation for disabilities, required identification or materials, and any options for taking the test remotely.

Test-takers must also complete a Pre-Assessment Activity. This mandatory activity explains the purpose and process of the TSI, provides practice questions and feedback, discusses developmental education options if you do not meet the cut-off scores for college readiness (see below), and offers other information about college resources. You must contact the college where you plan to take the TSI to arrange to take the Pre-Assessment Activity.

What's on the TSI?

The TSI assesses reading comprehension, writing, and mathematical skills. The questions are aligned with the Texas College and Career Readiness Standards, and gauge your readiness to tackle college-level coursework. Because the test is computer adaptive, you will encounter more difficult topics as you continue to correctly answer questions on the test.

What's on the TSI?

ASSESSMENT	*NUMBER OF QUESTIONS	STRANDS (CONTENT AREAS)	CONCEPTS
Mathematics	20 questions	Elementary algebra and functions	Operations with algebraic expressions; linear equations, inequalities, and systems; word problems
		Intermediate algebra and functions	Quadratic and polynomial equations, expressions, and functions; working with powers, roots, and radicals; rational and exponential expressions, equations, and functions

ASSESSMENT	*NUMBER OF QUESTIONS	STRANDS (CONTENT AREAS)	CONCEPTS
Mathematics (continued)	20 questions	Geometry and measurement	Plane geometry; linear, area, and three-dimensional measurements; symmetry and transformations
		Data analysis, statistics, and probability	Data interpretation, statistics, probability
Reading	24 questions	Literary analysis	Identifying and analyzing elements and ideas in literary texts
		Main idea and supporting details	Identifying the main ideas and supporting ideas of a passage; identifying details in a passage
		Inferences in a text or texts	Appropriately connecting ideas between two passages; comparing two passages; drawing inferences about a single passage
		Author's use of language	Identifying the author's purpose, tone, use of language, organization, and rhetorical strategies; using evidence to determine the meaning of words in context
Writing (multiple-choice questions)	20 questions	Essay revision	Improving organization, coherence, word choice, and rhetorical effectiveness; using evidence
		Agreement	Performing subject-verb agreement, pronoun agreement; determining verb tenses
		Sentence structure	Determining and resolving errors in punctuation and sentence structure
		Sentence logic	Properly placing and using transitions and modifying clauses in sentences
Writing (essay)	1 essay (300 – 600 words)		Effective, organized writing with supported and well-developed ideas, strong sentence structure, and few mechanical errors, following the conventions of Standard English

*Number of questions is approximate.

How is the TSI Scored?

The TSI is a diagnostic assessment; as such, there is no way to pass or fail it. Rather, the Texas Coordinating Board has determined cut-off scores for college readiness. As these are subject to change annually, check with the College Board and the Texas Coordinating Board for details.

The separate mathematics, writing, and reading assessments are computer adaptive. That is, they adapt to the student's skill level: a student's response to a question determines the difficulty level of the next one. If you answer a question correctly, the next one will be harder; however answering a question incorrectly yields an easier question.

The essay is scored on a scale of 8 – 0 based on clarity of purpose, organization, coherence and focus, demonstration of critical thinking, strength of argument and development, sentence variety, style, and proper use of mechanics (grammar and punctuation).

Depending on how you score, you may be asked to test further. The questions on each assessment cover four different content areas, or strands (see above). If you score below a certain threshold in one or more strands, you will be asked to answer more questions in that content area in order to best gauge your preparation for college-level coursework. These additional questions are part of the DE Diagnostic Test. Depending on your DE Diagnostic results, you may be asked to answer more questions as part of the Adult Basic Education (ABE) Tests, which also include reading, writing, and mathematics diagnostics. This process will help you and your advisors target any specific areas for improvement, ensuring you are absolutely ready for college.

About This Guide

This guide will help you master the most important test topics and develop critical test-taking skills. We have built features into our books to prepare you for your tests and increase your score. Along with a detailed summary of the test's format, content, and scoring, we offer an in-depth overview of the content knowledge required to pass the test. In the review you'll find sidebars that provide interesting information, highlight key concepts, and review content so that you can solidify your understanding of the exam's concepts. You can also test your knowledge with sample questions throughout the text and practice questions that reflect the content and format of the TSI. We're pleased you've chosen Accepted, Inc. to be a part of your journey!

CHAPTER ONE
Numbers and Operations

This chapter provides a review of the basic yet critical components of mathematics such as manipulating fractions, comparing numbers, and using units. These concepts will provide the foundation for more complex mathematical operations in later chapters.

Types of Numbers

Numbers are placed in categories based on their properties.

- A **NATURAL NUMBER** is greater than 0 and has no decimal or fraction attached. These are also sometimes called counting numbers {1, 2, 3, 4, ...}.
- **WHOLE NUMBERS** are natural numbers and the number 0 {0, 1, 2, 3, 4, ...}.
- **INTEGERS** include positive and negative natural numbers and 0 {..., –4, –3, –2, –1, 0, 1, 2, 3, 4, ...}.
- A **RATIONAL NUMBER** can be represented as a fraction. Any decimal part must terminate or resolve into a repeating pattern. Examples include –12, $-\frac{4}{5}$, 0.36, $7.\overline{7}$, $26\frac{1}{2}$, etc.
- An **IRRATIONAL NUMBER** cannot be represented as a fraction. An irrational decimal number never ends and never resolves into a repeating pattern. Examples include $-\sqrt{7}$, π, and 0.34567989135...
- A **REAL NUMBER** is a number that can be represented by a point on a number line. Real numbers include all the rational and irrational numbers.
- An **IMAGINARY NUMBER** includes the imaginary unit i, where $i = \sqrt{-1}$ Because $i^2 = -1$, imaginary numbers produce a negative value when squared. Examples of imaginary numbers include $-4i$, $0.75i$, $i\sqrt{2}$ and $\frac{8}{3}i$.

▸ A COMPLEX NUMBER is in the form $a + bi$, where a and b are real numbers. Examples of complex numbers include $3 + 2i$, $-4 + i$, $\sqrt{3} - i\sqrt[3]{5}$ and $\frac{5}{8} - \frac{7i}{8}$. All imaginary numbers are also complex.

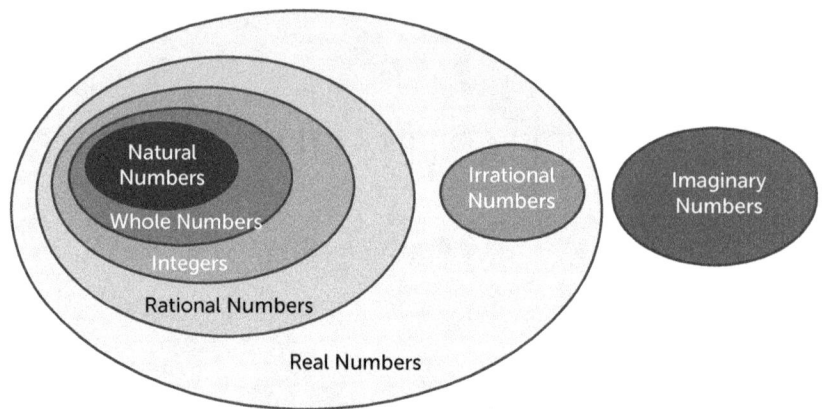

Figure 1.1. Types of Numbers

DID YOU KNOW?
If a real number is a natural number (e.g., 50), then it is also a whole number, an integer, and a rational number.

The FACTORS of a natural number are all the numbers that can multiply together to make the number. For example, the factors of 24 are 1, 2, 3, 4, 6, 8, 12, and 24. Every natural number is either prime or composite. A PRIME NUMBER is a number that is only divisible by itself and 1. (The number 1 is not considered prime.) Examples of prime numbers are 2, 3, 7, and 29. The number 2 is the only even prime number. A COMPOSITE NUMBER has more than two factors. For example, 6 is composite because its factors are 1, 6, 2, and 3. Every composite number can be written as a unique product of prime numbers, called the PRIME FACTORIZATION of the number. For example, the prime factorization of 90 is $90 = 2 \times 3^2 \times 5$. All integers are either even or odd. An even number is divisible by 2; an odd number is not.

PROPERTIES of NUMBER SYSTEMS

A system is CLOSED under an operation if performing that operation on two elements of the system results in another element of that system. For example, the integers are closed under the operations of addition, subtraction, and multiplication but not division. Adding, subtracting, or multiplying two integers results in another integer. However, dividing two integers could result in a rational number that is not an integer ($-2 \div 3 = \frac{-2}{3}$).

▸ The rational numbers are closed under all four operations (except for division by 0).

▸ The real numbers are closed under all four operations.

▸ The complex numbers are closed under all four operations.

▸ The irrational numbers are NOT closed under ANY of the four operations.

The **COMMUTATIVE PROPERTY** holds for an operation if order does not matter when performing the operation. For example, multiplication is commutative for integers: $(-2)(3) = (3)(-2)$.

The **ASSOCIATIVE PROPERTY** holds for an operation if elements can be regrouped without changing the result. For example, addition is associative for real numbers: $-3 + (-5 + 4) = (-3 + -5) + 4$.

The **DISTRIBUTIVE PROPERTY** of multiplication over addition allows a product of sums to be written as a sum of products: $a(b + c) = ab + ac$. The value a is distributed over the sum $(b + c)$. The acronym FOIL (First, Outer, Inner, Last) is a useful way to remember the distributive property.

When an operation is performed with an **IDENTITY ELEMENT** and another element a, the result is a. The identity element for multiplication on real numbers is $a \times 1 = a$), and for addition is 0 ($a + 0 = a$).

An operation of a system has an **INVERSE ELEMENT** if applying that operation with the inverse element results in the identity element. For example, the inverse element of a for addition is $-a$ because $a + (-a) = 0$. The inverse element of a for multiplication is $\frac{1}{a}$ because $a \times \frac{1}{a} = 1$.

EXAMPLES

1. Classify the following numbers as natural, whole, integer, rational, or irrational. (The numbers may have more than one classification.)

    [A] 72

    [B] $-\frac{2}{3}$

    [C] $\sqrt{5}$

2. Determine the real and imaginary parts of the following complex numbers.

    [A] 20

    [B] $10 - i$

    [C] $15i$

3. Answer True or False for each statement:

    [A] The natural numbers are closed under subtraction.

    [B] The sum of two irrational numbers is irrational.

    [C] The sum of a rational number and an irrational number is irrational.

4. Answer true or false for each statement:

    [A] The associative property applies for multiplication in the real numbers.

    [B] The commutative property applies to all real numbers and all operations.

Scientific Notation

Scientific notation is a method of representing very large and small numbers in the form $a \times 10^n$, where a is a value between 1 and 10, and n is a nonzero integer. For example, the number 927,000,000 is written in scientific notation as 9.27×10^8. Multiplying 9.27 by 10 eight times gives 927,000,000. When performing operations with scientific notation, the final answer should be in the form $a \times 10^n$.

When adding and subtracting numbers in scientific notation, the power of 10 must be the same for all numbers. This results in like terms in which the a terms are added or subtracted and the 10^n remains unchanged. When multiplying numbers in scientific notation, multiply the a factors, and then multiply that answer by 10 to the sum of the exponents. For division, divide the a factors and subtract the exponents.

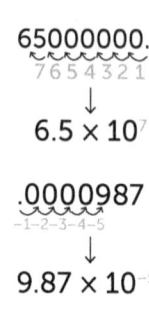

Figure 1.2. Scientific Notation

DID YOU KNOW?
When multiplying numbers in scientific notation, add the exponents. When dividing, subtract the exponents.

EXAMPLES

5. Simplify: $(3.8 \times 10^3) + (4.7 \times 10^2)$

6. Simplify: $(8.1 \times 10^{-5})(1.4 \times 10^7)$

Positive and Negative Numbers

Positive numbers are greater than 0, and **negative numbers** are less than 0. Both positive and negative numbers can be shown on a **number line**.

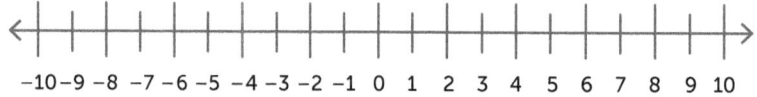

Figure 1.3. Number Line

The **absolute value** of a number is the distance the number is from 0. Since distance is always positive, the absolute value of a number is always positive. The absolute value of a is denoted $|a|$. For example, $|-2| = 2$ since -2 is two units away from 0.

Positive and negative numbers can be added, subtracted, multiplied, and divided. The sign of the resulting number is governed by a specific set of rules shown in the Table 1.1.

Table 1.1. Operations with Positive and Negative Numbers

Adding Real Numbers		Subtracting Real Numbers	
Positive + Positive = Positive	7 + 8 = 15	Negative − Positive = Negative	−7 − 8 = −7 + (−8) = −15
Negative + Negative = Negative	−7 + (−8) = −15	Positive − Negative = Positive	7 − (−8) = 7 + 8 = 15
Negative + Positive OR Positive + Negative = Keep the sign of the number with larger absolute value	−7 + 8 = 1 7 + −8 = −1	Negative − Negative = Change the subtraction to addition and change the sign of the second number; then use addition rules.	−7 − (−8) = −7 + 8 = 1 −8 − (−7) = −8 + 7 = −1

Multiplying Real Numbers		Dividing Real Numbers	
Positive × Positive = Positive	8 × 4 = 32	Positive ÷ Positive = Positive	8 ÷ 4 = 2
Negative × Negative = Positive	−8 × (−4) = 32	Negative ÷ Negative = Positive	−8 ÷ (−4) = 2
Positive × Negative OR Negative × Positive = Negative	8 × (−4) = −32 −8 × 4 = −32	Positive ÷ Negative OR Negative ÷ Positive = Negative	8 ÷ (−4) = −2 −8 ÷ 4 = −2

EXAMPLES

7. Add or subtract the following real numbers:

   [A] −18 + 12

   [B] −3.64 + (−2.18)

   [C] 9.37 − 4.25

   [D] 86 − (−20)

8. Multiply or divide the following real numbers:

   (A) $(\frac{10}{3})(-\frac{9}{5})$

   [B] $\frac{-64}{-10}$

   [C] (2.2)(3.3)

   [D] −52 ÷ 13

Order of Operations

The **ORDER OF OPERATIONS** is simply the order in which operations are performed. Multiplication and division, and addition and subtraction, are performed together from left to right. So, performing multiple operations on a set of numbers is a four-step process. **PEMDAS** is a common way to remember the order of operations:

1. **P**arentheses: Calculate expressions inside parentheses, brackets, braces, etc.
2. **E**xponents: Calculate exponents and square roots.
3. **M**ultiplication: Calculate any remaining multiplication and division in order from left to right.
4. **D**ivision: Calculate any remaining multiplication and division in order from left to right.
5. **A**ddition: Calculate any remaining addition and subtraction in order from left to right.
6. **S**ubtraction: Calculate any remaining addition and subtraction in order from left to right.

Always work from left to right within each step when simplifying expressions.

EXAMPLES

9. Simplify: $2(21 - 14) + 6 \div (-2) \times 3 - 10$

10. Simplify: $-(3)^2 + 4(5) + (5 - 6)^2 - 8$

11. Simplify: $\dfrac{(7 - 9)^3 + 8(10 - 12)}{4^2 - 5^2}$

Ratios

A **RATIO** is a comparison of two numbers and can be represented as $\frac{a}{b}$, $a:b$, or a to b. The two numbers represent a constant relationship, not a specific value: for every a number of items in the first group, there will be b number of items in the second. For example, if the ratio of blue to red candies in a bag is 3:5, the bag will contain 3 blue candies for every 5 red candies. So, the bag might contain 3 blue candies and 5 red candies, or it might contain 30 blue candies and 50 red candies, or 36 blue candies and 60 red candies. All of these values are representative of the ratio 3:5 (which is the ratio in its lowest, or simplest, terms).

To find the "whole" when working with ratios, simply add the values in the ratio. For example, if the ratio of boys to girls in a class is 2:3, the "whole" is five: 2 out of every 5 students are boys, and 3 out of every 5 students are girls.

EXAMPLES

12. There are 10 boys and 12 girls in a first-grade class. What is the ratio of boys to the total number of students? What is the ratio of girls to boys?

13. A family spends $600 a month on rent, $400 on utilities, $750 on groceries, and $550 on miscellaneous expenses. What is the ratio of the family's rent to their total expenses?

Proportions

A **PROPORTION** is an equation which states that two ratios are equal. A proportion is given in the form $\frac{a}{b} = \frac{c}{d}$, where the a and d terms are the extremes and the b and c terms are the means. A proportion is solved using cross-multiplication ($ad = bc$) to create an equation with no fractional components. A proportion must have the same units in both numerators and both denominators.

EXAMPLES

14. Solve the proportion for x: $\frac{3x-5}{2} = \frac{x-8}{3}$.

15. A map is drawn such that 2.5 inches on the map equates to an actual distance of 40 miles. If the distance measured on the map between two cities is 17.25 inches, what is the actual distance between them in miles?

16. A factory knows that 4 out of 1000 parts made will be defective. If in a month there are 125,000 parts made, how many of these parts will be defective?

Percentages

A **PERCENT** (or percentage) means per hundred and is expressed with a percent symbol (%). For example, 54% means 54 out of every 100. A percent can be converted to a decimal by removing the % symbol and moving the decimal point two places to the left, while a decimal can be converted to a percent by moving the decimal point two places to the right and attaching the % sign. A percent can be converted to a fraction by writing the percent as a fraction with 100 as the denominator and reducing. A fraction can be converted to a percent by performing the indicated division, multiplying the result by 100, and attaching the % sign.

The equation for finding percentages has three variables: the part, the whole, and the percent (which is expressed in the equation as a decimal). The equation, as shown below, can be rearranged to solve for any of these variables.

- part = whole × percent
- percent = $\frac{part}{whole}$
- whole = $\frac{part}{percent}$

This set of equations can be used to solve percent word problems. All that's needed is to identify the part, whole, and/or percent, and then to plug those values into the appropriate equation and solve.

EXAMPLES

17. Change the following values to the indicated form:
   - **[A]** 18% to a fraction
   - **[B]** $\frac{3}{5}$ to a percent
   - **[C]** 1.125 to a percent
   - **[D]** 84% to a decimal

18. In a school of 650 students, 54% of the students are boys. How many students are girls?

PERCENT CHANGE

Percent change problems involve a change from an original amount. Often percent change problems appear as word problems that include discounts, growth, or markups. In order to solve percent change problems, it's necessary to identify the percent change (as a decimal), the amount of change, and the original amount. (Keep in mind that one of these will be the value being solved for.) These values can then be plugged into the equations below:

DID YOU KNOW?
Key terms associated with percent change problems include *discount*, *sales tax*, and *markup*.

- amount of change = original amount × percent change
- percent change = $\frac{amount\ of\ change}{original\ amount}$
- original amount = $\frac{amount\ of\ change}{percent\ change}$

EXAMPLES

19. An HDTV that originally cost $1,500 is on sale for 45% off. What is the sale price for the item?

20. A house was bought in 2000 for $100,000 and sold in 2015 for $120,000. What was the percent growth in the value of the house from 2000 to 2015?

Exponents and Radicals

EXPONENTS

An expression in the form b^n is in an exponential notation where b is the **BASE** and n is an **EXPONENT**. To perform the operation, multiply the base by itself the number of times indicated by the exponent. For example, 2^3 is equal to $2 \times 2 \times 2$ or 8.

Table 1.2. Operations with Exponents

Rule	Example	Explanation
$a^0 = 1$	$5^0 = 1$	Any base (except 0) to the 0 power is 1.
$a^{-n} = \frac{1}{a^n}$	$5^{-3} = \frac{1}{5^3}$	A negative exponent becomes positive when moved from numerator to denominator (or vice versa).
$a^m a^n = a^{m+n}$	$5^3 5^4 = 5^{3+4} = 5^7$	Add the exponents to multiply two powers with the same base.
$(a^m)^n = a^{m \times n}$	$(5^3)^4 = 5^{3(4)} = 5^{12}$	Multiply the exponents to raise a power to a power.
$\frac{a^m}{a^n} = a^{m-n}$	$\frac{5^4}{5^3} = 5^{4-3} = 5^1$	Subtract the exponents to divide two powers with the same base.
$(ab)^n = a^n b^n$	$(5 \times 6)^3 = 5^3 6^3$	Apply the exponent to each base to raise a product to a power.
$\left(\frac{a}{b}\right)^n = \frac{a^n}{b^n}$	$\left(\frac{5}{6}\right)^3 = \frac{5^3}{6^3}$	Apply the exponent to each base to raise a quotient to a power.
$\left(\frac{a}{b}\right)^{-n} = \left(\frac{b}{a}\right)^n$	$\left(\frac{5}{6}\right)^{-3} = \left(\frac{6}{5}\right)^3$	Invert the fraction and change the sign of the exponent to raise a fraction to a negative power.
$\frac{a^m}{b^n} = \frac{b^{-n}}{a^{-m}}$	$\frac{5^3}{6^4} = \frac{6^{-4}}{5^{-3}}$	Change the sign of the exponent when moving a number from the numerator to denominator (or vice versa).

EXAMPLES

21. Simplify: $\frac{(10^2)^3}{(10^2)^2}$

22. Simplify: $\frac{(x^{-2}y^2)^2}{x^3 y}$

RADICALS

RADICALS are expressed as $\sqrt[b]{a}$, where b is called the **INDEX** and a is the **RADICAND**. A radical is used to indicate the inverse operation of an exponent: finding the base which can be raised to b to yield a. For example, $\sqrt[3]{125}$ is equal to 5 because $5 \times 5 \times 5$ equals 125. The same operation can be expressed using a fraction exponent, so $\sqrt[b]{a} = a^{\frac{1}{b}}$. Note that when no value is indicated for b, it is assumed to be 2 (square root).

When b is even and a is positive, $\sqrt[b]{a}$ is defined to be the positive real value n such that $nb = a$ (example: $\sqrt{16} = 4$ only, and not –4, even though (–4)(–4) = 16). If b is even and a is negative, $\sqrt[b]{a}$ will be a complex number (example: $\sqrt{-9} = 3i$). Finally if b is odd, $\sqrt[b]{a}$ will always be a real number regardless of the sign of a. If a is negative, $\sqrt[b]{a}$ will be negative since a number to an odd power is negative (example: $\sqrt[5]{-32} = -2$ since $(-2)^5 = -32$).

$\sqrt[n]{x}$ is referred to as the *n*th root of *x*.

▶ $n = 2$ is the square root
▶ $n = 3$ is the cube root
▶ $n = 4$ is the fourth root
▶ $n = 5$ is the fifth root

The following table of operations with radicals holds for all cases EXCEPT the case where b is even and a is negative (the complex case).

Table 1.3. Operations with Radicals

Rule	Example	Explanation
$\sqrt[b]{ac} = \sqrt[b]{a}\sqrt[b]{c}$	$\sqrt[3]{81} = \sqrt[3]{27}\sqrt[3]{3} = 3\sqrt[3]{3}$	The values under the radical sign can be separated into values that multiply to the original value.
$\sqrt[b]{\dfrac{a}{c}} = \dfrac{\sqrt[b]{a}}{\sqrt[b]{c}}$	$\sqrt{\dfrac{4}{81}} = \dfrac{\sqrt{4}}{\sqrt{81}} = \dfrac{2}{9}$	The b-root of the numerator and denominator can be calculated when there is a fraction under a radical sign.
$\sqrt[b]{a^c} = (\sqrt[b]{a})^c = a^{\frac{c}{b}}$	$\sqrt[3]{6^2} = (\sqrt[3]{6})^2 = 6^{\frac{2}{3}}$	The b-root can be written as a fractional exponent. If there is a power under the radical sign, it will be the numerator of the fraction.
$\dfrac{c}{\sqrt[b]{a}} \times \dfrac{\sqrt[b]{a}}{\sqrt[b]{a}} = \dfrac{c\sqrt[b]{a}}{a}$	$\dfrac{5}{\sqrt{2}} \dfrac{\sqrt{2}}{\sqrt{2}} = \dfrac{5\sqrt{2}}{2}$	To rationalize the denominator, multiply the numerator and denominator by the radical in the denominator until the radical has been canceled out.
$\dfrac{c}{b - \sqrt{a}} \times \dfrac{b + \sqrt{a}}{b + \sqrt{a}}$ $= \dfrac{c(b + \sqrt{a})}{b^2 - a}$	$\dfrac{4}{3 - \sqrt{2}} \dfrac{3 + \sqrt{2}}{3 + \sqrt{2}}$ $= \dfrac{4(3 + \sqrt{2})}{9 - 2} = \dfrac{12 + 4\sqrt{2}}{7}$	To rationalize the denominator, the numerator and denominator are multiplied by the conjugate of the denominator.

EXAMPLES

23. Simplify: $\sqrt{48}$

24. Simplify: $\dfrac{6}{\sqrt{8}}$

Answer Key

1. [A] **The number is natural, whole, an integer, and rational.**

   [B] **The fraction is rational.**

   [C] **The number is irrational.** (It cannot be written as a fraction, and written as a decimal is approximately 2.2360679...)

2. A complex number is in the form of $a + bi$, where a is the real part and bi is the imaginary part.

   [A] $20 = 20 + 0i$

   The real part is 20, and there is no imaginary part.

   [B] $10 - i = 10 - 1i$

   The real part is 10, and $-1i$ is the imaginary part.

   [C] $15i = 0 + 15i$

   The real part is 0, and the imaginary part is $15i$.

3. **[A] is false.** Subtracting the natural number 7 from 2 results in $2 - 7 = -5$, which is an integer, but not a natural number.

   [B] is false. For example, $(5 - 2\sqrt{3}) + (2 + 2\sqrt{3}) = 7$. The sum of two irrational numbers in this example is a whole number, which is not irrational. The sum of a rational number and an irrational number is sometimes rational and sometimes irrational.

   [C] is true. Because irrational numbers have decimal parts that are unending and with no pattern, adding a repeating or terminating decimal will still result in an unending decimal without a pattern.

4. **[A] is true.** For all real numbers, $a \times (b \times c) = (a \times b) \times c$. Order of multiplication does not change the result.

   [B] is false. The commutative property does not work for subtraction or division on real numbers. For example, $12 - 5 = 7$, but $5 - 12 = -7$, and $10 \div 2 = 5$, but $2 \div 10 = \frac{1}{5}$.

5. $(3.8 \times 10^3) + (4.7 \times 10^2)$

   To add, the exponents of 10 must be the same.

   $3.8 \times 10^3 = 3.8 \times 10 \times 10^2 = 38 \times 10^2$

   Add the a terms together.

   $38 \times 10^2 + 4.7 \times 10^2 = 42.7 \times 10^2$

   Write the number in proper scientific notation.

   $= \mathbf{4.27 \times 10^3}$

6. $(8.1 \times 10^{-5})(1.4 \times 10^7)$

   Multiply the a factors and add the exponents on the base of 10.

   $8.1 \times 1.4 = 11.34$

   $-5 + 7 = 2$

   $= 11.34 \times 10^2$

   Write the number in proper scientific notation.

   $= \mathbf{1.134 \times 10^3}$

7. [A] Since $|-18| > |12|$, the answer is negative: $|-18| - |12| = 6$. So the answer is **−6**.

   [B] Adding two negative numbers results in a negative number. Add the values: **−5.82**.

   [C] The first number is larger than the second, so the final answer is positive: **5.12**.

   [D] Change the subtraction to addition, change the sign of the second number, and then add: 86 − (−20) = 86 + (+20) = **106**.

8. [A] Multiply the numerators, multiply the denominators, and simplify: $\frac{-90}{15}$ = **−6**.

   [B] A negative divided by a negative is a positive number: **6.4**.

   [C] Multiplying positive numbers gives a positive answer: **7.26**.

   [D] Dividing a negative by a positive number gives a negative answer: **−4**.

9. 2(21 − 14) + 6 ÷ (−2) × 3 − 10

   Calculate expressions inside parentheses.

   = 2(7) + 6 ÷ (−2) × 3 − 10

   There are no exponents or radicals, so perform multiplication and division from left to right.

   = 14 + 6 ÷ (−2) × 3 − 10

   = 14 + (−3) × 3 − 10

   = 14 + (−9) − 10

   Perform addition and subtraction from left to right.

   = 5 − 10 = **−5**

10. −(3)² + 4(5) + (5 − 6)² − 8

    Calculate expressions inside parentheses.

    = −(3)² + 4(5) + (−1)² − 8

    Simplify exponents and radicals.

    = −9 + 4(5) + 1 − 8

    Perform multiplication and division from left to right.

    = −9 + 20 + 1 − 8

    Perform addition and subtraction from left to right.

    = 11 + 1 − 8

    = 12 − 8 = **4**

11. Simplify: $\frac{(7-9)^3 + 8(10-12)}{4^2 - 5^2}$

    Calculate expressions inside parentheses.

    $= \frac{(-2)^3 + 8(-2)}{4^2 - 5^2}$

    Simplify exponents and radicals.

    $= \frac{-8 + (-16)}{16 - 25}$

    Perform addition and subtraction from left to right.

    $= \frac{-24}{-9}$

    Simplify.

    $= \frac{8}{3}$

12. Identify the variables.

    number of boys: 10

    number of girls: 12

    number of students: 22

    Write out and simplify the ratio of boys to total students.

    number of boys : number of students

    = 10 : 22 = $\frac{10}{22}$ = $\frac{5}{11}$

    Write out and simplify the ratio of girls to boys.

    number of girls : number of boys

    = 12 : 10 = $\frac{12}{10}$ = $\frac{6}{5}$

13. Identify the variables.

    rent = 600

    utilities = 400

    groceries = 750

    miscellaneous = 550

    total expenses =

    600 + 400 + 750 + 550 = 2300

    Write out and simplify the ratio of rent to total expenses.

    rent : total expenses

    = 600 : 2300 = $\frac{60}{2300}$ = $\frac{6}{23}$

14. $\frac{(3x-5)}{2} = \frac{(x-8)}{3}$

    Cross-multiply.

$3(3x - 5) = 2(x - 8)$

Solve the equation for x.

$9x - 15 = 2x - 16$

$7x - 15 = -16$

$7x = -1$

$x = -\frac{1}{7}$

15. Write a proportion where x equals the actual distance and each ratio is written as inches : miles.

$\frac{2.5}{40} = \frac{17.25}{x}$

Cross-multiply and divide to solve for x.

$2.5x = 690$

$x = 276$

The two cities are **276 miles apart**.

16. Write a proportion where x is the number of defective parts made and both ratios are written as defective : total.

$\frac{4}{1000} = \frac{x}{125,000}$

Cross-multiply and divide to solve for x.

$1000x = 500,000$

$x = 500$

There are **500 defective parts** for the month.

17. [A] The percent is written as a fraction over 100 and reduced:

$\frac{18}{100} = \frac{9}{50}$

[B] Dividing 5 by 3 gives the value 0.6, which is then multiplied by 100: **60%**.

[C] The decimal point is moved two places to the right: $1.125 \times 100 =$ **112.5%**.

[D] The decimal point is moved two places to the left: $84 \div 100 =$ **0.84**.

18. Identify the variables.

Percent of students who are girls = $100\% - 54\% = 46\%$

percent = $46\% = 0.46$

whole = 650 students

part = ?

Plug the variables into the appropriate equation.

part = whole × percent

= $0.46 \times 650 = 299$

There are 299 girls.

19. Identify the variables.

original amount = $1,500

percent change = $45\% = 0.45$

amount of change = ?

Plug the variables into the appropriate equation.

amount of change = original amount × percent change

= $1500 \times 0.45 = 675$

To find the new price, subtract the amount of change from the original price.

$1500 - 675 = 825$

The final price is $825.

20. Identify the variables.

original amount = $100,000

amount of change = $120,000 - 100,000 = 20,000$

percent change = ?

Plug the variables into the appropriate equation.

percent change = $\frac{\text{amount of change}}{\text{original amount}}$

= $\frac{20,000}{100,000} = 0.20$

To find the percent growth, multiply by 100.

$0.20 \times 100 =$ **20%**

Numbers and Operations

21. $\dfrac{(10^2)^3}{(10^2)^2}$

Multiply the exponents raised to a power.

$= \dfrac{10^6}{10^{-4}}$

Subtract the exponent in the denominator from the one in the numerator.

$= 10^{6-(-4)}$

Simplify.

$= 10^{10} = $ **10,000,000,000**

22. $\dfrac{(x^{-2}y^2)^2}{x^3y}$

Multiply the exponents raised to a power.

$= \dfrac{x^{-4}y^4}{x^3y}$

Subtract the exponent in the denominator from the one in the numerator.

$= x^{-4-3}y^{4-1} = x^{-7}y^3$

Move negative exponents to the denominator.

$= \dfrac{y^3}{x^7}$

23. $\sqrt{48}$

Determine the largest square number that is a factor of the radicand (48) and write the radicand as a product using that square number as a factor.

$= \sqrt{16 \times 3}$

Apply the rules of radicals to simplify.

$= \sqrt{16}\sqrt{3} = 4\sqrt{3}$

24. $\dfrac{6}{\sqrt{8}}$

Apply the rules of radicals to simplify.

$= \dfrac{6}{\sqrt{4}\sqrt{2}} = \dfrac{6}{2\sqrt{2}}$

Multiply by $\dfrac{\sqrt{2}}{\sqrt{2}}$ to rationalize the denominator.

$= \dfrac{6}{2\sqrt{2}}\left(\dfrac{\sqrt{2}}{\sqrt{2}}\right) = \dfrac{3\sqrt{2}}{2}$

CHAPTER TWO
Algebra

Algebra, meaning "restoration" in Arabic, is the mathematical method of finding the unknown. The first algebraic book in Egypt was used to figure out complex inheritances that were to be split among many individuals. Today, algebra is just as necessary when dealing with unknown amounts.

Algebraic Expressions

The foundation of algebra is the **VARIABLE**, an unknown number represented by a symbol (usually a letter such as x or a). Variables can be preceded by a **COEFFICIENT**, which is a constant (i.e., a real number) in front of the variable, such as $4x$ or $-2a$. An **ALGEBRAIC EXPRESSION** is any sum, difference, product, or quotient of variables and numbers (for example $3x^2$, $2x + 7y - 1$, and $\frac{5}{x}$ are algebraic expressions). **TERMS** are any quantities that are added or subtracted (for example, the terms of the expression $x^2 - 3x + 5$ are x^2, $3x$, and 5). A **POLYNOMIAL EXPRESSION** is an algebraic expression where all the exponents on the variables are whole numbers. A polynomial with only two terms is known as a **BINOMIAL**, and one with three terms is a **TRINOMIAL**. A **MONOMIAL** has only one term.

EVALUATING EXPRESSIONS is another way of saying "find the numeric value of an expression if the variable is equal to a certain number." To evaluate the expression, simply plug the given value(s) for the variable(s) into the equation and simplify. Remember to use the order of operations when simplifying:

1. **P**arentheses
2. **E**xponents
3. **M**ultiplication

DID YOU KNOW?
Simplified expressions are ordered by variable terms alphabetically with highest exponent first then down to constants.

4. Division
5. Addition
6. Subtraction

EXAMPLE

1. If $m = 4$, find the value of the following expression: $5(m - 2)^3 + 3m^2 - \frac{m}{4} - 1$

Operations with Expressions
ADDING and SUBTRACTING

Expressions can be added or subtracted by simply adding and subtracting **LIKE TERMS**, which are terms with the same variable part (the variables must be the same, with the same exponents on each variable). For example, in the expressions $2x + 3xy - 2z$ and $6y + 2xy$, the like terms are $3xy$ and $2xy$. Adding the two expressions yields the new expression $2x + 6xy - 2z + 6y$. Note that the other terms did not change; they cannot be combined because they have different variables.

EXAMPLE

2. If $a = 12x + 7xy - 9y$ and $b = 8x - 9xz + 7z$, what is $a + b$?

DISTRIBUTING and FACTORING

Distributing and factoring can be seen as two sides of the same coin. **DISTRIBUTION** multiplies each term in the first factor by each term in the second factor to get rid of parentheses. **FACTORING** reverses this process, taking a polynomial in standard form and writing it as a product of two or more factors.

DID YOU KNOW?
Operations with polynomials can always be checked by evaluating equivalent expressions for the same value.

When distributing a monomial through a polynomial, the expression outside the parentheses is multiplied by each term inside the parentheses. Using the rules of exponents, coefficients are multiplied and exponents are added.

When simplifying two polynomials, each term in the first polynomial must multiply each term in the second polynomial. A binomial (two terms) multiplied by a binomial, will require 2 × 2 or 4 multiplications. For the binomial × binomial case, this process is sometimes called **FOIL**, which stands for first, outside, inside, and last. These terms refer to the placement of each term of the expression: multiply the first term in each expression, then the outside terms, then the inside terms, and finally the last terms. A binomial (two terms) multiplied by a trinomial (three terms), will require 2 × 3 or 6 products to simplify. The first term in the first polynomial multiplies each of the three terms in the second polynomial, then the second term in the first polynomial multiplies each of the three terms in the second polynomial. A trinomial (three terms) by a trinomial will require 3 × 3 or 9 products, and so on.

Factoring is the reverse of distributing: the first step is always to remove ("undistribute") the GCF of all the terms, if there is a GCF (besides 1). The GCF is the product of any constants and/or variables that every term shares. (For example, the GCF of $12x^3$, $15x^2$ and $6xy^2$ is $3x$ because $3x$ evenly divides all three terms.) This shared factor can be taken out of each term and moved to the outside of the parentheses, leaving behind a polynomial where each term is the original term divided by the GCF. (The remaining terms for the terms in the example would be $4x^2$, $5x$, and $2xy$.) It may be possible to factor the polynomial in the parentheses further, depending on the problem.

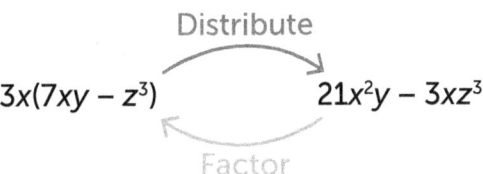

Figure 2.1. Distribution and Factoring

EXAMPLES

3. Expand the following expression: $5x(x^2 - 2c + 10)$

4. Expand the following expression: $(x^2 - 5)(2x - x^3)$

5. Factor the expression $16z^2 + 48z$

6. Factor the expression $6m^3 + 12m^3n - 9m^2$

FACTORING TRINOMIALS

If the leading coefficient is $a = 1$, the trinomial is in the form $x^2 + bx + c$ and can often be rewritten in the factored form, as a product of two binomials: $(x + m)(x + n)$. Recall that the product of two binomials can be written in expanded form $x^2 + mx + nx + mn$. Equating this expression with $x^2 + bx + c$, the constant term c would have to equal the product mn. Thus, to work backward from the trinomial to the factored form, consider all the numbers m and n that multiply to make c. For example, to factor $x^2 + 8x + 12$, consider all the pairs that multiply to be 12 (12 = 1 × 12 or 2 × 6 or 3 × 4). Choose the pair that will make the coefficient of the middle term (8) when added. In this example 2 and 6 add to 8, so making $m = 2$ and $n = 6$ in the expanded form gives:

$$x^2 + 8x + 12 = x^2 + 2x + 6x + 12$$

$= (x^2 + 2x) + (6x + 12)$	Group the first two terms and the last two terms.

$= x(x + 6) + 2(x + 6)$	Factor the GCF out of each set of parentheses.
$= (x + 6)(x + 2)$	The two terms now have the common factor $(x + 6)$, which can be removed, leaving $(x + 2)$ and the original polynomial is factored.

In general:

$x^2 + bx + c = x^2 + mx + nx + mn$, where $c = mn$ and $b = m + n$

$= (x^2 + mx) + (nx + mn)$	Group.
$= x(x + m) + n(x + m)$	Factor each group.
$= (x + m)(x + n)$	Factor out the common binomial.

Note that if none of the factors of c add to the value b, then the trinomial cannot be factored, and is called PRIME.

If the leading coefficient is not 1 ($a \neq 1$), first make sure that any common factors among the three terms are factored out. If the a-value is negative, factor out –1 first as well. If the a-value of the new polynomial in the parentheses is still not 1, follow this rule: Identify two values r and s that multiply to be ac and add to be b. Then write the polynomial in this form: $ax^2 + bx + c = ax^2 + rx + sx + c$, and proceed by grouping, factoring, and removing the common binomial as above.

There are a few special factoring cases worth memorizing: difference of squares, binomial squared, and the sum and difference of cubes.

- ▶ **DIFFERENCE OF SQUARES** (each term is a square and they are subtracted):
  - ▷ $a^2 - b^2 = (a + b)(a - b)$
  - ▷ Note that a SUM of squares is never factorable.
- ▶ **BINOMIAL SQUARED:** $a^2 + 2ab + b^2 = (a + b)(a + b) = (a + b)^2$
- ▶ **SUM AND DIFFERENCE OF CUBES:**
  - ▷ $a^3 + b^3 = (a + b)(a^2 - ab + b^2)$
  - ▷ $a^3 - b^3 = (a - b)(a^2 + ab + b^2)$
  - ▷ Note that the second factor in these factorizations will never be able to be factored further.

EXAMPLES

7. Factor: $16x^2 + 52x + 30$

8. Factor: $-21x^2 - x + 10$

Linear Equations

An **EQUATION** states that two expressions are equal to each other. Polynomial equations are categorized by the highest power of the variables they contain: the highest power of any exponent of a linear equation is 1, a quadratic equation has a variable raised to the second power, a cubic equation has a variable raised to the third power, and so on.

SOLVING LINEAR EQUATIONS

Solving an equation means finding the value or values of the variable that make the equation true. To solve a linear equation, it is necessary to manipulate the terms so that the variable being solved for appears alone on one side of the equal sign while everything else in the equation is on the other side.

The way to solve linear equations is to "undo" all the operations that connect numbers to the variable of interest. Follow these steps:

1. Eliminate fractions by multiplying each side by the least common multiple of any denominators.
2. Distribute to eliminate parentheses, braces, and brackets.
3. Combine like terms.
4. Use addition or subtraction to collect all terms containing the variable of interest to one side, and all terms not containing the variable to the other side.
5. Use multiplication or division to remove coefficients from the variable of interest.

DID YOU KNOW?
On multiple choice tests, it is often easier to plug the possible values into the equation and determine which solution makes the equation true than to solve the equation.

Sometimes there are no numeric values in the equation or there are a mix of numerous variables and constants. The goal is to solve the equation for one of the variables in terms of the other variables. In this case, the answer will be an expression involving numbers and letters instead of a numeric value.

EXAMPLES

9. Solve for x: $\frac{100(x + 5)}{20} = 1$

10. Solve for x: $2(x + 2)^2 - 2x^2 + 10 = 42$

11. Solve the equation for D: $\frac{A(3B + 2D)}{2N} = 5M - 6$

GRAPHS of LINEAR EQUATIONS

The most common way to write a linear equation is **SLOPE-INTERCEPT FORM**, $y = mx + b$. In this equation, m is the slope, which describes how steep the line is, and b is the *y*-intercept. Slope is often described as "rise over run" because it is calculated as the difference in *y*-values (rise) over the difference in *x*-values (run). The slope of the line is also the rate of change of the dependent variable *y* with respect to the independent variable *x*. The *y*-intercept is the point where the line crosses the *y*-axis, or where *x* equals zero.

DID YOU KNOW?
Use the phrase "Begin, Move" to remember that *b* is the *y*-intercept (where to begin) and *m* is the slope (how the line moves).

To graph a linear equation, identify the *y*-intercept and place that point on the *y*-axis. If the slope is not written as a fraction, make it a fraction by writing it over 1 ($\frac{m}{1}$). Then use the slope to count up (or down, if negative) the "rise" part of the slope and over the "run" part of the slope to find a second point. These points can then be connected to draw the line.

To find the equation of a line, identify the *y*-intercept, if possible, on the graph and use two easily identifiable points to find the slope. If the *y*-intercept is not easily identified, identify the slope by choosing easily identifiable points; then choose one point on the graph, plug the point and the slope values into the equation, and solve for the missing value *b*.

▶ standard form: $Ax + By = C$
▶ $m = -\frac{A}{B}$
▶ *x*-intercept = $\frac{C}{A}$
▶ *y*-intercept = $\frac{C}{B}$

DID YOU KNOW?
slope-intercept form:
$y = mx + b$
slope: $m = \frac{y_2 - y_1}{x_2 - x_1}$

Another way to express a linear equation is standard form: $Ax + By = C$. In order to graph equations in this form, it is often easiest to convert them to point-slope form. Alternately, it is easy to find the *x*- or *y*-intercept from this form, and once these two points are known, a line can be drawn through them. To find the *x*-intercept, simply make $y = 0$ and solve for *x*. Similarly, to find the *y*-intercept, make $x = 0$ and solve for *y*.

EXAMPLES

12. What is the equation of the following line?

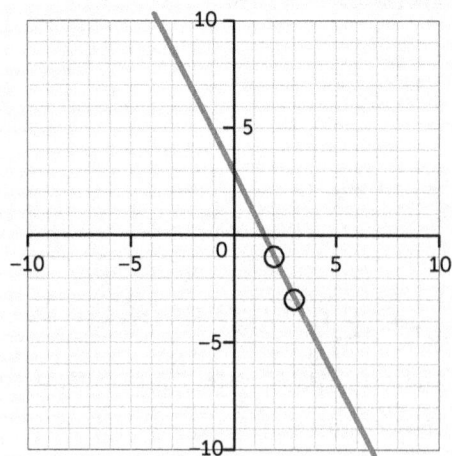

13. What is the slope of the line whose equation is $6x - 2y - 8 = 0$?

14. Write the equation of the line which passes through the points $(-2,5)$ and $(-5,3)$.

15. What is the equation of the following graph?

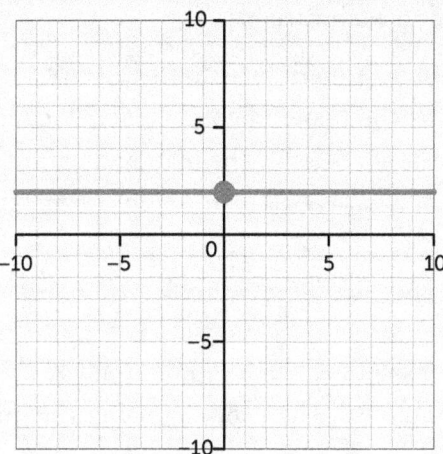

SYSTEMS of LINEAR EQUATIONS

Systems of equations are sets of equations that include two or more variables. These systems can only be solved when there are at least as many equations as there are variables. Systems involve working with more than one equation to solve for more than one variable. For a system of linear equations, the solution to the system is the set of values for the variables that satisfies every equation in the system. Graphically, this will be the point where every line meets. If the lines are parallel (and hence do not intersect), the system will have no solution. If the lines are multiples of each other, meaning they share all coordinates, then the system has infinitely many solutions (because every point on the line is a solution).

DID YOU KNOW?
Plug answers back into both equations to ensure the system has been solved properly.

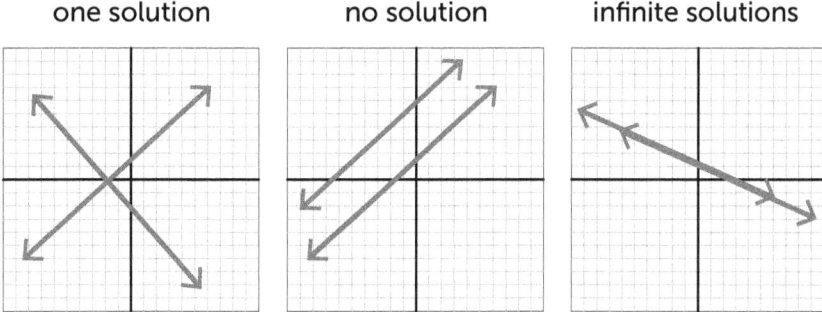

Figure 2.2. Systems of Equations

There are three common methods for solving systems of equations. To perform **SUBSTITUTION**, solve one equation for one variable, and then plug in the resulting expression for that variable in the second equation. This process works best for systems of two equations with two variables where the coefficient of one or more of the variables is 1.

To solve using **ELIMINATION**, add or subtract two equations so that one or more variables are eliminated. It's often necessary to multiply one or both of the equations by a scalar (constant) in order to make the variables cancel. Equations can be added or subtracted as many times as necessary to find each variable.

Yet another way to solve a system of linear equations is to use a **MATRIX EQUATION**. In the matrix equation $AX = B$, A contains the system's coefficients, X contains the variables, and B contains the constants (as shown below). The matrix equation can then be solved by multiplying B by the inverse of A: $X = A^{-1}B$

$$\begin{matrix} ax + by = e \\ cx + dy = f \end{matrix} \rightarrow A = \begin{bmatrix} a & b \\ c & d \end{bmatrix} \quad X = \begin{bmatrix} x \\ y \end{bmatrix} \quad B = \begin{bmatrix} e \\ f \end{bmatrix} \rightarrow AX = B$$

This method can be extended to equations with three or more variables. Technology (such as a graphing calculator) is often employed when solving using this method if more than two variables are involved.

EXAMPLES

16. Solve for *x* and *y*:
    $2x - 4y = 28$
    $4x - 12y = 36$

17. Solve for the system for *x* and *y*:
    $3 = -4x + y$
    $16x = 4y + 2$

18. Solve the system of equations:
    $6x + 10y = 18$
    $4x + 15y = 37$

19. Solve the following systems of equations using matrix arithmetic:
    $2x - 3y = -5$
    $3x - 4y = -8$

BUILDING EQUATIONS

In word problems, it is often necessary to translate a verbal description of a relationship into a mathematical equation. No matter the problem, this process can be done using the same steps:

1. Read the problem carefully and identify what value needs to be solved for.
2. Identify the known and unknown quantities in the problem, and assign the unknown quantities a variable.

3. Create equations using the variables and known quantities.
4. Solve the equations.
5. Check the solution: Does it answer the question asked in the problem? Does it make sense?

DID YOU KNOW?
Use the acronym STAR to remember word-problem strategies: Search the problem, Translate into an expression or equation, Answer, and Review.

EXAMPLES

20. A school is holding a raffle to raise money. There is a $3 entry fee, and each ticket costs $5. If a student paid $28, how many tickets did he buy?

21. Kelly is selling shirts for her school swim team. There are two prices: a student price and a nonstudent price. During the first week of the sale, Kelly raised $84 by selling 10 shirts to students and 4 shirts to nonstudents. She earned $185 in the second week by selling 20 shirts to students and 10 shirts to nonstudents. What is the student price for a shirt?

Linear Inequalities
SOLVING LINEAR INEQUALITIES

An inequality shows the relationship between two expressions, much like an equation. However, the equal sign is replaced with an inequality symbol that expresses the following relationships:

- < less than
- \> greater than
- ≤ less than or equal to
- ≥ greater than or equal to

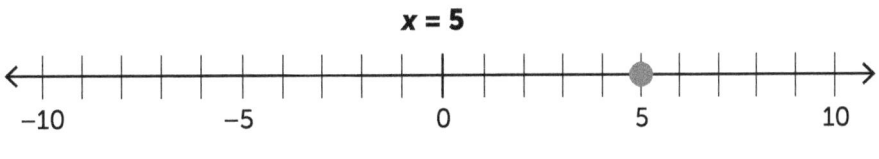
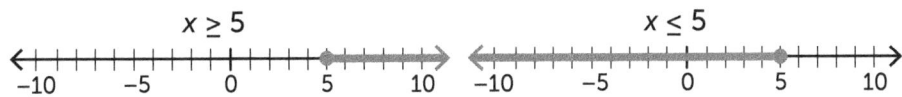
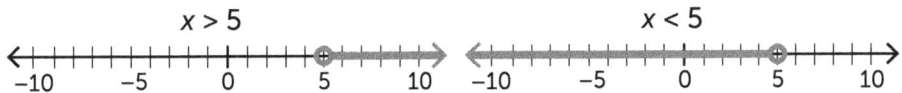

Figure 2.3. Inequalities on a Number Line

Inequalities are read from left to right. For example, the inequality $x \leq 8$ would be read as "x is less than or equal to 8," meaning x has a value smaller than or equal to 8. The set of solutions of an inequality can be expressed using a number line. The shaded region on the number line represents the set of all the numbers that make an inequality true. One major difference between equations and inequalities is that equations generally have a finite number of solutions, while inequalities generally have infinitely many solutions (an entire interval on the number line containing infinitely many values).

Linear inequalities can be solved in the same way as linear equations, with one exception. When multiplying or dividing both sides of an inequality by a negative number, the direction of the inequality sign must reverse—"greater than" becomes "less than" and "less than" becomes "greater than."

EXAMPLES

22. Solve for z: $3z + 10 < -z$

23. Solve for x: $2x - 3 > 5(x - 4) - (x - 4)$

COMPOUND INEQUALITIES

Compound inequalities have more than one inequality expression. Solutions of compound inequalities are the sets of all numbers that make *all* the inequalities true. Some compound inequalities may not have any solutions, some will have solutions that contain some part of the number line, and some will have solutions that include the entire number line.

Table 2.1. Unions and Intersections

Inequality	Meaning in Words	Number Line
$a < x < b$	All values x that are greater than a and less than b	open circles at a and b, shaded between
$a \leq x \leq b$	All values x that are greater than or equal to a and less than or equal to b	closed circles at a and b, shaded between
$x < a$ or $x > b$	All values of x that are less than a or greater than b	open circles at a and b, shaded outside
$x \leq a$ or $x \geq b$	All values of x that are less than or equal to a or greater than or equal to b	closed circles at a and b, shaded outside

Compound inequalities can be written, solved, and graphed as two separate inequalities. For compound inequalities in which the word *and* is used, the solution to the compound inequality will be the set of numbers on the number line where both inequalities have solutions (where both are shaded). For compound inequalities where *or* is used, the solution to the compound inequality will be *all* the shaded regions for *either* inequality.

EXAMPLES

24. Solve the compound inequalities: $2x + 4 < -18$ *or* $4(x + 2) > 18$

25. Solve the inequality: $-1 \leq 3(x + 2) - 1 \leq x + 3$

GRAPHING LINEAR INEQUALITIES in TWO VARIABLES

Linear inequalities in two variables can be graphed in much the same way as linear equations. Start by graphing the corresponding equation of a line (temporarily replace the inequality with an equal sign, and then graph). This line creates a boundary line of two half-planes. If the inequality is a "greater/less than," the boundary should not be included and a dotted line is used. A solid line is used to indicate that the boundary should be included in the solution when the inequality is "greater/less than or equal to."

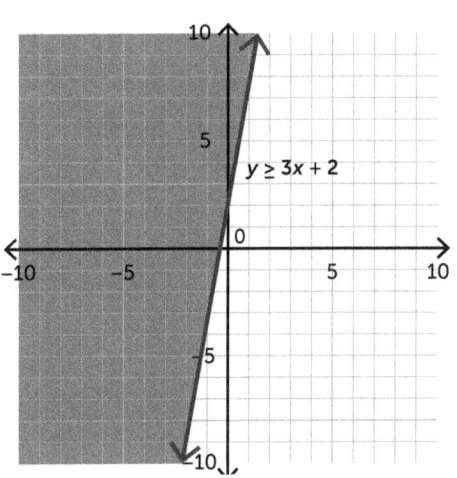

Figure 2.4. Graphing Inequalities

One side of the boundary is the set of all points (x, y) that make the inequality true. This side is shaded to indicate that all these values are solutions. If y is greater than the expression containing x, shade above the line; if it is less than, shade below. A point can also be used to check which side of the line to shade.

A set of two or more linear inequalities is a **SYSTEM OF INEQUALITIES**. Solutions to the system are all the values of the variables that make every inequality in the system true. Systems of inequalities are solved graphically by graphing all the inequalities in the same plane. The region where all the shaded solutions overlap is the solution to the system.

DID YOU KNOW?
A dotted line is used for "greater/less than" because the solution may approach that line, but the coordinates on the line can never be a solution.

EXAMPLES

26. Graph the following inequality: $3x + 6y \leq 12$.

27. Graph the system of inequalities: $-x + y \leq 1, x \geq -1, y > 2x - 4$

Algebra 25

28. What is the inequality represented on the graph below?

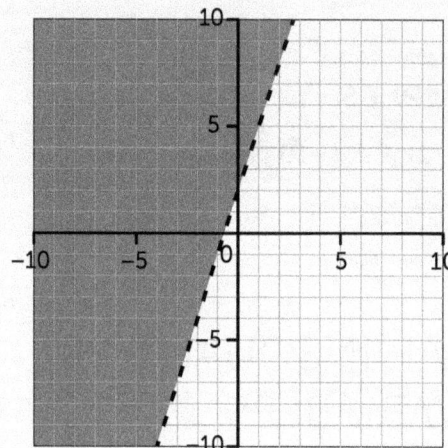

Quadratic Equations and Inequalities

Quadratic equations are degree 2 polynomials; the highest power on the dependent variable is two. While linear functions are represented graphically as lines, the graph of a quadratic function is a **PARABOLA**. The graph of a parabola has three important components. The **VERTEX** is where the graph changes direction. In the parent graph $y = x^2$, the origin $(0,0)$ is the vertex. The **AXIS OF SYMMETRY** is the vertical line that cuts the graph into two equal halves. The line of symmetry always passes through the vertex. On the parent graph, the y-axis is the axis of symmetry. The **ZEROS** or **ROOTS** of the quadratic are the x-intercepts of the graph.

FORMS of QUADRATIC EQUATIONS

Quadratic equations can be expressed in two forms:

- **STANDARD FORM:** $y = ax^2 + bx + c$
  - Axis of symmetry: $x = -\frac{b}{2a}$
  - Vertex: $(-\frac{b}{2a}, f(-\frac{b}{2a}))$
- **VERTEX FORM:** $y\ a(x - h)^2 + k$
  - Vertex: (h, k)
  - Axis of symmetry: $x = h$

In both equations, the sign of a determines which direction the parabola opens: if a is positive, then it opens upward; if a is negative, then it opens downward. The wideness or narrowness is also determined by a. If the absolute value of a is less than one (a proper fraction), then the parabola will get wider the closer $|a|$ is to zero. If the absolute value of a is greater than one, then the larger $|a|$ becomes, the narrower the parabola will be.

Equations in vertex form can be converted to standard form by squaring out the $(x - h)^2$ part (using FOIL), distributing the a, adding k, and simplifying the result.

Equations can be converted from standard form to vertex form by **COMPLETING THE SQUARE**. Take an equation in standard form, $y = ax^2 + bc + c$.

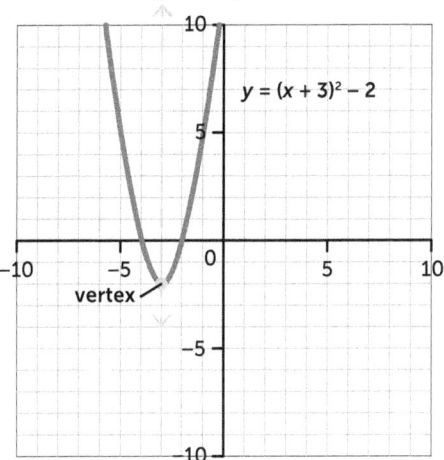

Figure 2.5. Parabola

1. Move c to the left side of the equation.
2. Divide the entire equation through by a (to make the coefficient of x^2 be 1).
3. Take half of the coefficient of x, square that number, and then add the result to both sides of the equation.
4. Convert the right side of the equation to a perfect binomial squared, $(x + m)^2$.
5. Isolate y to put the equation in proper vertex form.

EXAMPLES

29. What is the line of symmetry for $y = -2(x + 3)^2 + 2$?

30. What is the vertex of the parabola $y = -3x^2 + 24x - 27$?

31. Write $y = -3x^2 + 24x - 27$ in vertex form by completing the square.

SOLVING QUADRATIC EQUATIONS

Solving the quadratic equation $ax^2 + bx + c = 0$ finds x-intercepts of the parabola (by making $y = 0$). These are also called the **ROOTS** or **ZEROS** of the quadratic function. A quadratic equation may have zero, one, or two real solutions. There are several ways of finding the zeros. One way is to factor the quadratic into a product of two binomials, and then use the zero product property. (If $m \times n = 0$, then either $m = 0$ or $n = 0$.) Another way is to complete the square and square root both sides. One way that works every time is to memorize and use the **QUADRATIC FORMULA**:

$$x = \frac{-b \pm \sqrt{b^2 - 4ac}}{2a}$$

The a, b, and c come from the standard form of quadratic equations above. (Note that to use the quadratic equation, the right-hand side of the equation must be equal to zero.)

The part of the formula under the square root radical ($b^2 - 4ac$) is known as the **DISCRIMINANT**. The discriminant tells how many and what type of roots will result without actually calculating the roots.

DID YOU KNOW?
With all graphing problems, putting the function into the $y =$ window of a graphing calculator will aid the process of elimination when graphs are examined and compared to answer choices with a focus on properties like axis of symmetry, vertices, and roots of formulas.

Table 2.2. Discriminants

If $B^2 - 4AC$ is	There will be	And the parabola
zero	only 1 real root	has its vertex on the x-axis
positive	2 real roots	has two x-intercepts
negative	0 real roots 2 complex roots	has no x-intercepts

EXAMPLES

32. Find the zeros of the quadratic equation: $y = -(x + 3)^2 + 1$.

33. Find the root(s) for: $z^2 - 4z + 4 = 0$

34. Write a quadratic function that has zeros at $x = -3$ and $x = 2$ that passes through the point $(-2, 8)$.

GRAPHING QUADRATIC EQUATIONS

The final expected quadratic skills are graphing a quadratic function given its equation and determining the equation of a quadratic function from its graph. The equation's form determines which quantities are easiest to obtain:

Table 2.3. Obtaining Quantities from Quadratic Functions

Name of Form	Equation of Quadratic	Easiest Quantity to Find	How to Find Other Quantities
vertex form	$y = a(x - h)^2 + k$	vertex at (h, k) and axis of symmetry $x = h$	Find zeros by making $y = 0$ and solving for x.
factored form	$y = a(x - m)(x - n)$	x-intercepts at $x = m$ and $x = n$	Find axis of symmetry by averaging m and n: $x = \frac{m + n}{2}$. This is also the x-value of the vertex.
standard form	$y = ax^2 + bx + c$	y-intercept at $(0, c)$	Find axis of symmetry and x-value of the vertex using $x = \frac{-b}{2a}$. Find zeros using quadratic formula.

To graph a quadratic function, first determine if the graph opens up or down by examining the a-value. Then determine the quantity that is easiest to find based on the form given, and find the vertex. Then other values can be found, if necessary, by choosing x-values and finding the corresponding y-values. Using symmetry instantly doubles the number of points that are known.

Given the graph of a parabola, the easiest way to write a quadratic equation is to identify the vertex and insert the *h*- and *k*-values into the vertex form of the equation. The *a*-value can be determined by finding another point the graph goes through, plugging these values in for *x* and *y*, and solving for *a*.

EXAMPLES

35. Graph the quadratic $y = 2(x - 3)^2 + 4$.

36. What is the vertex form of the equation shown on the following graph?

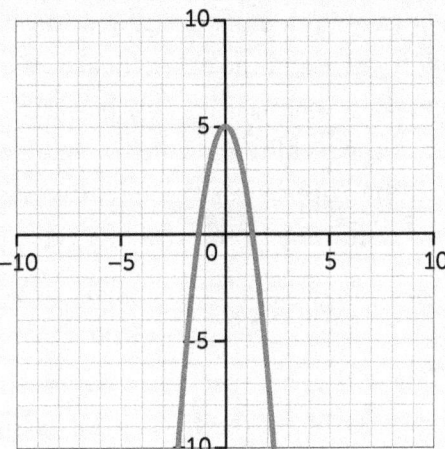

QUADRATIC INEQUALITIES

Quadratic inequalities with two variables, such as $y < (x + 3)^2 - 2$ can be graphed much like linear inequalities: graph the equation by treating the inequality symbol as an equal sign, then shade the graph. Shade above the graph when *y* is greater is than, and below the graph when *y* is less than.

Quadratic inequalities with only one variable, such as $x^2 - 4x > 12$, can be solved by first manipulating the inequality so that one side is zero. The zeros can then be found and used to determine where the inequality is greater than zero (positive) or less than zero (negative). Often it helps to set up intervals on a number line and test a value within each range created by the zeros to identify the values that create positive or negative values.

EXAMPLE

37. Find the values of *x* such that $x^2 - 4x > 12$.

Algebra 29

Absolute Value Equations and Inequalities

The **ABSOLUTE VALUE** of a number means the distance between that number and zero. The absolute value of any number is positive since distance is always positive. The notation for absolute value of a number is two vertical bars:

$|-27| = 27$ The distance from −27 to 0 is 27.
$|27| = 27$ The distance from 27 to 0 is 27.

Solving equations and simplifying inequalities with absolute values usually requires writing two equations or inequalities, which are then solved separately using the usual methods of solving equations. To write the two equations, set one equation equal to the positive value of the expression inside the absolute value and the other equal to the negative value. Two inequalities can be written in the same manner. However, the inequality symbol should be flipped for the negative value. The formal definition of the absolute value is

$$|x| = \begin{cases} -x, & x < 0 \\ x, & x \geq 0 \end{cases}$$

This is true because whenever x is negative, the opposite of x is the answer (for example, $|-5| = -(-5) = 5$, but when x is positive, the answer is just x. This type of function is called a **PIECE-WISE FUNCTION**. It is defined in two (or more) distinct pieces. To graph the absolute value function, graph each piece separately. When $x < 0$ (that is, when it is negative), graph the line $y = -x$. When $x > 0$ (that is, when x is positive), graph the line $y = x$. This creates a V-shaped graph that is the parent function for absolute value functions.

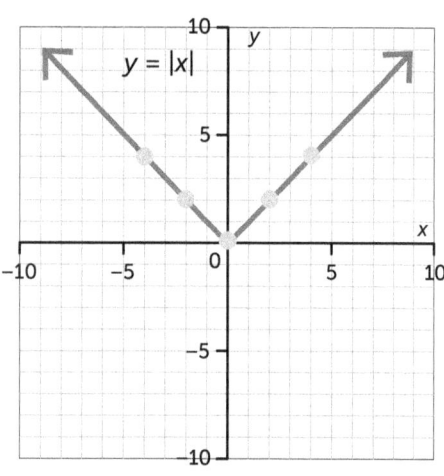

Figure 2.6. Absolute Value Parent Function

EXAMPLES

38. Solve for x: $|x - 3| = 27$

39. Solve for r: $\frac{|r - 7|}{5} = 27$

40. Find the solution set for the following inequality: $\left|\frac{3x}{7}\right| \geq 4 - x$.

Functions
WORKING with FUNCTIONS

Functions can be thought of as a process: when something is put in, an action (or operation) is performed, and something different comes out. A **FUNCTION** is a relationship between two quantities (for example x and y) in which, for every value of the independent variable (usually x), there is exactly one value of the dependent variable (usually y). Briefly, each input has *exactly one* output. Graphically this means the graph passes the **VERTICAL LINE TEST**: anywhere a vertical line is drawn on the graph, the line hits the curve at exactly one point.

The notation $f(x)$ or $g(t)$, etc., is often used when a function is being considered. This is **FUNCTION NOTATION**. The input value is x and the output value y is written as $y = f(x)$. Thus, $f(2)$ represents the output value (or y value) when $x = 2$, and $f(2) = 5$ means that when $x = 2$ is plugged into the $f(x)$ function, the output (y value) is 5. In other words, $f(2) = 5$ represents the point $(2, 5)$ on the graph of $f(x)$.

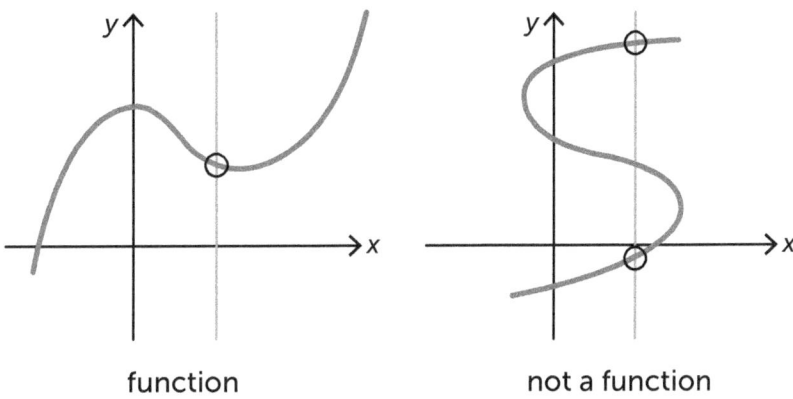

Figure 2.7. Vertical Line Test

Every function has an **INPUT DOMAIN** and **OUTPUT RANGE**. The domain is the set of all the possible x values that can be used as input values (these are found along the horizontal axis on the graph), and the range includes all the y values or output values that result from applying $f(x)$ (these are found along the vertical axis on the graph). Domain and range are usually intervals of numbers and are often expressed as inequalities, such as $x < 2$ (the domain is all values less than 2) or $3 < x < 15$ (all values between 3 and 15).

A function $f(x)$ is **EVEN** if $f(-x) = f(x)$. Even functions have symmetry across the y-axis. An example of an even function is the parent quadratic $y = x^2$, because any value of x (for example, 3) and its opposite $-x$ (for example, -3) have the same y value (for

Algebra 31

example, $3^2 = 9$ and $(-3)^2 = 9$). A function is **ODD** if $f(-x) = -f(x)$. Odd functions have symmetry about the origin. For example, $f(x) = x^3$ is an odd function because $f(3) = 27$, and $f(-3) = -27$. A function may be even, odd, or neither.

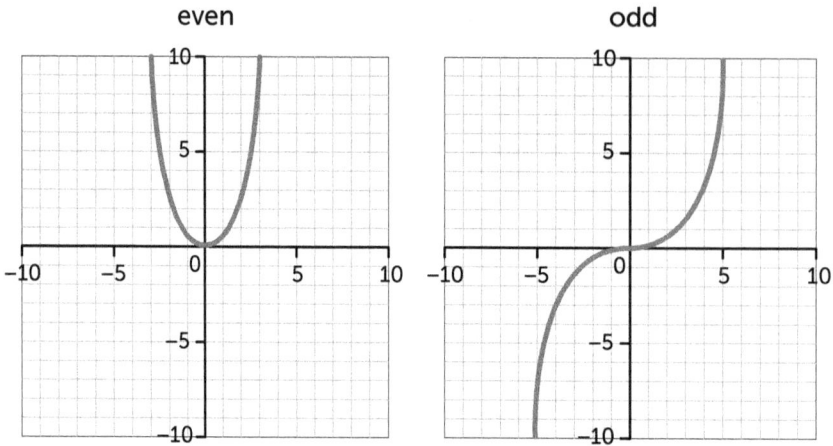

Figure 2.8. Even and Odd Functions

EXAMPLES

41. What are the domain and range of the following function?

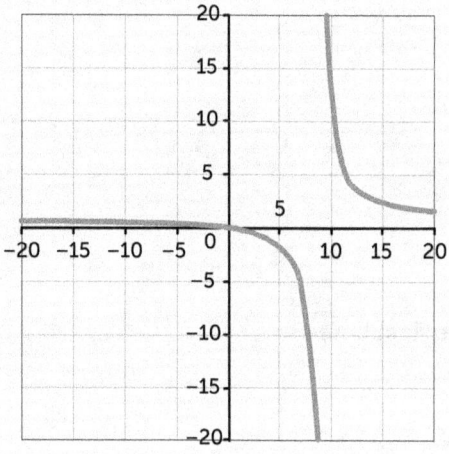

42. What is the domain and the range of the following graph?

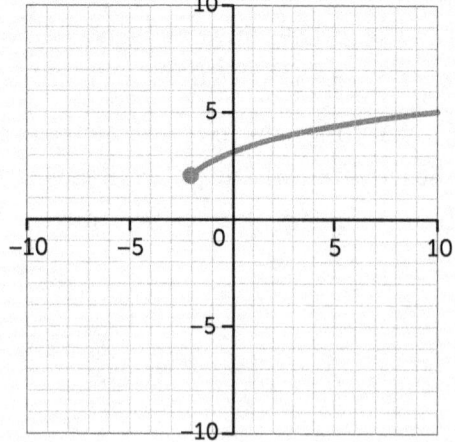

43. Evaluate: $f(4)$ if $f(x) = x^3 - 2x + \sqrt{x}$

44. Which of the following represents a function?

A)

x	g(x)
0	0
1	1
2	2
1	3

B)

x	f(x)
0	1
0	2
0	3
0	4

C)

t	f(t)
1	1
2	2
3	3
4	4

D)

x	f(x)
0	0
5	1
0	2
5	3

INVERSE FUNCTIONS

INVERSE FUNCTIONS switch the inputs and the outputs of a function. If $f(x) = k$ then the inverse of that function would read $f^{-1}(k) = x$. The domain of $f^{-1}(x)$ is the range of $f(x)$, and the range of $f^{-1}(x)$ is the domain of $f(x)$. If point (a, b) is on the graph of $f(x)$, then point (b, a) will be on the graph of $f^{-1}(x)$. Because of this fact, the graph of $f^{-1}(x)$ is a

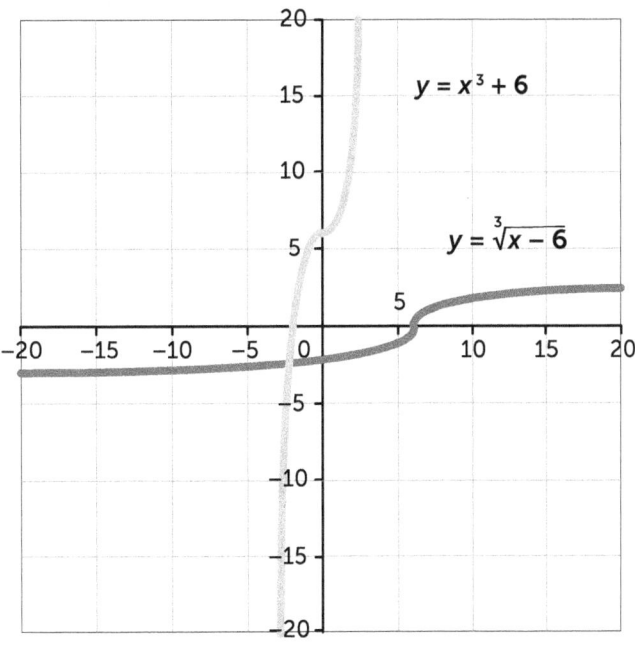

Figure 2.9. Inverse Functions

reflection of the graph of $f(x)$ across the line $y = x$. Inverse functions "undo" all the operations of the original function.

> **DID YOU KNOW?**
> Inverse graphs can be tested by taking any point on one graph and flipping coordinates to see if that new point is on the other curve. For example, the coordinate point (5,–2) is on the function and (–2,5) is a point on its inverse.

The steps for finding an inverse function are:

1. Replace $f(x)$ with y to make it easier manipulate the equation.
2. Switch the x and y.
3. Solve for y.
4. Label the inverse function as $f^{-1}(x) =$.

EXAMPLES

45. What is the inverse of function of $f(x) = 5x + 5$?

46. Find the inverse of the graph of $f(x) = -1 - \frac{1}{5}x$.

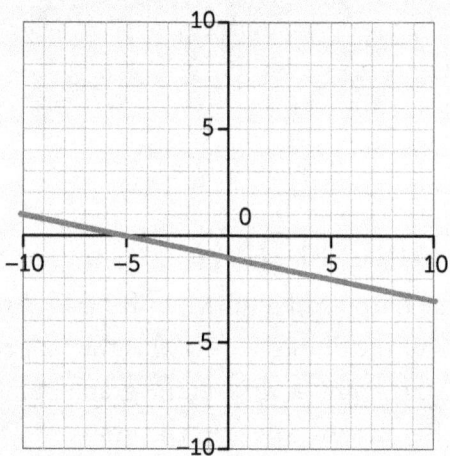

COMPOUND FUNCTIONS

COMPOUND FUNCTIONS take two or more functions and combine them using operations or composition. Functions can be combined using addition, subtraction, multiplication, or division:

- addition: $(f + g)(x) = f(x) + g(x)$
- subtraction: $(f - g)(x) = f(x) - g(x)$
- multiplication: $(fg)(x) = f(x)g(x)$
- division: $(\frac{f}{g})(x) = \frac{f(x)}{g(x)}$ (note that $g(x) \neq 0$)

Functions can also be combined using **COMPOSITION**. Composition of functions is indicated by the notation $(f \circ g)(x)$. Note that the $\circ$ symbol does NOT mean multiply. It means take the output of $g(x)$ and make it the input of $f(x)$:

$$(f \circ g)(x) = f(g(x))$$

This equation is read *f* of *g* of *x*, and will be a new function of *x*. Note that order is important. In general, $f(g(x)) \neq g(f(x))$. They *will* be equal when $f(x)$ and $g(x)$ are inverses of each other, however, as both will simplify to the original input *x*. This is because performing a function on a value and then using that output as the input to the inverse function should bring you back to the original value.

The domain of a composition function is the set of *x* values that are in the domain of the "inside" function $g(x)$ such that $g(x)$ is in the domain of the outside function $f(x)$. For example, if $f(x) = \frac{1}{x}$ and $g(x) = \sqrt{x}$, $f(g(x))$ has a domain of $x > 0$ because $g(x)$ has a domain of $x \geq 0$. But when $f(x)$ is applied to the $\sqrt{x}$ function, the composition function becomes $\frac{1}{\sqrt{x}}$ and the value $x = 0$ is no longer allowed because it would result in 0 in the denominator, so the domain must be further restricted.

EXAMPLES

47. If $z(x) = 3x - 3$ and $y(x) = 2x - 1$, find $(y \circ z)(-4)$.

48. Find $(k \circ t)(x)$ if $k(x) = \frac{1}{2}x - 3$ and $t(x) = \frac{1}{2}x - 2$.

49. The wait (*W*) (in minutes) to get on a ride at an amusement park depends on the number of people (*N*) in the park. The number of people in the park depends on the number of hours, *t*, that the park has been open. Suppose $N(t) = 400t$ and $W(N) = 5(1.2)\frac{N}{100}$. What is the value and the meaning in context of $N(4)$ and $W(N(4))$?

TRANSFORMING FUNCTIONS

Many functions can be graphed using simple transformation of parent functions. Transformations include reflections across axes, vertical and horizontal translations (or shifts), and vertical or horizontal stretches or compressions. The table gives the effect of each transformation to the graph of any function $y = f(x)$.

Table 2.4. Effects of Transformations

Equation	Effect on Graph
$y = -f(x)$	reflection across the *x*-axis (vertical reflection)
$y = f(x) + k$	vertical shift up *k* units ($k > 0$) or down *k* units ($k < 0$)
$y = kf(x)$	vertical stretch (if $k > 1$) or compression (if $k < 1$)
$y = f(-x)$	reflection across the *y*-axis (horizontal reflection)
$y = f(x + k)$	horizontal shift right *k* units ($k < 0$) or left *k* units ($k > 0$)
$y = f(kx)$	horizontal stretch ($k < 1$) or compression ($k > 1$)

Note that the first three equations have an operation applied to the *outside* of the function $f(x)$ and these all cause *vertical changes* to the graph of the function that are INTUITIVE (for example, adding a value moves it up). The last three equations have an operation applied to the *inside* of the function $f(x)$ and these all cause HORIZONTAL CHANGES to the graph of the function that are COUNTERINTUITIVE (for example, multiplying the x's by a fraction results in stretch, not compression, which would seem more intuitive). It is helpful to group these patterns together to remember how each transformation affects the graph.

EXAMPLES

50. Graph: $y = |x + 1| + 4$

51. Graph: $y = -3|x - 2| + 2$

Exponential and Logarithmic Functions

EXPONENTIAL FUNCTIONS

An **EXPONENTIAL FUNCTION** has a constant base and a variable in the exponent: $f(x) = b^x$ is an exponential function with base b and exponent x. The value b is the quantity that the y value is multiplied by each time the x value is increased by 1. When looking at a table of values, an exponential function can be identified because the $f(x)$ values are being multiplied. (In contrast, linear $f(x)$ values are being added to.)

DID YOU KNOW?
To solve an exponential equation, start by looking for a common base:
$4^{(x-2)} = \sqrt{8}$
can be rewritten as
$(2^2)^{(x-2)} = (2^3)^{\frac{1}{2}}$
If no common base can be found, logarithms can be used to move the variable out of the exponent position.

The graph of the exponential parent function does not cross the x-axis, which is the function's horizontal asymptote. The y-intercept of the function is at $(0, 1)$.

The general formula for an exponential function, $f(x) = ab^{(x-h)} + k$, allows for transformations to be made to the function. The value h moves the function left or right (moving the y-intercept) while the value k moves the function up or down (moving both the y-intercept and the horizontal asymptote). The value a stretches or compresses the function (moving the y-intercept).

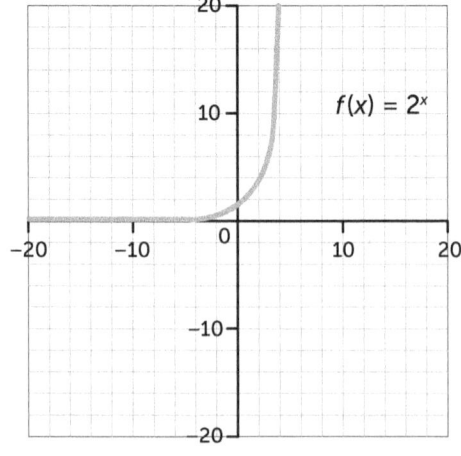

Figure 2.10. Exponential Parent Function

Exponential equations have at least one variable in an exponent position. One way to solve these equations is to make the bases on both side of the equation equivalent, and then equate the exponents. Many exponential equations do not have a solution. Negative numbers often lead to no solutions: for example, $2^x = -8$. The domain of exponential functions is only positive numbers, as seen above, so there is no x value that will result in a negative output.

EXAMPLES

52. Graph the exponential function $f(x) = 5^x - 2$.

53. If the height of grass in a yard in a humid summer week grows by 5% every day, how much taller would the grass be after six days?

54. Solve for x: $4^{x+1} = \frac{1}{256}$

LOGARITHMIC FUNCTIONS

The **LOGARITHMIC FUNCTION (LOG)** is the inverse of the exponential function.

A log is used to find out to what power an input is raised to get a desired output. In the table, the base is 3. The log function determines to what power 3 must be raised so that $\frac{1}{9}$ is the result in the table (the answer is −2). As with all inverse functions, these exponential and logarithmic functions are reflections of each other across the line $y = x$.

A **NATURAL LOGARITHM (LN)** has the number e as its base. Like π, e is an irrational number that is a nonterminating decimal. It is usually shortened to 2.71 when doing calculations. Although the proof of e is beyond the scope of this book, e is to be understood as the upper limit of the range of this rational function: $(1 + \frac{1}{n})^n$.

$y = \log_3 x \Rightarrow 3^y = x$

x	y
$\frac{1}{9}$	−2
$\frac{1}{3}$	−1
1	0
3	1
9	2
27	3

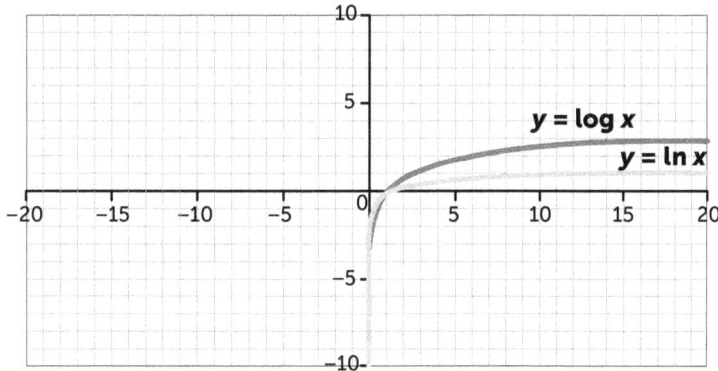

Figure 2.11. Logarithmic Parent Functions

In order to make use of and solve logarithmic functions, log rules are often employed that allow simplification:

Table 2.5. Properties of Logarithms

Change of base	$\log_b(m) = \frac{\log(m)}{\log(b)}$
Logs of products	$\log_b(mn) = \log_b(m) + \log_b(n)$
Logs of quotients	$\log_b(\frac{m}{n}) = \log_b(m) - \log_b(n)$
Log of a power	$\log_b(m^n) = n \times \log_b(m)$
Equal logs/equal arguments	$\log_b M = \log_b N \Leftrightarrow M = N$

Note that when the base is not written out, such as in log(*m*), it is understood that the base is 10. Just like a 1 is not put in front of a variable because its presence is implicitly understood, 10 is the implicit base whenever a base is not written out.

EXAMPLES

55. Expand $\log_5(\frac{25}{x})$

56. Solve for *x*: $\ln x + \ln 4 = 2\ln 4 - \ln 2$

57. Solve for *x*: $2^x = 40$

SPECIAL EQUATIONS

There are three exponential function formulas that frequently show up in word problems:

THE GROWTH FORMULA: $y = a(1 + r)^t$
Initial amount *a* increases at a rate of *r* per time period

THE DECAY FORMULA: $y = a(1 - r)^t$
Initial amount *a* decreases at a rate of *r* per time period

In these formulas, *a* is the initial amount (at time *t* = 0), *r* is the rate of growth or decay (written as a decimal in the formula), and *t* is the number of growth or decay cycles that have passed.

A special case of the growth function is known as:

THE COMPOUND-INTEREST FORMULA: $A = P(1 + \frac{r}{n})^{nt}$

In this formula, *A* is the future value of an investment, *P* is the initial deposit (or principal), *r* is the interest rate as a percentage, *n* is the number of times interest is compounded within a time period, or how often interest is applied to the account in a year (once per year, $n = 1$; monthly, $n = 12$; etc.), and t is the number of compounding cycles (usually years).

EXAMPLES

58. In the year 2000, the number of text messages sent in a small town was 120. If the number of text messages grew every year afterward by 124%, how many years would it take for the number of text messages to surpass 36,000?

59. The half-life of a certain isotope is 5.5 years. If there were 20 grams of one such isotope left after 22 years, what was its original weight?

60. If there were a glitch at a bank and a savings account accrued 5% interest five times per week, what would be the amount earned on a $50 deposit after twelve weeks?

Polynomial Functions

A polynomial is any equation or expression with two or more terms with whole number exponents. All polynomials with only one variable are functions. The zeros, or roots, of a polynomial function are where the function equals zero and crosses the x-axis.

A linear function is a degree 1 polynomial and always has one zero. A quadratic function is a degree 2 polynomial and always has exactly two roots (including complex roots and counting repeated roots separately). This pattern is extended in the **FUNDAMENTAL THEOREM OF ALGEBRA**:

DID YOU KNOW?
All polynomials where n is an odd number will have at least one real zero or root. Complex zeros always come in pairs (specifically, complex conjugate pairs).

A polynomial function with degree $n > 0$ such as $f(x) = ax^n + bx^{n-1} + cx^{n-2} + \ldots + k$, has exactly n (real or complex) roots (some roots may be repeated). Simply stated, whatever the degree of the polynomial is, that is how many roots it will have.

Table 2.6. Zeros of Polynomial Functions

Polynomial Degree, N	Number and Possible Types of Zeros
1	1 real zero (guaranteed)
2	0, 1, or 2 real zeros possible 2 real *or* complex zeros (guaranteed)
3	1, 2, or 3 real zeros possible (there must be at least one real zero) Or 1 real zero (guaranteed) and 2 complex zeros (guaranteed)

4	0, 1, 2, 3, or 4 real zeros (possible) Or 2 real zeros and 2 complex zeros or 4 complex zeros
...	...

All the zeros of a polynomial satisfy the equation $f(x) = 0$. That is, if k is a zero of a polynomial, then plugging in $x = k$ into the polynomial results in 0. This also means that the polynomial is evenly divisible by the factor $(x - k)$.

EXAMPLE

61. Find the roots of the polynomial: $y = 3t^4 - 48$

Rational Functions
WORKING with RATIONAL FUNCTIONS

Rational functions are ratios of polynomial functions in the form $f(x) = \frac{g(x)}{h(x)}$. Just like rational numbers, rational functions form a closed system under addition, subtraction, multiplication, and division by a nonzero rational expression. This means adding two rational functions, for example, results in another rational function.

To add or subtract rational expressions, the least common denominator of the factors in the denominator must be found. Then, numerators are added, just like adding rational numbers. To multiply rational expressions, factors can be multiplied straight across, canceling factors that appear in the numerator and denominator. To divide rational functions, use the "invert and multiply" rule.

Rational equations are solved by multiplying through the equation by the least common denominator of factors in the denominator. Just like with radical equations, this process can result in extraneous solutions, so all answers need to be checked by plugging them into the original equation.

EXAMPLES

62. If $f(x) = \frac{2}{3x^2y}$ and $g(x) = \frac{5}{21y}$, find the difference between the functions, $f(x) - g(x)$.

63. If $f(x) = \frac{(x-1)(x+2)^2}{5x^2 + 10x}$ and $g(x) = \frac{x^2 + x - 2}{x + 5}$, find the quotient $\frac{f(x)}{g(x)}$.

64. Solve the rational equation $\frac{x}{x+2} + \frac{2}{x^2 + 5x + 6} = \frac{5}{x+3}$.

GRAPHING RATIONAL FUNCTIONS

Rational functions are graphed by examining the function to find key features of the graph, including asymptotes, intercepts, and holes.

A **VERTICAL ASYMPTOTE** exists at any value that makes the denominator of a (simplified) rational function equal zero. A vertical asymptote is a vertical line through an x value that is not in the domain of the rational function (the function is undefined at this value because division by 0 is not allowed). The function approaches, but never crosses, this line, and the y values increase (or decrease) without bound (or "go to infinity") as this x value is approached.

To find x-intercepts and vertical asymptotes, factor the numerator and denominator of the function. Cancel any terms that appear in the numerator and denominator (if there are any). These values will appear as **HOLES** on the final graph. Since a fraction only equals 0 when its numerator is 0, set the simplified numerator equal to 0 and solve to find the x-intercepts. Next, set the denominator equal to 0 and solve to find the vertical asymptotes.

HORIZONTAL ASYMPTOTES are horizontal lines that describe the "end behavior" of a rational function. In other words, the horizontal asymptote describes what happens to the y-values of the function as the x-values

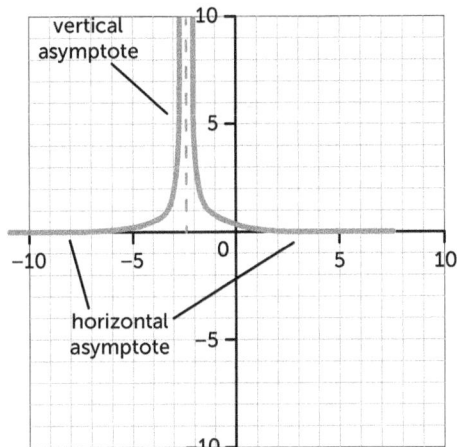

Figure 2.12. Graphing Rational Functions

get very large ($x \to \infty$) or very small ($x \to -\infty$). A horizontal asymptote occurs if the degree of the numerator of a rational function is less than or equal to the degree in the denominator. The table summarizes the conditions for horizontal asymptotes:

Table 2.7. Conditions for Horizontal Asymptotes

For polynomials with first terms $\frac{ax^n}{bx^d}$ ...

$n < d$	as $x \to \infty$, $y \to 0$ as $x \to -\infty$, $y \to 0$	The x-axis ($y = 0$) is a horizontal asymptote.
$n = d$	as $x \to \pm\infty$, $y \to \frac{a}{b}$	There is a horizontal asymptote at $y = \frac{a}{b}$.
$n > d$	as $x \to \infty$, $y \to \infty$ or $-\infty$ as $x \to -\infty$, $y \to \infty$ or $-\infty$	There is no horizontal asymptote.

EXAMPLES

65. Create a function that has an x-intercept at (5, 0) and vertical asymptotes at $x = 1$ and $x = -1$.

66. Graph the function: $f(x) = \frac{3x^2 - 12x}{x^2 - 2x - 3}$.

Radical Functions

RADICAL FUNCTIONS have rational (fractional) exponents, or include the radical symbol. For example, $f(x) = 2(x - 5)^{\frac{1}{3}}$ and $g(t) = \sqrt[4]{5 - x}$ are radical functions. The domain of even root parent functions is $0 \leq x \leq \infty$ and the range is $y \geq 0$. For odd root parent functions, the domain is all real numbers (because you can take cube roots, etc., of negative numbers). The range is also all real numbers.

To solve equations involving radical functions, first isolate the radical part of the expression. Then "undo" the fractional exponent by raising both sides to the reciprocal of the fractional exponent (for example, undo square roots by squaring both sides). Then solve the equation using inverse operations, as always. All answers should be checked by plugging them back into the original equation, as **EXTRANEOUS SOLUTIONS** result when an equation is raised to powers on both sides. This means there may be some answers that are not actually solutions, and should be eliminated.

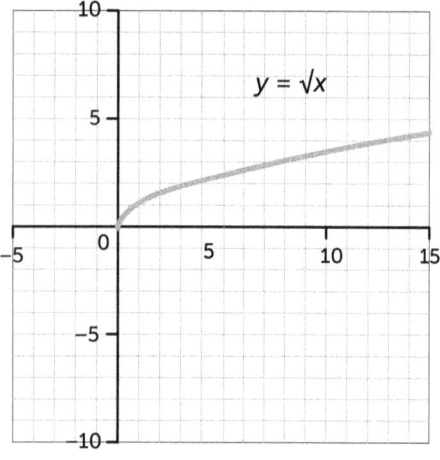

Figure 2.13. Radical Parent Function

EXAMPLES

67. Solve the equation: $\sqrt{2x - 5} + 4 = x$

68. Solve the equation: $2(x^2 - 7x)^{\frac{2}{3}} = 8$

Answer Key

1. $5(m - 2)^3 + 3m^2 - \frac{m}{4} - 1$

   Plug the value 4 in for m in the expression.

   $= 5(4 - 2)^3 + 3(4)^2 - \frac{4}{4} - 1$

   Calculate all the expressions inside the parentheses.

   $= 5(2)^3 + 3(4)^2 - \frac{4}{4} - 1$

   Simplify all exponents.

   $= 5(8) + 3(16) - \frac{4}{4} - 1$

   Perform multiplication and division from left to right.

   $= 40 + 48 - 1 - 1$

   Perform addition and subtraction from left to right.

   = 86

2. The only like terms in both expressions are $12x$ and $8x$, so these two terms will be added, and all other terms will remain the same.

   $a + b = (12x + 8x) + 7xy - 9y - 9xz + 7z =$ **$20x + 7xy - 9y - 9xz + 7z$**

3. $5x(x^2 - 2c + 10)$

   Distribute and multiply the term outside the parentheses to all three terms inside the parentheses.

   $(5x)(x^2) = 5x^3$

   $(5x)(-2c) = -10xc$

   $(5x)(10) = 50x$

   $= 5x^3 - 10xc + 50x$

4. $(x^2 - 5)(2x - x^3)$

   Apply FOIL: first, outside, inside, and last.

   $(x^2)(2x) = 2x^3$

   $(x^2)(-x^3) = -x^5$

   $(-5)(2x) = -10x$

   $(-5)(-x^3) = 5x^3$

   Combine like terms and put them in order.

   $= 2x^3 - x^5 - 10x + 5x^3$

   $= -x^5 + 7x^3 - 10x$

5. $16z^2 + 48z$

   Both terms have a z, and 16 is a common factor of both 16 and 48. So the greatest common factor is $16z$. Factor out the GCF.

   $16z^2 + 48z$

   $= 16z(z + 3)$

6. $6m^3 + 12m^3n - 9m^2$

   All the terms share the factor m^2, and 3 is the greatest common factor of 6, 12, and 9. So, the GCF is $3m^2$.

   $= 3m^2(2m + 4mn - 3)$

7. $16x^2 + 52x + 30$

   Remove the GCF of 2.

   $= 2(8x^2 + 26x + 15)$

   To factor the polynomial in the parentheses, calculate $ac = (8)(15) = 120$, and consider all the pairs of numbers that multiply to be 120: 1×120, 2×60, 3×40, 4×30, 5×24, 6×20, 8×15, and 10×12. Of these pairs, choose the pair that adds to be the b-value 26 (6 and 20).

   $= 2(8x^2 + 6x + 20x + 15)$

   Group.

   $= 2[(8x^2 + 6x) + (20x + 15)]$

   Factor out the GCF of each group.

   $= 2[2x(4x + 3) + 5(4x + 3)]$

   Factor out the common binomial.

   $= 2[(4x + 3)(2x + 5)]$

   $= 2(4x + 3)(2x + 5)$

If there are no values *r* and *s* that multiply to be *ac* and add to be *b*, then the polynomial is prime and cannot be factored.

8. $-21x^2 - x + 10$

   Factor out the negative.

   $= -(21x^2 + x - 10)$

   Factor the polynomial in the parentheses.

   $ac = 210$ and $b = 1$

   The numbers 15 and −14 can be multiplied to get 210 and subtracted to get 1.

   $= -(21x^2 - 14x + 15x - 10)$

   Group.

   $= -[(21x^2 - 14x) + (15x - 10)]$

   Factor out the GCF of each group.

   $= -[7x(3x - 2) + 5(3x - 2)]$

   Factor out the common binomial.

   $= -(3x - 2)(7x + 5)$

9. $\frac{100(x + 5)}{20} = 1$

   Multiply both sides by 20 to cancel out the denominator.

   $(20)\left(\frac{100(x + 5)}{20}\right) = (1)(20)$

   $100(x + 5) = 20$

   Distribute 100 through the parentheses.

   $100x + 500 = 20$

   "Undo" the +500 by subtracting 500 on both sides of the equation to isolate the variable term.

   $100x = -480$

   "Undo" the multiplication by 100 by dividing by 100 on both sides to solve for *x*.

   $x = \frac{-480}{100}$

   $x = -4.8$

10. $2(x + 2)^2 - 2x^2 + 10 = 42$

    Eliminate the exponents on the left side.

    $2(x + 2)(x + 2) - 2x^2 + 10 = 42$

    Apply FOIL.

    $2(x^2 + 4x + 4) - 2x^2 + 10 = 42$

    Distribute the 2.

    $2x^2 + 8x + 8 - 2x^2 + 10 = 42$

    Combine like terms on the left-hand side.

    $8x + 18 = 42$

    Isolate the variable. "Undo" +18 by subtracting 18 on both sides.

    $8x = 24$

    "Undo" multiplication by 8 by dividing both sides by 8.

    $x = 3$

11. $\frac{A(3B + 2D)}{2N} = 5M - 6$

    Multiply both sides by 2*N* to clear the fraction, and distribute the *A* through the parentheses.

    $3AB + 2AD = 10MN - 12N$

    Isolate the term with the *D* in it by moving 3*AB* to the other side of the equation.

    $2AD = 10MN - 12N - 3AB$

    Divide both sides by 2*A* to get *D* alone on the right-hand side.

    $D = \frac{(10MN - 12N - 3AB)}{2A}$

12. The *y*-intercept can be identified on the graph as (0,3).

    $b = 3$

    To find the slope, choose any two points and plug the values into the slope equation. The two points chosen here are (2,−1) and (3,−3).

    $m = \frac{(-3) - (-1)}{3 - 2} = \frac{-2}{1} = -2$

    Replace *m* with −2 and *b* with 3 in $y = mx + b$.

    $y = -2x + 3$

13. $6x - 2y - 8 = 0$

Rearrange the equation into slope-intercept form by solving the equation for y.

$-2y = -6x + 8$

$y = \frac{-6x + 8}{-2}$

$y = 3x - 4$

The slope is 3, the value attached to x.

$m = 3$

14. $(-2,5)$ and $(-5,3)$

Calculate the slope.

$m = \frac{3 - 5}{(-5) - (-2)} = \frac{-2}{-3} = \frac{2}{3}$

To find b, plug into the equation $y = mx + b$ the slope for m and a set of points for x and y.

$5 = \frac{2}{3}(-2) + b$

$5 = \frac{-4}{3} + b$

$b = \frac{19}{3}$

Replace m and b to find the equation of the line.

$y = \frac{2}{3}x + \frac{19}{3}$

15. The line has a rise of 0 and a run of 1, so the slope is $\frac{0}{1} = 0$. There is no x-intercept. The y-intercept is $(0,2)$, meaning that the b-value in the slope-intercept form is 2.

$y = 0x + 2$, or $y = 2$

16. Solve the system with substitution. Solve one equation for one variable.

$2x - 4y = 28$

$x = 2y + 14$

Plug in the resulting expression for x in the second equation and simplify.

$4x - 12y = 36$

$4(2y + 14) - 12y = 36$

$8y + 56 - 12y = 36$

$-4y = -20$

$y = 5$

Plug the solved variable into either equation to find the second variable.

$2x - 4y = 28$

$2x - 4(5) = 28$

$2x - 20 = 28$

$2x = 48$

$x = 24$

The answer is $y = 5$ and $x = 24$ or **(24,5)**.

17. Isolate the variable in one equation.

$3 = -4x + y$

$y = 4x + 3$

Plug the expression into the second equation.

Both equations have slope 4. This means the graphs of the equations are parallel lines, so no intersection (solution) exists.

$16x = 4y + 2$

$16x = 4(4x + 3) + 2$

$16x = 16x + 12 + 2$

$0 = 14$

No solution exists.

18. Because solving for x or y in either equation will result in messy fractions, this problem is best solved using elimination. The goal is to eliminate one of the variables by making the coefficients in front of one set of variables the same, but with different signs, and then adding both equations.

To eliminate the x's in this problem, find the least common multiple of coefficients 6 and 4. The smallest number that both 6 and 4 divide into evenly is 12.

Algebra   45

Multiply the top equation by −2, and the bottom equation by 3.

$6x + 10y = 18 \xrightarrow{(-2)} -12x - 20y = -36$

$4x + 15y = 37 \xrightarrow{(3)} 12x + 45y = 111$

Add the two equations to eliminate the x's.

$25y = 75$

Solve for y.

$y = 3$

Replace y with 3 in either of the original equations.

$6x + 10(3) = 18$

$6x + 30 = 18$

$x = -2$

The solution is **(−2,3)**.

19. Write the system in matrix form, $AX = B$.

$\begin{bmatrix} 2 & -3 \\ 3 & -4 \end{bmatrix} \begin{bmatrix} x \\ y \end{bmatrix} = \begin{bmatrix} -5 \\ -8 \end{bmatrix}$

Calculate the inverse of Matrix **A**.

$\begin{bmatrix} 2 & -3 \\ 3 & -4 \end{bmatrix}^{-1} = \frac{1}{(2)(-4) - (-3)(3)} \begin{bmatrix} -4 & 3 \\ -3 & 2 \end{bmatrix}$

$= \begin{bmatrix} -4 & 3 \\ -3 & 2 \end{bmatrix}$

Multiply **B** by the inverse of **A**.

$\begin{bmatrix} x \\ y \end{bmatrix} = \begin{bmatrix} -4 & 3 \\ -3 & 2 \end{bmatrix} \begin{bmatrix} -5 \\ -8 \end{bmatrix} = \begin{bmatrix} -4 \\ -1 \end{bmatrix}$

Match up the 2 × 1 matrices to identify x and y.

x = −4

y = −1

20. Identify the quantities.

Number of tickets = x

Cost per ticket = 5

Cost for x tickets = 5x

Total cost = 28

Entry fee = 3

Set up equations. The total cost for x tickets will be equal to the cost for x tickets plus the $3 flat fee.

$5x + 3 = 28$

Solve the equation for x.

$5x + 3 = 28$

$5x = 25$

$x = 5$

The student bought **5 tickets**.

21. Assign variables.

Student price = s

Nonstudent price = n

Create two equations using the number of shirts Kelly sold and the money she earned.

$10s + 4n = 84$

$20s + 10n = 185$

Solve the system of equations using substitution.

$10s + 4n = 84$

$10n = -20s + 185$

$n = -2s + 18.5$

$10s + 4(-2s + 18.5) = 84$

$10s - 8s + 74 = 84$

$2s + 74 = 84$

$2s = 10$

$s = 5$

The student cost for shirts is **$5**.

22. $3z + 10 < -z$

Collect nonvariable terms to one side.

$3z < -z - 10$

Collect variable terms to the other side.

$4z < -10$

Isolate the variable.

z < −2.5

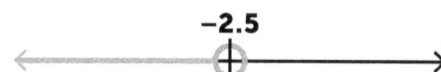

23. $2x - 3 > 5(x - 4) - (x - 4)$

    Distribute 5 through the parentheses and −1 through the parentheses.

    $2x - 3 > 5x - 20 - x + 4$

    Combine like terms.

    $2x - 3 > 4x - 16$

    Collect x-terms to one side, and constant terms to the other side.

    $-2x > -13$

    Divide both sides by −2; since dividing by a negative, reverse the direction of the inequality.

    $x < 6.5$

24. $2x + 4 < -18$ or $4(x + 2) > 18$

    Solve each inequality independently.

    $2x < -14$ $4x + 8 > 18$
    $x < -7$ $4x > 10$
                  $x > 2.5$

    The solution to the original compound inequality is **the set of all x for which $x < -7$ or $x > 2.5$**.

25. $-1 \le 3(x + 2) - 1 \le x + 3$

    Break up the compound inequality into two inequalities.

    $-1 \le 3(x + 2) - 1$ and
    $3(x + 2) - 1 \le x + 3$

    Solve separately.

    $-1 \le 3x + 6 - 1$ $3x + 6 - 1 \le x + 3$
    $-6 \le 3x$ $2x \le -2$
    $-2 \le x$ and $x \le -1$

    The only values of x that satisfy *both* inequalities are the values between −2 and −1 (inclusive).

    $-2 \le x \le -1$

26. Find the x- and y-intercepts.

    $3x + 6y \le 12$

    $3(0) + 6y = 12$

    $y = 2$

    y-intercept: (0,2)

    $3x + 6(0) \le 12$

    $x = 4$

    x-intercept: (4,0)

    Graph the line using the intercepts, and shade below the line.

    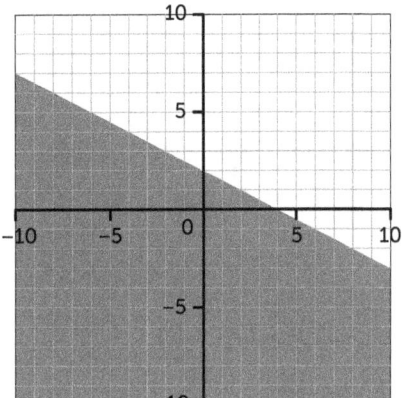

27. To solve the system, graph all three inequalities in the same plane; then identify the area where the three solutions overlap. All

    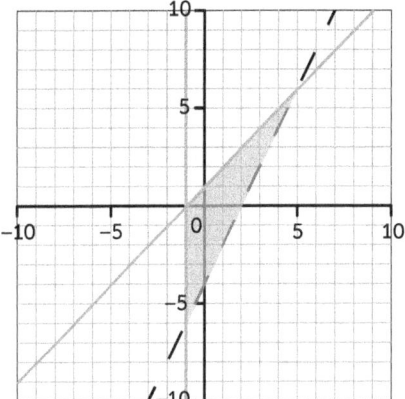

    points (x,y) in this area will be solutions to the system since they satisfy all three inequalities.

28. Determine the equation of the boundary line.

y-intercept: (0,2)

slope: 3

y = 3x + 2

Replace the equal sign with the appropriate inequality: the line is dotted and the shading is above the line, indicating that the symbol should be "greater than." Check a point: for example (1,5) is a solution since 5 > 3(–1) + 2.

y > 3x + 2

29. This quadratic is given in vertex form, with $h = -3$ and $k = 2$. The vertex of this equation is (–3,2). The line of symmetry is the vertical line that passes through this point. Since the x-value of the point is –3, the line of symmetry is **x = –3**.

30. $y = -3x^2 + 24x - 27$

    This quadratic equation is in standard form. Use the formula for finding the x-value of the vertex.

    $x = -\frac{b}{2a}$ where $a = -3$, $b = 24$

    $x = -\frac{24}{2(-3)} = 4$

    Plug $x = 4$ into the original equation to find the corresponding y-value.

    $y = -3(4)^2 + 24(4) - 27 = 21$

    The vertex is at **(4, 21)**.

31. $y = -3x^2 + 24x - 27$

    Move c to the other side of the equation.

    $y + 27 = -3x^2 + 24x$

    Divide through by a (–3 in this example).

    $\frac{y}{-3} - 9 = x^2 - 8x$

    Take half of the new b, square it, and add that quantity to both sides: $\frac{1}{2}(-8) = -4$. Squaring it gives $(-4)^2 = 16$.

    $\frac{y}{-3} - 9 + 16 = x^2 - 8x + 16$

    Simplify the left side, and write the right side as a binomial squared.

    $\frac{y}{-3} + 7 = (x - 4)^2$

    Subtract 7, and then multiply through by –3 to isolate y.

    y = –3(x – 4)² + 21

32. Method 1: Make $y = 0$; isolate x by square rooting both sides:

    Make $y = 0$.

    $0 = -(x + 3)^2 + 1$

    Subtract 1 from both sides.

    $-1 = -(x + 3)^2$

    Divide by –1 on both sides.

    $1 = (x + 3)^2$

    Square root both sides. Don't forget to write plus OR minus 1.

    $(x + 3) = \pm 1$

    Write two equations using +1 and –1.

    $(x + 3) = 1$ or $(x + 3) = -1$

    Solve both equations. These are the zeros.

    x = –2 or x = –4

    Method 2: Convert vertex form to standard form, and then use the quadratic formula.

    Put the equation in standard form by distributing and combining like terms.

    $y = -(x + 3)^2 + 1$

    $y = -(x^2 + 6x + 9) + 1$

    $y = -x^2 - 6x - 8$

    Find the zeros using the quadratic formula.

    $x = \frac{-b \pm \sqrt{(b^2 - 4ac)}}{2a}$

    $x = \frac{-(-6) \pm \sqrt{(-6)^2 - 4(-1)(-8)}}{2(-1)}$

    $x = \frac{6 \pm \sqrt{36 - 32}}{-2}$

$$x = \frac{6 \pm \sqrt{4}}{-2}$$

x = −4, −2

33. This polynomial can be factored in the form $(z − 2)(z − 2) = 0$, so the only root is $z = 2$. There is only one x-intercept, and the vertex of the graph is *on* the x-axis.

34. If the quadratic has zeros at $x = −3$ and $x = 2$, then it has factors of $(x + 3)$ and $(x − 2)$. The quadratic function can be written in the factored form $y = a(x + 3)(x − 2)$. To find the a-value, plug in the point $(−2, 8)$ for x and y:

    $8 = a(−2 + 3)(−2 − 2)$

    $8 = a(−4)$

    $a = −2$

    The quadratic function is:

    y = −2(x + 3)(x − 2).

35. Start by marking the vertex at (3,4) and recognizing this parabola opens upward. The line of symmetry is $x = 3$. Now, plug in an easy value for x to get one point on the curve; then use symmetry to find another point. In this case, choose $x = 2$ (one unit to the left of the line of symmetry) and solve for y:

    $y = 2(2 − 3)^2 + 4$

    $y = 2(1) + 4$

    $y = 6$

    Thus the point (2,6) is on the curve. Then use symmetry to find the corresponding point one unit to the right of the line of symmetry, which must also have a y value of 6. This point is (4,6). Draw a parabola through the points.

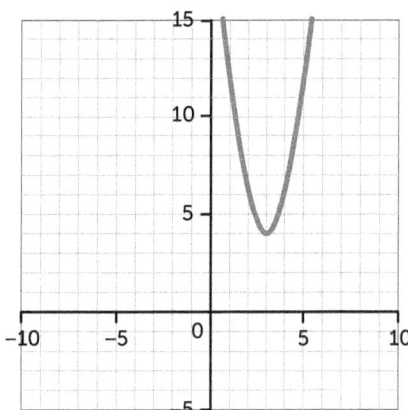

36. Locate the vertex and plug values for h and k into the vertex form of the quadratic equation.

    $(h, k) = (0, 5)$

    $y = a(x − h)^2 + k$

    $y = a(x − 0)^2 + 5$

    $y = ax^2 + 5$

    Choose another point on the graph to plug into this equation to solve for a.

    $(x, y) = (1, 2)$

    $y = ax^2 + 5$

    $2 = a(1)^2 + 5$

    $a = −3$

    Plug a into the vertex form of the equation.

    y = −3x² + 5

37. Find the zeros of the inequality.

    $x^2 − 4x = 12$

    $x^2 − 4x − 12 = 0$

    $(x + 2)(x − 6) = 0$

    $x = −2, 6$

    Create a table or number line with the intervals created by the zeros. Use a test value to determine whether the expression is positive or negative.

Algebra

x	$(x+2)(x-6)$
$-\infty < x < -2$	+
$-2 < x < 6$	−
$6 < x < \infty$	+

Identify the values of x which make the expression positive.

$x < -2$ or $x > 6$

38. Set the quantity inside the parentheses equal to 27 or −27, and solve:

$x - 3 = -27$

$x = -24$

$x - 3 = 27$

$x = 30$

39. The first step is to isolate the absolute value part of the equation. Multiplying both sides by 5 gives:

$|r - 7| = 135$

If the quantity in the absolute value bars is 135 or −135, then the absolute value would be 135:

$r - 7 = -135$

$r = -128$

$r - 7 = 135$

$r = 142$

40. $\left|\frac{3x}{7}\right| \geq 4 - x$

Simplify the equation.

$\frac{|3x|}{7} \geq 4 - x$

$|3x| \geq 28 - 7x$

Create and solve two inequalities. When including the negative answer, flip the inequality.

$3x \geq 28 - 7x$

$10x \geq 28$

$x \geq \frac{28}{10}$

$-(3x) \leq 28 - 7x$

$-3x \leq 28 - 7x$

$4x \leq 28$

$x \leq 7$

Combine the two answers to find the solution set.

$\frac{28}{10} \leq x \leq 7$

41. This function has an asymptote at $x = 9$, so is not defined there. Otherwise, the function is defined for all other values of x.

D: $-\infty < x < 9$ or $9 < x < \infty$

Interval notation can also be used to show domain and range. Round brackets indicate that an end value is not included, and square brackets show that it is. The symbol ∪ means *or*, and the symbol ∩ means *and*. For example, the statement (−infinity, 4) ∪ (4, infinity) describes the set of all real numbers except 4.

Since the function has a horizontal asymptote at $y = 1$ that it never crosses, the function never takes the value 1, so the range is all real numbers except 1:

R: $-\infty < y < 1$ or $1 < y < \infty$.

42. For the domain, this graph goes on to the right to positive infinity. Its leftmost point, however, is $x = -2$. Therefore, its domain is all real numbers equal to or greater than −2, **D: − 2 ≤ x < ∞**, or **[−2,∞)**.

The lowest range value is $y = 2$. Although it has a decreasing slope, this function continues to rise. Therefore, the domain is all real numbers greater than 2, **R: 2 ≤ y < ∞ or [2,∞)**.

43. $f(4)$ if $f(x) = x^3 - 2x + \sqrt{x}$

Plug in 4.

$f(4) = (4)^3 - 2(4) + \sqrt{(4)}$

Follow the PEMDAS order of operations.

= 64 − 8 + 2 = **58**

44. For a set of numbers to represent a function, every input must generate a unique output. Therefore, if the same input (x) appears more than once in the table, determine if that input has two different outputs. If so, then the table does not represent a function.

   A) This table is not a function because input value 1 has two different outputs (1 and 3).
   B) Table B is not function because 0 is the only input and results in four different values.
   C) This table shows a function because each input has one output.
   D) This table also has one input going to two different values, so it is not a function.

45. Replace f(x) with y.
   y = 5x + 5
   Switch the places of y and x.
   x = 5y + 5
   Solve for y.
   x = 5y + 5
   x − 5 = 5y
   y = $\frac{x}{5}$ − 1
   $f^{-1}(x) = \frac{x}{5} - 1$

46. This is a linear graph with some clear coordinates: (−5,0), (0,−1), (5,−2), and (10,−3). This means the inverse function will have coordinate (0,−5), (−1,0), (−2,5), and (−3,10). The inverse function is reflected over the line y = x and is the line $f^{-1}(x) = -5(x + 1)$ on the graph.

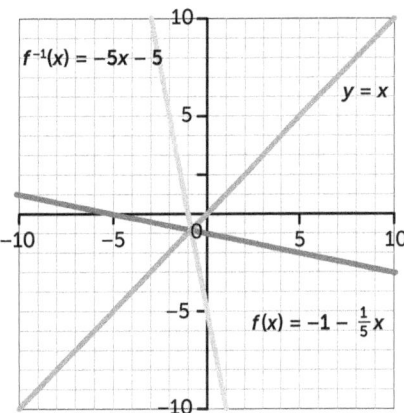

47. (y ∘ z)(−4) = y(z(−4))
   Starting on the inside, evaluate z.
   z(−4)
   = 3(−4) − 3 = −12 − 3 = −15
   Replace z(−4) with −15, and simplify.
   y(z(−4))
   = y(−15) = 2(−15) − 1
   = −30 − 1 = **−31**

48. Replace x in the k(x) function with ($\frac{1}{2}$x − 2)
   (k ∘ t)(x) = k(t(x))
   = k($\frac{1}{2}$x − 2) = $\frac{1}{2}$($\frac{1}{2}$x − 2) − 3
   Simplify.
   = $\frac{1}{4}$x − 1 − 3 = $\frac{1}{4}$x − 4
   (k O t)(x) = $\frac{1}{4x}$ − 4

49. N(4) = 400(4) = 1600 and means that 4 hours after the park opens there are 1600 people in the park. W(N(4)) = W(1600) = 96 and means that 4 hours after the park opens the wait time is about **96 minutes** for the ride.

50. This function is the absolute value function with a vertical shift up of 4 units (since the 4 is outside the absolute value bars), and a horizontal shift left of 1 unit (since it is inside the bars). The vertex of the graph is at (–1,4) and the line $x = -1$ is an axis of symmetry.

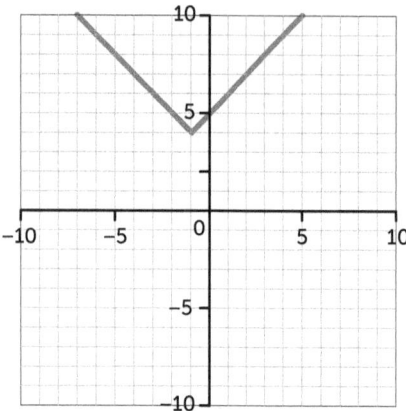

51. The negative sign in front of the absolute value means the graph will be reflected across the *x*-axis, so it will open down. The 3 causes a vertical stretch of the function, which results in a narrower graph. The basic curve is shifted 2 units right (since the –2 is an inside change) and 2 units up (since the +2 is an outside change), so the vertex is at (2,2).

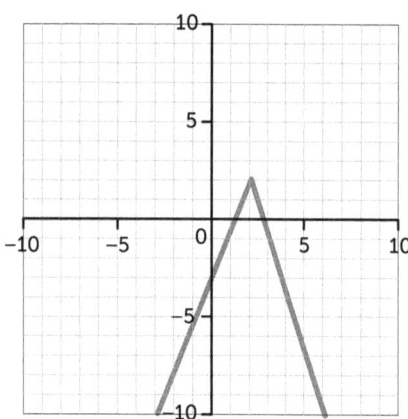

52. One way to do this is to use a table:

x	$5^x - 2$
–2	$\frac{1}{25} - 2 = -\frac{49}{25}$
–1	$\frac{1}{5} - 2 = -\frac{9}{5}$
0	$1 - 2 = -1$
1	$5 - 2 = 3$
2	$25 - 2 = 23$

Another way to graph this is simply to see this function as the parent function $y = b^x$ (with $b = 5$), shifted down by a vertical shift of 2 units. Thus the new horizontal asymptote will be at $y = 2$, and the new *y*-intercept will be $y = -1$.

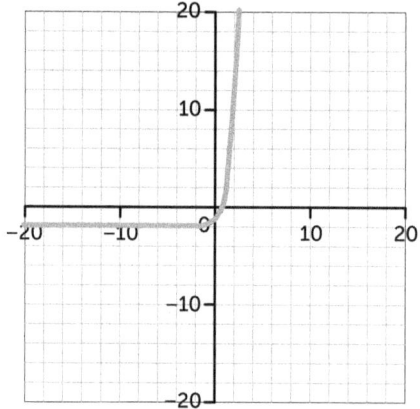

53. Any time a question concerns growth or decay, an exponential function must be created to solve it. In this case, create a table with initial value *a*, and a daily growth rate of $(1+0.05) = 1.05$ per day.

Days (x)	Height (h)
0	a
1	1.05a
2	$1.05(1.05a) = (1.05)^2 a$
3	$(1.05)^2(1.05a) = (1.05)^3 a$
x	$(1.05)^x a$

After six days the height of the grass is $(1.05)^6 =$ **1.34 times as tall**. The grass would grow 34% in one week.

54. $4^{x+1} = \frac{1}{256}$

Find a common base and rewrite the equation.

$4^{x+1} = 4^{-4}$

Set the exponents equal and solve for x.

$x + 1 = -4$

$x = -5$

55. Since division of a term can be written as a subtraction problem, this simplifies to:

$\log_5(25) - \log_5(x)$

The first term asks "what power of 5 gives 25?" The power is 2. Therefore, the most expanded form is: **$2 - \log_5(x)$**

56. $\ln x + \ln 4 = 2\ln 4 - \ln 2$

Apply the log of product and log of exponent rules.

$\ln(4x) = \ln 4^2 - \ln 2$

$\ln(4x) = \ln 16 - \ln 2$

Follow log of quotient rule.

$\ln(4x) = \ln 8$

Set the arguments equal to each other.

$4x = 8$

$x = 2$

57. $2^x = 40$

Take the $\log_2$ of both sides.

$\log_2 2^x = \log_2 40$

Drop the x down using properties of logs.

$x \log_2 2 = \log_2 40$

$\log_2 2$ simplifies to 1.

$x = \log_2 40$

Use the change of base rule or a calculator to calculate the value of $\log_2(40)$.

≈ 5.32

58. Plug the given values into the growth equation.

$y = a(1 + r)^t$

$36{,}000 = 120(1 + 1.24)^t$

Use the properties of logarithms to solve the equation.

$300 = (2.24)^t$

$\log_{2.24} 300 = \log_{2.24}(2.24)^t$

$7.07 \approx t$

The number of text messages will pass 36,000 in **7.07 years**.

59. Identify the variables.

$t = \frac{22}{5.5} = 4$

$r = 0.5$

$a = ?$

Plug these values into the decay formula and solve.

$20 = a(1 - 0.50)^4$

$20 = a(0.5)^4$

$20 = a(\frac{1}{2})^4$

$20 = a(\frac{1}{16})$

$320 = a$

The original weight is **320 grams**.

60. Identify the variables.

$r = 0.05$

$n = 5$

$t = 12$

$P = 50$

Use the compound-interest formula, since this problem has many steps of growth within a time period.

$A = 50(1 + \frac{0.05}{5})^{5(12)}$

$A = 50(1.01)^{60}$

$A = 50(1.82) = 90.83$

Subtract the original deposit to find the amount of interest earned.

$90.83 - 50 =$ **$40.83**

61. $y = 3t^4 - 48$

Factor the polynomial. Remove the common factor of 3 from each term and make $y = 0$.

$3(t^4 - 16) = 0$

Factor the difference of squares. $t^2 - 4$ is also a difference of squares.

$3(t^2 - 4)(t^2 + 4) = 0$

$3(t + 2)(t - 2)(t^2 + 2) = 0$

Set each factor equal to zero. Solve each equation.

$t + 2 = 0$	$t - 2 = 0$	$t^2 + 2 = 0$
$t = -2$	$t = 2$	$t^2 = -2$
$t = \pm\sqrt{-2} = \pm 2i$		

This degree 4 polynomial has four roots, two real roots: **2 or −2**, and two complex roots: **2i or −2i**. The graph will have two x-intercepts at (−2,0) and (2,0).

62. Write the difference.

$f(x) - g(x) = \dfrac{2}{3x^2 y} - \dfrac{5}{21y}$

Figure out the least common denominator. Every factor must be represented to the highest power it appears in either denominator. So, the LCD = $3(7)x^2 y$.

$= \dfrac{2}{3x^2 y}\left(\dfrac{7}{7}\right) - \dfrac{5}{21y}\left(\dfrac{x^2}{x^2}\right)$

$= \dfrac{14}{21x^2 y} - \dfrac{5x^2}{21x^2 y}$

Subtract the numerators the find the answer.

$f(x) - g(x) = \dfrac{\mathbf{14 - 5x^2}}{\mathbf{21x^2 y}}$

63. Write the quotient; then invert and multiply.

$\dfrac{f(x)}{g(x)} = \dfrac{\frac{(x-1)(x+2)^2}{5x^2 + 10x}}{\frac{x^2 + x - 2}{x + 5}}$

$= \dfrac{(x-1)(x+2)^2}{5x^2 + 10x} \times \dfrac{x+5}{x^2 + x - 2}$

Factor all expressions, and then cancel any factors that appear in both the numerator and the denominator.

$= \dfrac{(x-1)(x+2)^2}{5x(x+2)} \times \dfrac{x+5}{(x+2)(x-1)}$

$= \dfrac{\mathbf{x + 5}}{\mathbf{5x}}$

64. $\dfrac{x}{x+2} + \dfrac{2}{x^2 + 5x + 6} = \dfrac{5}{x+3}$

Factor any denominators that need factoring.

$\dfrac{x}{x+2} + \dfrac{2}{(x+3)(x+2)} = \dfrac{5}{x+3}$

Multiply through by the LCM of the denominators, which is $(x+2)(x+3)$.

$x(x+3) + 2 = 5(x+2)$

Simplify the expression.

$x^2 + 3x + 2 - 5x - 10 = 0$

$x^2 - 2x - 8 = 0$

Factor the quadratic.

$(x-4)(x+2) = 0$

Plugging $x = -2$ into the original equation results in a 0 in the denominator. So this solution is an extraneous solution and must be thrown out.

Plugging in $x = 4$ gives:

$\dfrac{4}{6} + \dfrac{2}{16 + 20 + 6} = \dfrac{5}{7}$.

So **x = 4** is a solution to the equation.

65. The numerator will have a factor of $(x - 5)$ in order to have a zero at $x = 5$. The denominator will need factors of $(x - 1)$ and $(x + 1)$ in order for the denominator to be 0 when x is 1 or −1. Thus, one function that would have these features is

$y = \dfrac{(x-5)}{(x+1)(x-1)} = \dfrac{\mathbf{x - 5}}{\mathbf{x^2 - 1}}$

66. $f(x) = \dfrac{3x^2 - 12x}{x^2 - 2x - 3}$.

Factor the equation.

$y = \dfrac{3x^2 - 12x}{x^2 - 2x - 3} = \dfrac{3x(x-4)}{(x-3)(x+1)}$

Find the roots by setting the numerator equal to zero.

$3x(x - 4) = 0$

$x = 0, 4$

Find the vertical asymptotes by setting the denominator equal to zero.

$(x - 3)(x + 1) = 0$

$x = -1, 3$

Find the horizontal asymptote by looking at the degree of the numerator and the denominator.

The degree of the numerator and denominator are equal, so the asymptote is the ratio of the coefficients:

$y = \frac{3}{1} = 3$

Use the roots and asymptotes to graph the function.

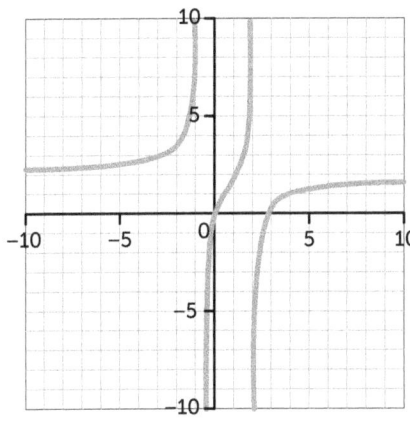

67. $\sqrt{2x - 5} + 4 = x$

Isolate the $\sqrt{2x - 5}$ by subtracting 4.

$\sqrt{2x - 5} = x - 4$

Square both sides to clear the $\sqrt{}$.

$2x - 5 = x^2 - 8x + 16$

Collect all variables to one side.

$x^2 - 10x + 21 = 0$

Factor and solve.

$(x - 7)(x - 3) = 0$

$x = 7$ or $x = 3$

Check solutions by plugging into the original, as squaring both sides can cause extraneous solutions.

True, $x = 7$ is a solution.

False, $x = 3$ is NOT a solution (extraneous solution).

$\sqrt{2(7) - 5} + 4 = 7$

$\sqrt{2(3) - 5} + 4 = 3$

$\sqrt{9} + 4 = 7$

$\sqrt{1} + 4 = 3$

$x = 7$

68. $2(x^2 - 7x)^{\frac{2}{3}} = 8$

Divide by 2 to isolate the radical.

$(x^2 - 7x)^{\frac{2}{3}} = 4$

Raise both sides to the $\frac{3}{2}$ power to clear the $\frac{2}{3}$ exponent.

$x^2 - 7x = 4^{\frac{3}{2}}$

$x^2 - 7x = 8$

This is a quadratic, so collect all terms to one side.

$x^2 - 7x - 8 = 0$

Factor and solve for x.

$(x - 8)(x + 1) = 0$

$x = 8$ or $x = -1$

Plugging both solutions into the original equation confirms that both are solutions.

CHAPTER THREE
Geometry

Properties of Shapes
BASIC DEFINITIONS

The basic figures from which many other geometric shapes are built are points, lines, and planes. A **POINT** is a location in a plane. It has no size or shape, but is represented by a dot. It is labeled using a capital letter.

A **LINE** is a one-dimensional collection of points that extends infinitely in both directions. At least two points are needed to define a line, and any points that lie on the same line are **COLINEAR**. Lines are represented by two points, such as *A* and *B*, and the line symbol: ($\overleftrightarrow{AB}$). Two lines on the same plane will intersect unless they are **PARALLEL**, meaning they have the same slope. Lines that intersect at a 90 degree angle are **PERPENDICULAR**.

A **LINE SEGMENT** has two endpoints and a finite length. The length of a segment, called the measure of the segment, is the distance from *A* to *B*. A line segment is a subset of a line, and is also denoted with two points, but with a segment symbol: ($\overline{AB}$). The **MIDPOINT** of a line segment is the point at which the segment is divided into two equal parts. A line, segment, or plane that passes through the midpoint of a segment is called a **BISECTOR** of the segment, since it cuts the segment into two equal segments.

A **RAY** has one endpoint and extends indefinitely in one direction. It is defined by its endpoint, followed by any other point on the ray: $\overrightarrow{AB}$. It is important that the first letter represents the endpoint. A ray is sometimes called a half line.

A **PLANE** is a flat sheet that extends indefinitely in two directions (like an infinite sheet of paper). A plane is a two-dimensional (2D) figure. A plane can always be defined through any three noncollinear points in three-dimensional (3D) space. A plane is named using any three points that are in the plane (for example, plane *ABC*). Any points lying in the same plane are said to be **COPLANAR**. When two planes intersect, the intersection is a line.

Table 3.1. Basic Geometric Figures

Term	Dimensions	Graphic	Symbol
point	zero	•	·A
line segment	one	A——B	$\overline{AB}$
ray	one	A——→B	$\overrightarrow{AB}$
line	one	←——→	$\overleftrightarrow{AB}$
plane	two	▱	Plane M

EXAMPLE

1. Which points and lines are not contained in plane *M* in the diagram below?

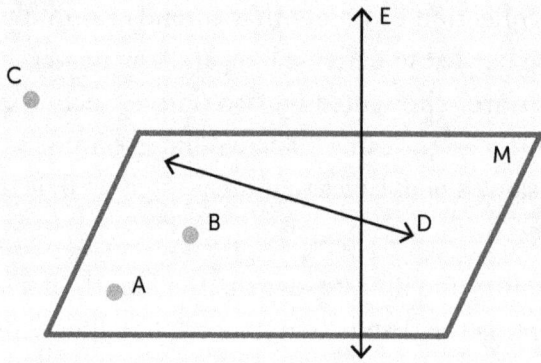

ANGLES

ANGLES are formed when two rays share a common endpoint. They are named using three letters, with the vertex point in the middle (for example ∠*ABC*, where *B* is the vertex). They can also be labeled with a number or named by their vertex alone (if it is clear to do so). Angles are also classified based on their angle measure. A **RIGHT ANGLE** has a measure of exactly 90°. **ACUTE ANGLES** have measures that are less than 90°, and **OBTUSE ANGLES** have measures that are greater than 90°.

Any two angles that add to make 90° are called **COMPLEMENTARY ANGLES**. A 30° angle would be complementary to a 60° angle.

DID YOU KNOW?
Angles can be measured in degrees or radian. Use the conversion factor 1 rad = 57.3 degrees to convert between them.

Supplementary angles add up to 180°. A supplementary angle to a 60° angle would be a 120° angle; likewise, 60° is the **supplement** of 120°. The complement and supplement of any angle must always be positive. For example, a 140 degree has no complement. Angles that are next to each other and share a common ray are called **adjacent angles**. Angles that are adjacent and supplementary are called a **linear pair** of angles. Their nonshared rays form a line (thus the *linear* pair). Note that angles that are supplementary do not need to be adjacent; their measures simply need to add to 180°.

Vertical angles are formed when two lines intersect. Four angles will be formed; the vertex of each angle is at the intersection point of the lines. The vertical angles across from each other will be equal in measure. The angles adjacent to each other will be linear pairs and therefore supplementary.

A ray, line, or segment that divides an angle into two equal angles is called an **angle bisector**.

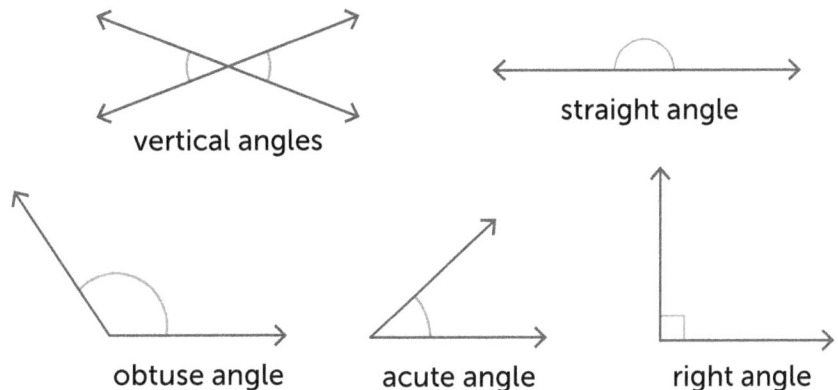

Figure 3.1. Types of Angles

EXAMPLES

2. How many linear pairs of angles are there in the following figure?

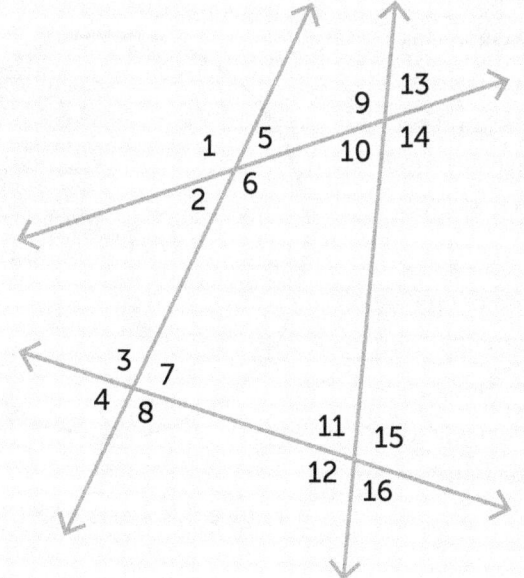

Geometry 59

3. If angles M and N are supplementary and ∠M is 30° less than twice ∠N, what is the degree measurement of each angle?

CIRCLES

A **CIRCLE** is the set of all the points in a plane that are the same distance from a fixed point called the **CENTER**. The distance from the center to any point on the circle is the **RADIUS** of the circle. The distance around the circle (the perimeter) is called the **CIRCUMFERENCE**.

DID YOU KNOW?
Trying to square a circle means attempting to create a square that has the same area as a circle. Because the area of a circle depends on ϖ, which is an irrational number, this task is impossible. The phrase is often used to describe trying to do something that can't be done.

The ratio of a circle's circumference to its diameter is a constant value called pi (π), an irrational number which is commonly rounded to 3.14. The formula to find a circle's circumference is $C = 2\pi r$. The formula to find the enclosed area of a circle is $A = \pi r^2$.

Circles have a number of unique parts and properties:

▶ The **DIAMETER** is the largest measurement across a circle. It passes through the circle's center, extending from one side of the circle to the other. The measure of the diameter is twice the measure of the radius.

▶ A line that cuts across a circle and touches it twice is called a **SECANT** line. The part of a secant line that lies within a circle is called a **CHORD**. Two chords within a circle are of equal length if they are are the same distance from the center.

▶ A line that touches a circle or any curve at one point is **TANGENT** to the circle or the curve. These lines are always exterior to the circle. A line tangent to a circle and a radius drawn to the point of tangency meet at a right angle (90°).

▶ An **ARC** is any portion of a circle between two points on the circle. The **MEASURE** of an arc is in degrees, whereas the **LENGTH OF THE ARC** will be in linear measurement (such as centimeters or inches). A **MINOR ARC** is the small arc between the two points (it measures less than 180°), whereas a **MAJOR ARC** is the large arc between the two points (it measures greater than 180°).

▶ An angle with its vertex at the center of a circle is called a **CENTRAL ANGLE**. For a central angle, the measure of the arc intercepted by the sides of the angle (in degrees) is the same as the measure of the angle.

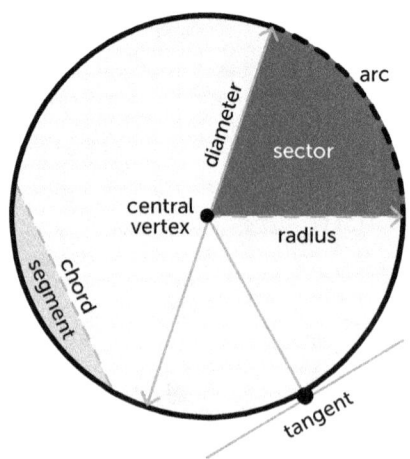

Figure 3.2. Parts of a Circle

- A **SECTOR** is the part of a circle *and* its interior that is inside the rays of a central angle (its shape is like a slice of pie).

	Area of Sector	Length of an Arc
Degrees	$A = \dfrac{\theta}{360°} \times \pi r^2$	$s = \dfrac{\theta}{360°} \times 2\pi r$
Radians	$A = \dfrac{1}{2} r^2 \theta$	$s = r\theta$

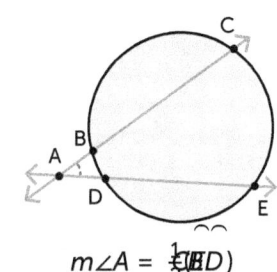

$m\angle A = \frac{1}{2}(CE - BD)$

Figure 3.3. Angles Outside a Circle

- An **INSCRIBED ANGLE** has a vertex on the circle and is formed by two chords that share that vertex point. The angle measure of an inscribed angle is one-half the angle measure of the central angle with the same endpoints on the circle.

- A **CIRCUMSCRIBED ANGLE** has rays tangent to the circle. The angle lies outside of the circle.

- Any angle outside the circle, whether formed by two tangent lines, two secant lines, or a tangent line and a secant line, is equal to half the difference of the intercepted arcs.

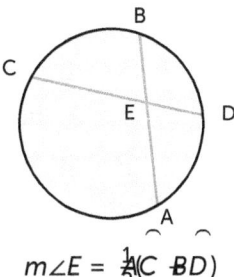

$m\angle E = \frac{1}{2}(AC + BD)$

Figure 3.4. Intersecting Chords

- Angles are formed within a circle when two chords intersect in the circle. The measure of the smaller angle formed is half the sum of the two smaller arc measures (in degrees). Likewise, the larger angle is half the sum of the two larger arc measures.

- If a chord intersects a line tangent to the circle, the angle formed by this intersection measures one half the measurement of the intercepted arc (in degrees).

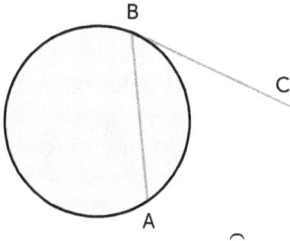

$m\angle ABC = \frac{1}{2} m\overset{\frown}{AB}$

Figure 3.5. Intersecting Chord and Tangent

EXAMPLES

4. Find the area of the sector *NHS* of the circle below with center at *H*:

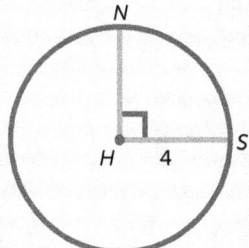

Geometry 61

5. In the circle below with center *O*, the minor arc *ACB* measures 5 feet. What is the measurement of *m∠AOB*?

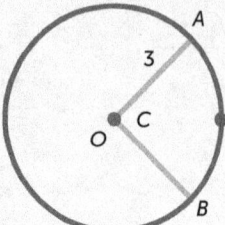

TRIANGLES

Much of geometry is concerned with triangles as they are commonly used shapes. A good understanding of triangles allows decomposition of other shapes (specifically polygons) into triangles for study.

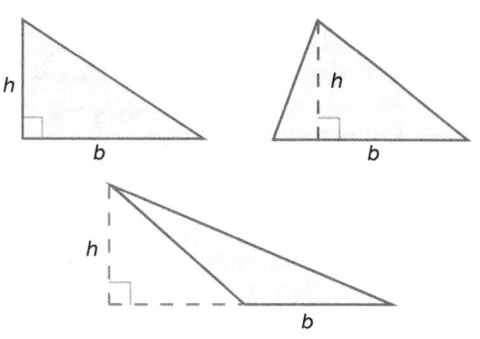

Figure 3.6. Finding the Base and Height of Triangles

Triangles have three sides, and the three interior angles always sum to 180°. The formula for the area of a triangle is $A = \frac{1}{2}bh$ or one-half the product of the base and height (or altitude) of the triangle.

Some important segments in a triangle include the angle bisector, the altitude, and the median. The **ANGLE BISECTOR** extends from the side opposite an angle to bisect that angle. The **ALTITUDE** is the shortest distance from a vertex of the triangle to the line containing the base side opposite that vertex. It is perpendicular to that line and can occur on the outside of the triangle. The **MEDIAN** extends from an angle to bisect the opposite side.

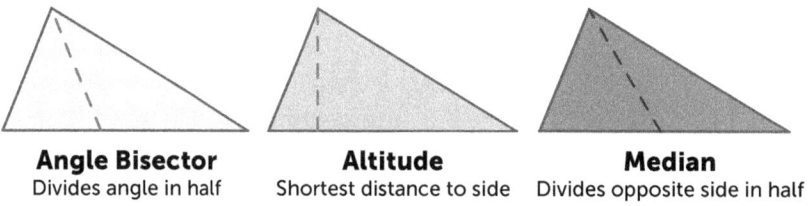

Angle Bisector
Divides angle in half

Altitude
Shortest distance to side

Median
Divides opposite side in half

Figure 3.7. Critical Segments in a Triangle

Triangles have two "centers." The **ORTHOCENTER** is formed by the intersection of a triangle's three altitudes. The **CENTROID** is where a triangle's three medians meet.

Triangles can be classified in two ways: by sides and by angles.

A **SCALENE TRIANGLE** has no equal sides or angles. An **ISOSCELES TRIANGLE** has two equal sides and two equal angles, often called **BASE ANGLES**. In an **EQUILATERAL TRIANGLE**, all three sides are equal as are all three angles. Moreover, because the sum of the angles of a triangle is always 180°, each angle of an equilateral triangle must be 60°.

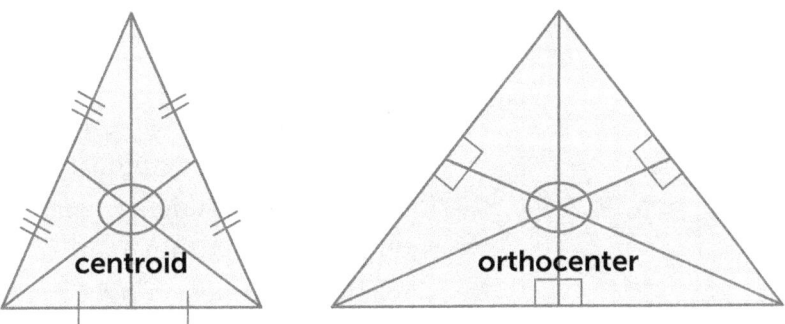

Figure 3.8. Centroid and Orthocenter of a Triangle

A RIGHT TRIANGLE has one right angle (90°) and two acute angles. An ACUTE TRIANGLE has three acute angles (all angles are less than 90°). An OBTUSE TRIANGLE has one obtuse angle (more than 90°) and two acute angles.

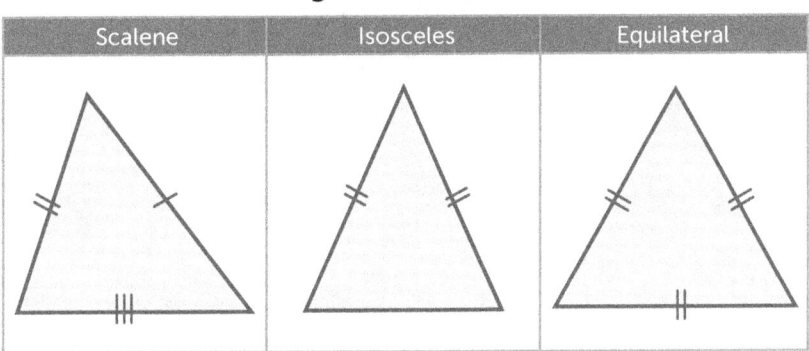

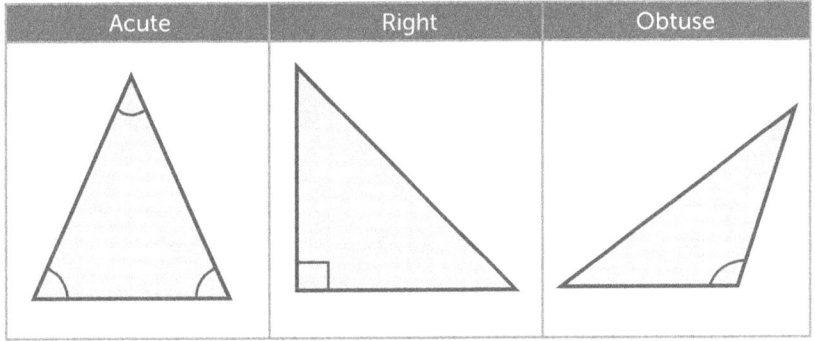

Figure 3.9. Types of Triangles

For any triangle, the side opposite the largest angle will have the longest length, while the side opposite the smallest angle will have the shortest length. The TRIANGLE INEQUALITY THEOREM states that the sum of any two sides of a triangle must be greater than the third side. If this inequality does not hold, then a triangle cannot be formed. A consequence of this theorem is the THIRD-SIDE RULE: if b and c are two sides of a triangle, then the measure of the third side a must be between

DID YOU KNOW?
Trigonometric functions can be employed to find missing sides and angles of a triangle.

the sum of the other two sides and the difference of the other two sides: $c - b < a < c + b$.

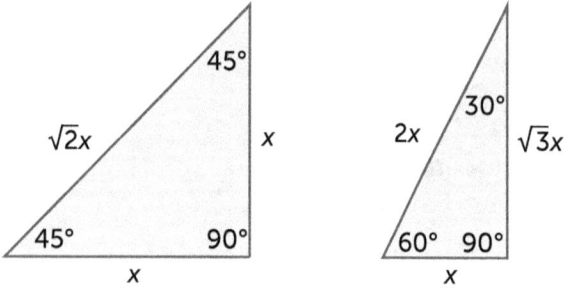

Figure 3.10. Special Right Triangles

Solving for missing angles or sides of a triangle is a common type of triangle problem. Often a right triangle will come up on its own or within another triangle. The relationship among a right triangle's sides is known as the **Pythagorean theorem**: $a^2 + b^2 = c^2$, where c is the hypotenuse and is across from the 90° angle. Right triangles with angle measurements of 90° – 45° – 45° and 90° – 60° – 30° are known as "special" right triangles and have specific relationships between their sides and angles.

EXAMPLES

6. What are the minimum and maximum values of *x* to the nearest hundredth?

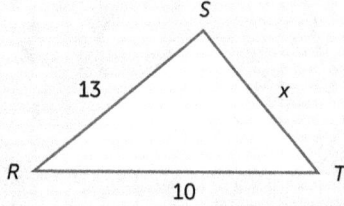

7. Given the diagram, if *XZ* = 100, *WZ* = 80, and *XU* = 70, then *WY* = ?

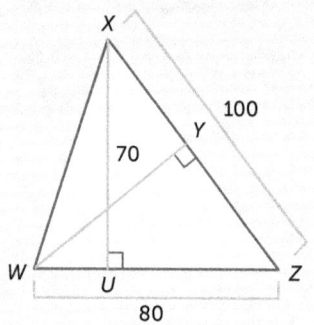

8. Examine and classify each of the following triangles:

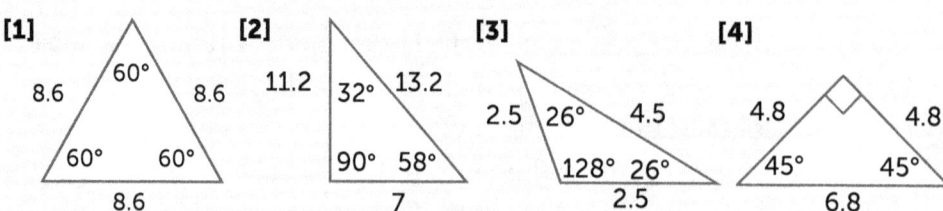

64 TSI Study Guide

QUADRILATERALS

All closed, four-sided shapes are **QUADRILATERALS**. The sum of all internal angles in a quadrilateral is always 360°. (Think of drawing a diagonal to create two triangles. Since each triangle contains 180°, two triangles, and therefore the quadrilateral, must contain 360°.) The **AREA OF ANY QUADRILATERAL** is $A = bh$, where b is the base and h is the height (or altitude).

A **PARALLELOGRAM** is a quadrilateral with two pairs of parallel sides. A rectangle is a parallelogram with two pairs of equal sides and four right angles. A **KITE** also has two pairs of equal sides, but its equal sides are consecutive. Both a **SQUARE** and a **RHOMBUS** have four equal sides. A square has four right angles, while a rhombus has a pair of acute opposite angles and a pair of obtuse opposite angles. A **TRAPEZOID** has exactly one pair of parallel sides.

DID YOU KNOW?
All squares are rectangles and all rectangles are parallelograms; however, not all parallelograms are rectangles and not all rectangles are squares.

Table 3.2 Properties of Parallelograms

Term	Shape	Properties
Parallelogram		Opposite sides are parallel. Consecutive angles are supplementary. Opposite angles are equal. Opposite sides are equal. Diagonals bisect each other.
Rectangle		All parallelogram properties hold. Diagonals are congruent *and* bisect each other. All angles are right angles.
Square		All rectangle properties hold. All four sides are equal. Diagonals bisect angles. Diagonals intersect at right angles and bisect each other.
Kite		One pair of opposite angles is equal. Two pairs of consecutive sides are equal. Diagonals meet at right angles.
Rhombus		All four sides are equal. Diagonals bisect angles. Diagonals intersect at right angles and bisect each other.
Trapezoid		One pair of sides is parallel. Bases have different lengths. Isosceles trapezoids have a pair of equal sides (and base angles).

EXAMPLES

9. In parallelogram *ABCD*, the measure of angle *m* is is $m° = 260°$. What is the measure of $n°$?

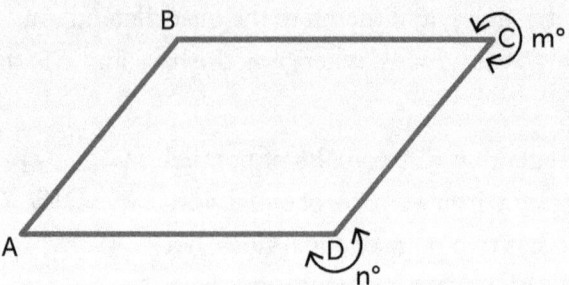

10. A rectangular section of a football field has dimensions of *x* and *y* and an area of 1000 square feet. Three additional lines drawn vertically divide the section into four smaller rectangular areas as seen in the diagram below. If all the lines shown need to be painted, calculate the total number of linear feet, in terms of *x*, to be painted.

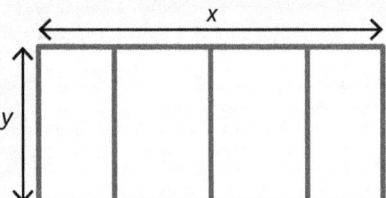

POLYGONS

Any closed shape made up of three or more line segments is a polygon. In addition to triangles and quadrilaterals, **HEXAGONS** and **OCTAGONS** are two common polygons.

DID YOU KNOW?
Breaking an irregular polygon down into triangles and quadrilaterals helps in finding its area.

The two polygons depicted in Figure 3.11 are **REGULAR POLYGONS**, meaning that they are equilateral (all sides having equal lengths) and equiangular (all angles having equal measurements). Angles inside a polygon are **INTERIOR ANGLES**, whereas those formed by one side of the polygon and a line extending outside the polygon are **EXTERIOR ANGLES**:

The sum of the all the exterior angles of a polygon is always 360°. Dividing 360° by the number of a polygon's sides finds the measure of the polygon's exterior angles.

To determine the sum of a polygon's interior angles, choose one vertex and draw diagonals from that

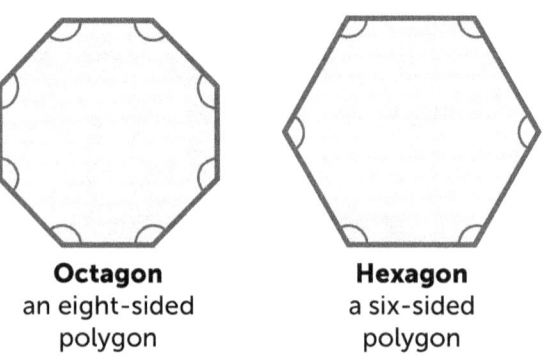

Octagon
an eight-sided polygon

Hexagon
a six-sided polygon

Figure 3.11. Common Polygons

vertex to each of the other vertices, decomposing the polygon into multiple triangles. For example, an octagon has six triangles within it, and therefore the sum of the interior angles is 6 × 180° = 1080°. In general, the formula for finding the sum of the angles in a polygon is *sum of angles* = $(n - 2) \times 180°$, where n is the number of sides of the polygon.

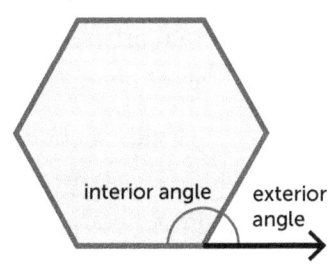

Figure 3.12. Interior and Exterior Angles

To find the measure of a single interior angle in a regular polygon, simply divide the sum of the interior angles by the number of angles (which is the same as the number of sides). So, in the octagon example, each angle is $\frac{1080}{8}$ = 135°.

In general, the formula to find the measure of a regular polygon's interior angles is: *interior angle* = $\frac{(n - 2)}{n} \times 180°$ where n is the number of sides of the polygon.

To find the area of a polygon, it is helpful to know the perimeter of the polygon (p), and the **APOTHEM** (a). The apothem is the shortest (perpendicular) distance from the polygon's center to one of the sides of the polygon. The formula for the area is: *area* = $\frac{ap}{2}$.

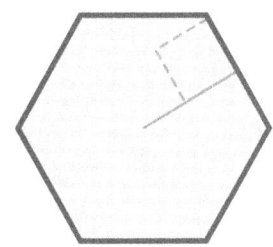

Figure 3.13. Apothem in a Hexagon

Finally, there is no universal way to find the perimeter of a polygon (when the side length is not given). Often, breaking the polygon down into triangles and adding the base of each triangle all the way around the polygon is the easiest way to calculate the perimeter.

EXAMPLES

11. What is the measure of an exterior angle and an interior angle of a regular 400-gon?

12. The circle and hexagon below both share center point *T*. The hexagon is entirely inscribed in the circle. The circle's radius is 5. What is the area of the shaded area?

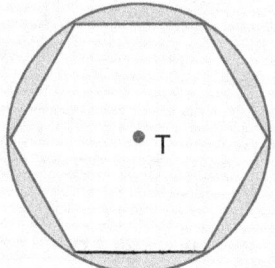

Three-Dimensional Shapes

THREE-DIMENSIONAL SHAPES have depth in addition to width and length. **VOLUME** is expressed as the number of cubic units any solid can hold—that is, what it takes to fill it up. SURFACE AREA is the sum of the areas of the two-dimensional figures that are found on its surface. Some three-dimensional shapes also have a unique property called a slant height (ℓ), which is the distance from the base to the apex along a lateral face.

Finding the surface area of a three-dimensional solid can be made easier by using a NET. This two-dimensional "flattened" version of a three-dimensional shape shows the component parts that comprise the surface of the solid.

Table 3.3. Three-Dimensional Shapes and Formulas

TERM	SHAPE	FORMULA	
Prism		$V = Bh$ $SA = 2lw + 2wh + 2lh$ $d^2 = a^2 + b^2 + c^2$	B = area of base h = height l = length w = width d = longest diagonal
Cube		$V = s^3$ $SA = 6s^2$	s = cube edge
Sphere		$V = \frac{4}{3}\pi r^3$ $SA = 4\pi r^2$	r = radius
Cylinder		$V = Bh = \pi r^2 h$ $SA = 2\pi r^2 + 2\pi rh$	B = area of base h = height r = radius
Cone		$V = \frac{1}{3}\pi r^2 h$ $SA = \pi r^2 + \pi rl$	r = radius h = height l = slant height
Pyramid		$V = \frac{1}{3}Bh$ $SA = B + \frac{1}{2}(p)l$	B = area of base h = height p = perimeter l = slant height

EXAMPLES

13. A sphere has a radius z. If that radius is increased by t, by how much is the surface area increased? Write the answer in terms of z and t.

14. A cube with volume 27 cubic meters is inscribed within a sphere such that all of the cube's vertices touch the sphere. What is the length of the sphere's radius?

Equality, Congruence, and Similarity

When discussing shapes in geometry, the term **CONGRUENT** is used to mean that two shapes have the same shape and size (but not necessarily the same orientation or location). This concept is slightly different from equality, which is used in geometry to describe numerical values. For example, if the length of two lines are equal, the two lines themselves are called congruent. Congruence is written using the symbol ≅. On figures, congruent parts are denoted with hash marks.

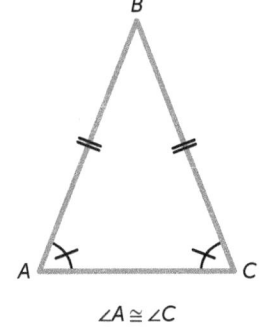

Figure 3.14. Congruent Parts of a Triangle

Shapes which are **SIMILAR** have the same shape but the not the same size, meaning their corresponding angles are the same but their lengths are not. For two shapes to be similar, the ratio of their corresponding sides must be a constant (usually written as k). Similarity is described using the symbol ~.

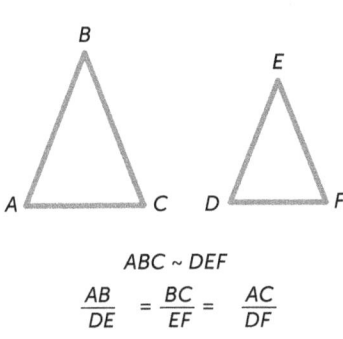

Figure 3.15. Similar Triangles

CONGRUENCE and SIMILARITY in TRIANGLES

Congruence and similarity in triangles is governed by a set of theorems that make it easy to determine the relationship between two triangles. These theorems can be used by looking at the number and location of congruent sides and angles shared by the triangles.

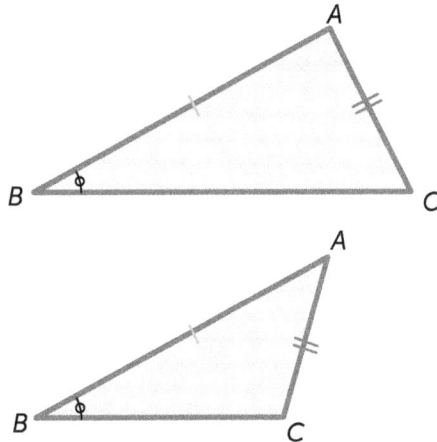

Figure 3.16. Two Possible Triangles Formed from Two Sides and One Non-Included Angle

Geometry 69

Table 3.4. Triangle Congruence

TRIANGLES ARE CONGRUENT IF...

SSS	all three corresponding sides are congruent.
SAS	two sides and the included angle are congruent.
AAS	two angles and one side are congruent.
ASA	two angles and the included side are congruent.

TRIANGLES ARE SIMILAR IF...

AA	two angles (and thus the third) are congruent.
SAS	two sides are proportional and included angle is congruent.
SSS	the ratio between all three corresponding sides is constant.

A note of caution about the SSA case (also known as the ASS case): Two triangles that have congruent (or proportional) sides and one congruent (but not included) angle are NOT necessarily congruent (or similar). This is because, given two side lengths and a nonincluded angle, it is often possible to draw an acute triangle and an obtuse triangle. Thus, there is NOT an SSA congruence theorem.

Right triangles, in general, have a couple of simpler similarity and congruence theorems. Since any pair of right triangles already has one angle that is the same (the right angle), any two pairs of corresponding sides that are either congruent or proportional will guarantee congruence or similarity between the triangles, respectively.

Table 3.5. Right Triangle Congruence

RIGHT TRIANGLES ARE CONGRUENT IF...

HL	the hypotenuse and one leg are congruent.
LL	the two pairs of corresponding legs are congruent.

RIGHT TRIANGLES ARE SIMILAR IF...

HL	the hypotenuse and one leg are proportional.
LL	two pairs of corresponding legs are similar.

EXAMPLES

15. Determine whether the following sets of triangles are congruent. If they are, state why.

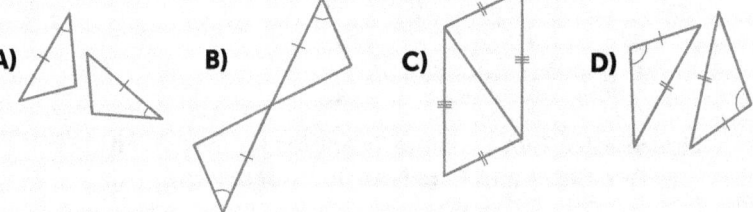

16. If △ABC ~ △DEF, what is the length of $\overline{DE}$?

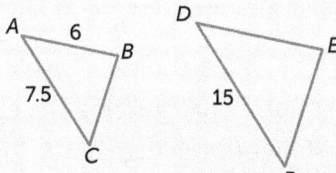

CONGRUENCE and SIMILARITY in THREE-DIMENSIONAL SHAPES

Three-dimensional shapes may also be congruent if they are the same size and shape, or similar if their corresponding parts are proportional. For example, a pair of cones is similar if the ratios of the cones' radii and heights are proportional. For rectangular prisms, all three dimensions must be proportional for the prisms to be similar. If two shapes are similar, their corresponding areas and volumes will also be proportional. If the constant of proportionality of the linear measurements of a 3D shape is k, the constant of proportionality between the areas will be k^2, and the constant of proportionality between the volumes will be k^3.

All spheres are similar as a dilation of the radius of a sphere will make it equivalent to any other sphere.

EXAMPLES

17. A square-based pyramid has a height of 10 cm. If the length of the side of the square is 6 cm, what is the surface area of the pyramid?

18. Given that two cones are similar and one cone's radius is three times longer than the other's radius, what is the volume of the smaller cone if the larger cone has a volume of 81π cubic inches and a height of 3 inches?

Transformations of Geometric Figures
BASIC TRANSFORMATIONS

Geometric figures are often drawn in the coordinate xy-plane, with the vertices or centers of the figures indicated by ordered pairs. These shapes can then be manipulated by performing **TRANSFORMATIONS**, which alter the size or shape of the figure using mathematical operations. The original shape is called the **PRE-IMAGE**, and the shape after a transformation is applied is called the **IMAGE**.

A **TRANSLATION** transforms a shape by moving it right or left, or up or down. Translations are sometimes called slides. After this transformation, the image is identical in size and shape to the pre-image. In other words, the image is **CONGRUENT**, or identical in size, to the pre-image. All corresponding pairs of angles are congruent, and all corresponding side lengths are congruent.

Translations are often in brackets: (x, y). The first number represents the change in the x direction (left/right), while the second number shows the change in the y direction (up/down).

DID YOU KNOW?
Transformation follow the order of operations. For example, to transform the function $y = a[f(x - h)] + k$:
1. Translate the function right/left h units.
2. Dilate the function by the scale factor a.
3. Reflect the graph if $a < 0$.
4. Translate the function up/down k units.

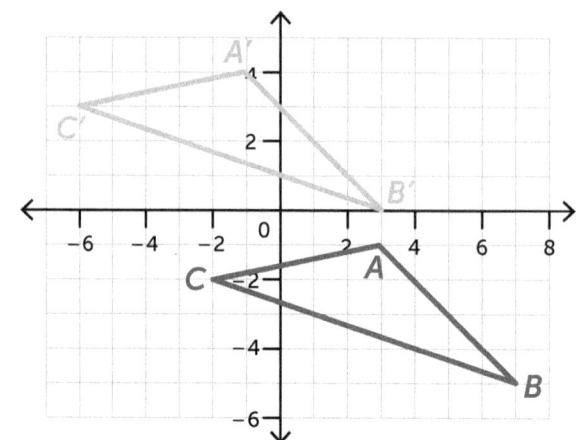

The translation moved triangle ABC left 4 units and up 6 units to produce triangle A'B'C'.

Figure 3.17. Translation

Similarly, rotations and reflections preserve the size and shape of the figure, so congruency is preserved. A **ROTATION** takes a pre-image and rotates it about a fixed point (often the origin) in the plane. Although the position or orientation of the shape changes, the angles and side lengths remain the same.

A **REFLECTION** takes each point in the pre-image and flips it over a point or line in the plane (often the x- or y-axis, but not necessarily). The image is congruent to the

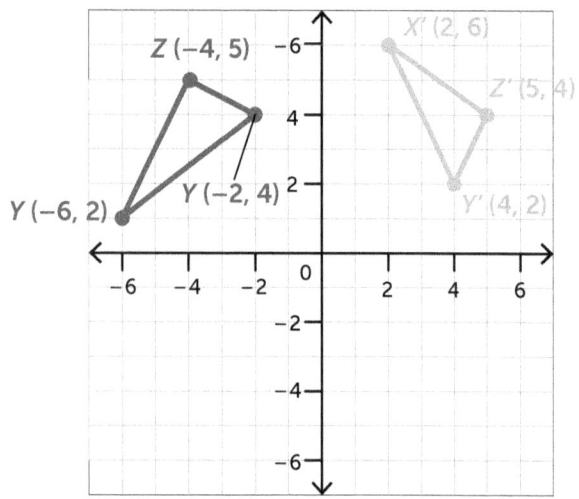

The triangle *XYZ* is rotated 90 in the clockwise direction about the origin (0, 0).

Figure 3.18. Rotation

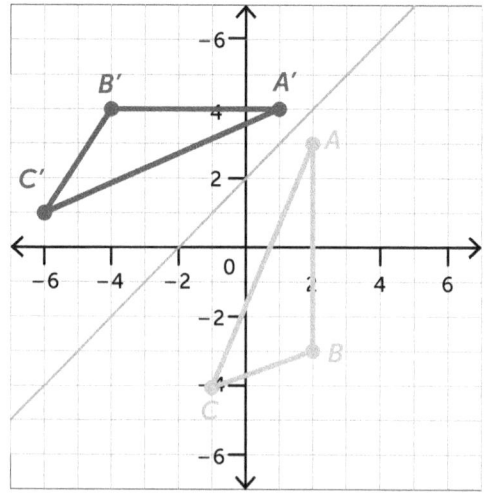

The triangle *ABC* is reflected over the line to produce the triangle *A'B'C'*.

Figure 3.19. Reflection

pre-image. When a figure is flipped across the *y*-axis, the signs of all *x*-coordinates will change. The *y*-coordinates change sign when a figure is reflected across the *x*-axis.

EXAMPLE

19. If quadrilateral *ABCD* has vertices *A* (−6,4), *B* (−6,8), *C* (2,8), and *D* (4,−4), what are the new vertices if *ABCD* is translated 2 units down and 3 units right?

DILATIONS and SIMILARITY

A **DILATION** increases (or decreases) the size of a figure by some **SCALE FACTOR**. Each coordinate of the points that make up the figure is multiplied by the same factor. If the factor is greater than 1, multiplying all the factors enlarges the shape; if the factor is less than 1 (but greater than 0), the shape is reduced in size.

DID YOU KNOW?
If two shapes are similar, their angle measurements will be equal and the ratio of equivalent sides will be the value *k*.

In addition to the scale factor, a dilation needs a **CENTER OF DILATION**, which is a fixed point in the plane about which the points are multiplied. Usually, but not always, the center of dilation is the origin (0,0). For dilations about the origin, the image coordinates are calculated by multiplying each coordinate by the scale factor *k*. Thus, point $(x, y) \rightarrow (kx, ky)$. Although dilations do not result in congruent figures, the orientation of the figure is preserved; consequently, corresponding line segments will be parallel.

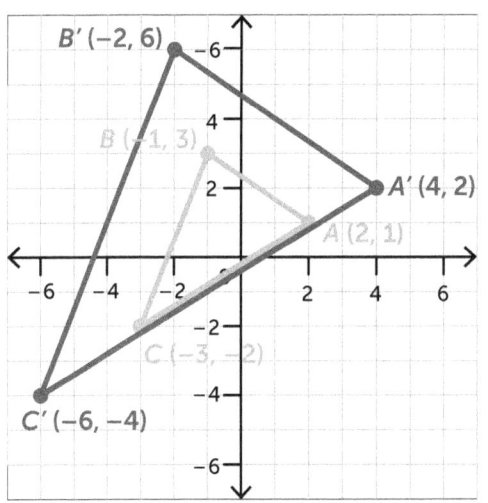

The triangle *ABC* is dilated by the scale factor 2 to produce triangle *A'B'C'*.

Figure 3.20. Dilation

Importantly, dilations do NOT create images that are congruent to the original because the size of each dimension is increased or decreased (the only exception being if the scale factor is exactly 1). However, the shape of the figure is maintained. The corresponding angle measures will be congruent, but the corresponding side lengths will be *proportional*. In other words, the image and pre-image will be **SIMILAR** shapes (described with the symbol ~).

EXAMPLE

20. If quadrilateral *ABCD* has vertices *A* (−6,4), *B* (−6,8), *C* (2,8), and *D* (4,−4), what are the new vertices if *ABCD* is increased by a factor of 5 about the origin?

TRANSFORMING COORDINATES

Transformations in a plane can actually be thought of as functions. An input pair of coordinates, when acted upon by a transformation, results in a pair of output coordinates. Each point is moved to a unique new point (a one-to-one correspondence).

Table 3.6. How Coordinates Change for Transformations in a Plane

Type of Transformation	Coordinate Changes
Translation right m units and up n units	$(x,y) \rightarrow (x+m, y+n)$
Rotations about the origin in positive (counterclockwise) direction **Rotation 90°** **Rotation 180°** **Rotation 270°**	$(x,y) \rightarrow (-y, x)$ $(x,y) \rightarrow (-x, -y)$ $(x,y) \rightarrow (y, -x)$
Reflections about the **x-axis** **y-axis** **line $y = x$**	$(x,y) \rightarrow (x, -y)$ $(x,y) \rightarrow (-x, y)$ $(x,y) \rightarrow (y, x)$
Dilations about the origin by a factor of k $0 < k < 1 \rightarrow$ **size reduced** $k > 1 \rightarrow$ **size enlarged**	$(x,y) \rightarrow (kx, ky)$

EXAMPLES

21. Triangle *ABC* with coordinates (2,8), (10,2), and (6,8) is transformed in the plane as shown in the diagram. What transformations result in the image triangle *A'B'C'*?

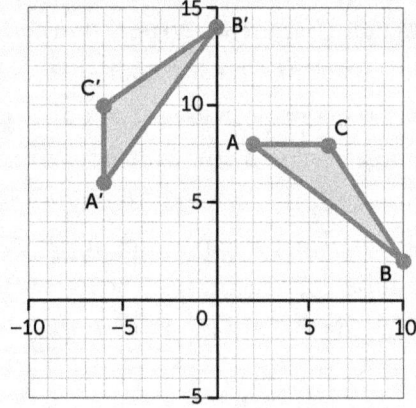

22. If quadrilateral *ABCD* has vertices *A* (−6,4), *B* (−6,8), *C* (2,8), and *D* (4,−4), what are the new vertices if *ABCD* is rotated 270° and then reflected across the *x*-axis?

Answer Key

1. Points A and B and line D are all on plane M. Point C is above the plane, and line E cuts through the plane and thus does not lie on plane M. The point at which line E intersects plane M is on plane M but the line as a whole is not.

2. Any two adjacent angles that are supplementary are linear pairs, so there are 16 linear pairs in the figure (∠1 and ∠5, ∠2 and ∠6, ∠5 and ∠6, ∠2 and ∠1, and so on).

3. Set up a system of equations.

   ∠M + ∠N = 180°

   ∠M = 2∠N − 30°

   Use substitution to solve for ∠N.

   ∠M + ∠N = 180°

   (2∠N − 30°) + ∠N = 180°

   3∠N − 30° = 180°

   3∠N = 210°

   ∠N = **70°**

   Solve for ∠M using the original equation.

   ∠M + ∠N = 180°

   ∠M + 70° = 180°

   ∠M = **110°**

4. Identify the important parts of the circle.

   $r = 4$

   ∠NHS = 90°

   Plug these values into the formula for the area of a sector.

   $A = \frac{\theta}{360°} \times \pi r^2$

   $= \frac{90}{360} \times \pi(4)^2 = \frac{1}{4} \times 16\pi$

   $= \mathbf{4\pi}$

5. Identify the important parts of the circle.

   $r = 3$

   length of $\overline{ACB} = 5$

   Plug these values into the formula for the length of an arc and solve for θ.

   $s = \frac{\theta}{360°} \times 2\pi r$

   $5 = \frac{\theta}{360°} \times 2\pi(3)$

   $\frac{5}{6\pi} = \frac{\theta}{360°}$

   $\theta = 95.5°$

   m∠AOB = 95.5°

6. The sum of two sides is 23 and their difference is 3. To connect the two other sides and enclose a space, x must be less than the sum and greater than the difference (that is, 3 < x < 23). Therefore, **x's minimum value to the nearest hundredth is 3.01 and its maximum value is 22.99.**

7. $WZ = b_1 = 80$

   $XU = h_1 = 70$

   $XZ = b_2 = 100$

   $WY = h_2 = ?$

   The given values can be used to write two equation for the area of △WXZ with two sets of bases and heights.

   $A = \frac{1}{2} bh$

   $A_1 = \frac{1}{2}(80)(70) = 2800$

   $A_2 = \frac{1}{2}(100)(h_2)$

   Set the two equations equal to each other and solve for WY.

   $2800 = \frac{1}{2}(100)(h_2)$

   $h_2 = 56$

   WY = 56

8. **Triangle 1 is an equilateral triangle** (all 3 sides are equal, and all 3 angles are equal)

   Triangle 2 is a scalene, right triangle (all 3 sides are different, and there is a 90° angle)

   Triangle 3 is an obtuse, isosceles triangle (there are 2 equal sides and, consequently, 2 equal angles)

   Triangle 4 is a right, isosceles triangle (there are 2 equal sides and a 90° angle)

9. Find $\angle C$ using the fact that the sum of $\angle C$ and m is 360°.

   $260° + m\angle C = 360°$

   $m\angle C = 100°$

   Solve for $\angle D$ using the fact that consecutive interior angles in a quadrilateral are supplementary.

   $m\angle C + m\angle D = 180°$

   $100° + m\angle D = 180°$

   $m\angle D = 80°$

   Solve for n by subtracting $m\angle D$ from 360°.

   $m\angle D + n = 360°$

   $n = \mathbf{280°}$

10. Find equations for the area of the field and length of the lines to be painted (L) in terms of x and y.

    $A = 1000 = xy$

    $L = 2x + 5y$

    Substitute to find L in terms of x.

    $y = \frac{1000}{x}$

    $L = 2x + 5y$

    $L = 2x + 5(\frac{1000}{x})$

    $L = 2x + \mathbf{\frac{5000}{x}}$

11. The sum of the exterior angles is 360°. Dividing this sum by 400 gives $\frac{360°}{400} = \mathbf{0.9°}$. Since an interior angle is supplementary to an exterior angle, all the interior angles have measure 180 − 0.9 = **179.1°**. Alternately, using the formula for calculating the interior angle gives the same result:

    interior angle $= \frac{400-2}{400} \times 180°$

    $= 179.1°$

12. The area of the shaded region will be the area of the circle minus the area of the hexagon. Use the radius to find the area of the circle.

    $A_C = \pi r^2 = \pi(5)^2 = 25\pi$

    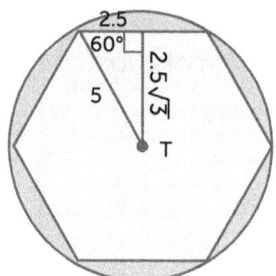

    To find the area of the hexagon, draw a right triangle from the vertex, and use special right triangles to find the hexagon's apothem. Then, use the apothem to calculate the area.

    $a = 2.5\sqrt{3}$

    $A_H = \frac{ap}{2} = \frac{(2.5\sqrt{3})(30)}{2} = 64.95$

    Subtract the area of the hexagon from the circle to find the area of the shaded region.

    $= A_C - A_H$

    $= 25\pi - 2.5\sqrt{3}$

    $\approx \mathbf{13.59}$

13. Write the equation for the area of the original sphere.

    $SA_1 = 4\pi z^2$

    Write the equation for the area of the new sphere.

    $SA_2 = 4\pi(z + t)^2$

$= 4π(z^2 + 2zt + t^2)$

$= 4πz^2 + 8πzt + 4πt^2$

To find the difference between the two, subtract the original from the increased surface area:

$A_2 - A_1 = 4πz^2 + 8πzt + 4πt^2 - 4πz^2$

$= \mathbf{4πt^2 + 8πzt}$

14. Since the cube's volume is 27, each side length is equal to $\sqrt[3]{27}$ = 3. The long diagonal distance from one of the cube's vertices to its opposite vertex will provide the sphere's diameter:

    $d = \sqrt{3^2 + 3^2 + 3^2} = \sqrt{27} = 5.2$

    Half of this length is the radius, which is **2.6 meters**.

15. A) Not enough information is provided to determine if the triangles are congruent.

    B) Congruent (ASA). The vertical angle shared by the triangles provides the second angle.

    C) Congruent (SSS). The shared side is the third congruent side.

    D) Not enough information is provided: SSA cannot be used to prove congruence.

16. Set up a proportion among the sides:

    $\frac{AB}{AC} = \frac{ED}{DF}$

    $\frac{6}{7.5} = \frac{DE}{15}$

    DE = 12

17. The surface area will be the area of the square base plus the area of the four triangles.

    Find the area of the square.

    $A = s^2 = 6^2 = 36$

    To find the area of the triangles, first find the pyramid's slant height.

$c^2 = a^2 + b^2$

$l^2 = 100 + 9$

$l = \sqrt{109}$

Find the area of the triangle face using the slant height as the height of the triangle face.

$A = \frac{1}{2} bh$

$A = \frac{1}{2}(6)(\sqrt{109})$

$A = 3\sqrt{109}$

Add the area of the square base and the four triangles to find the total surface area.

$SA = 36 + 4(3\sqrt{109}) ≈ \mathbf{161.3\ cm^2}$

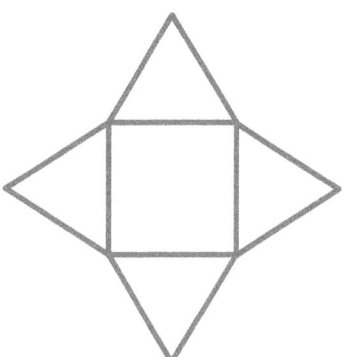

18. Identify the given variables.

    $V_1 = 81π$

    $h_1 = 3$

    Find the radius of the larger cone with the given information.

    $V_1 = \frac{1}{3} πr_1^2 h_1$

    $81π = \frac{1}{3} π(r_1)(3)$

    $r_1 = 9$

    Use the given scale factor to find the second cone's radius and height.

    $r_2 = \frac{1}{3} r_1$

    $r_2 = \frac{1}{3}(9)$

    $r_2 = 3$

    $h_2 = \frac{1}{3} h_1$

    $h_2 = \frac{1}{3}(3)$

    $h_2 = 1$

Find the area of the smaller cone.
$V_2 = \frac{1}{3}\pi r_2^2 h_2$
$V_2 = \frac{1}{3}\pi(3)^2(1)$
$V_2 = 3\pi$

19. Translating two units down decreases each y-value by 2, and moving 3 units to the right increases the x-value by 3. The new vertices are A (−3,2), B (−3,6), C (5,6), and D (7,−6).

20. Multiply each point by the scale factor of 5 to find the new vertices: **A (−30,20), B (−30,40), C (10,40), and D (20,−20).**

21. Since the orientation of the triangle is different from the original, it must have been rotated. A counterclockwise rotation of 90° about the point A (2,8) results in a triangle with the same orientation. Then the triangle must be translated to move it to the image location. Pick one point, say A, and determine the translation necessary to move it to point A'. In this case, each point on the pre-image must be translated 8 units left and 2 units down, or (−8,−2). (Note that this is one of many possible answers.)

22. When a figure is rotated 270°, the coordinates change: (a,b) → (b,−a). After the rotation, the new coordinates are (4,6), (8,6), (8,−2), and (−4,−4). Reflecting across the x-axis requires that every y-value is multiplied by −1 to arrive at the completely transformed quadrilateral with vertices of (4,−6), (8,−6), (8,2), and (−4,4).

CHAPTER FOUR
Statistics

Describing Sets of Data
MEASURES of CENTRAL TENDENCY

Measures of central tendency help identify the center, or most typical, value within a data set. There are three such central tendencies that describe the "center" of the data in different ways. The **MEAN** is the arithmetic average and is found by dividing the sum of all measurements by the number of measurements. The mean of a population is written as μ and the mean of a sample is written as $\bar{x}$.

$$\text{population mean} = \mu = \frac{x_1 + x_2 + \ldots xN}{N} = \frac{\Sigma x}{N}$$

$$\text{sample mean} = \bar{x} = \frac{x_1 + x_2 + \ldots xn}{n} = \frac{\Sigma x}{n}$$

The data points are represented by x's with subscripts; the sum is denoted using the Greek letter sigma (Σ); N is the number of data points in the entire population; and n is the number of data points in a sample set.

The **MEDIAN** divides the measurements into two equal halves. The median is the measurement right in the middle of an odd set of measurements or the average of the two middle numbers in an even data set. When calculating the median, it is important to order the data values from least to greatest before attempting to locate the middle value. The **MODE** is simply the measurement that occurs most often. There can be many modes in a data set, or no mode. Since measures of central tendency describe a *center* of the data, all three of these measures will be between the lowest and highest data values (inclusive).

DID YOU KNOW?
When the same value is added to each term in a set, the mean increases by that value and the standard deviation is unchanged.

When each term in a set is multiplied by the same value, both the mean and standard deviation will also be multiplied by that value.

Unusually large or small values, called **OUTLIERS**, will affect the mean of a sample more than the mode. If there is a high outlier, the mean will be greater than the median; if there is a low outlier, the mean will be lower than the median. When outliers are present, the median is a better measure of the data's center than the mean because the median will be closer to the terms in the data set.

EXAMPLES

1. What is the mean of the following data set? {1000, 0.1, 10, 1}

2. What is the median of the following data set? {1000, 10, 1, 0.1}

3. Josey has an average of 81 on four equally weighted tests she has taken in her statistics class. She wants to determine what grade she must receive on her fifth test so that her mean is 83, which will give her a B in the course, but she does not remember her other scores. What grade must she receive on her fifth test?

MEASURES of VARIATION

The values in a data set can be very close together (close to the mean), or very spread out. This is called the **SPREAD** or **DISPERSION** of the data. There are a few **MEASURES OF VARIATION** (or **MEASURES OF DISPERSION**) that quantify the spread within a data set. **RANGE** is the difference between the largest and smallest data points in a set:

$$R = \text{largest data point} - \text{smallest data point}$$

Notice range depends on only two data points (the two extremes). Sometimes these data points are outliers; regardless, for a large data set, relying on only two data points is not an exact tool.

The understanding of the data set can be improved by calculating **QUARTILES**. To calculate quartiles, first arrange the data in ascending order and find the set's median (also called quartile 2 or Q2). Then find the median of the lower half of the data, called quartile 1 (Q1), and the median of the upper half of the data, called quartile 3 (Q3). These three points divide the data into four equal groups of data (thus the word *quartile*). Each quartile contains 25% of the data.

INTERQUARTILE RANGE (IQR) provides a more reliable range that is not as affected by extremes. IQR is the difference between the third quartile data point and the first quartile data point and gives the spread of the middle 50% of the data:

$$IQR = Q_3 - Q_1$$

The **VARIANCE** of a data set is simply the square of the standard variation:

$$V = \sigma^2 = \frac{1}{N}\sum_{i=1}^{N}(x_i - \mu)^2$$

Variance measures how narrowly or widely the data points are distributed. A variance of zero means every data point is the same; a large variance means the data is widely spread out.

EXAMPLE

4. What are the range and interquartile range of the following set? {3, 9, 49, 64, 81, 100, 121, 144, 169}

Graphs, Charts, and Tables
PIE CHARTS

A pie chart simply states the proportion of each category within the whole. To construct a pie chart, the categories of a data set must be determined. The frequency of each category must be found and that frequency converted to a percent of the total. To draw the pie chart, determine the angle of each slice by multiplying the percentage by 360°.

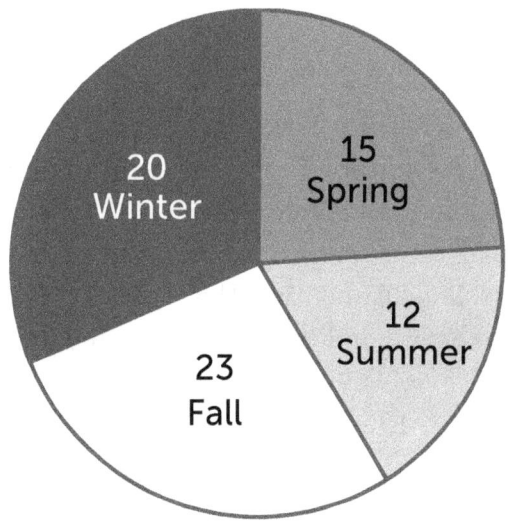

Figure 4.1. Pie Chart

EXAMPLE

5. A firm is screening applicants for a job by education-level attainment. There are 125 individuals in the pool: 5 have a doctorate, 20 have a master's degree, 40 have a bachelor's degree, 30 have an associate degree, and 30 have a high school degree. Construct a pie chart showing the highest level of education attained by the applicants.

SCATTER PLOTS

A scatter plot is displayed in the first quadrant of the *xy*-plane where all numbers are positive. Data points are plotted as ordered pairs, with one variable along the horizontal axis and the other along the vertical axis. Scatter plots can show if there is a correlation between two variables. There is a **POSITIVE CORRELATION** (expressed as a positive slope) if increasing one variable appears to result in an increase in the other variable. A **NEGATIVE CORRELATION** (expressed as a negative slope) occurs when an increase in one variable causes a decrease in the other. If the scatter plot shows no discernible pattern, then there is no correlation (a zero, mixed, or indiscernible slope).

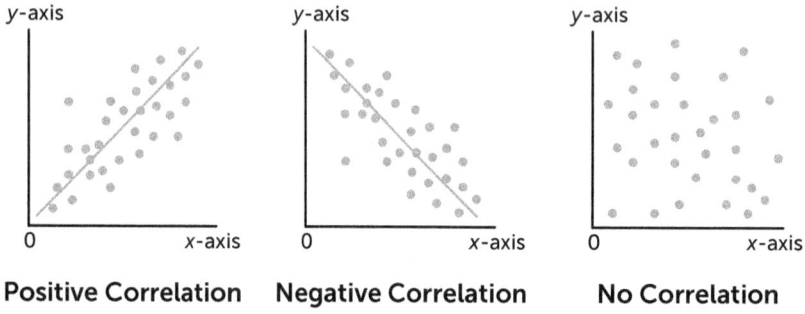

Figure 4.2. Scatter Plots and Correlation

Calculators or other software can be used to find the linear regression equation, which describes the general shape of the data. Graphing this equation produces the regression line, or line of best fit. The equation's **CORRELATION COEFFICIENT** (r) can be used to determine how closely the equation fits the data. The value of r is between −1 and 1. The closer r is to 1 (if the line has a positive slope) or −1 (if the line has a negative slope), the better the regression line fits the data. The closer the r value is to 0, the weaker the correlation between the line and the data. Generally, if the absolute value of the correlation coefficient is 0.8 or higher, then it is considered to be a strong correlation, while an $|r|$ value of less than 0.5 is considered a weak correlation.

To determine which curve is the "best fit" for a set of data, **RESIDUALS** are calculated. The calculator automatically calculates and saves these values to a list called RESID. These values are all the differences between the actual *y*-value of data points and the *y*-value calculated by the best-fit line or curve for that *x*-value. These values can be plotted on an *xy*-plane to produce a **RESIDUAL PLOT**. The residual plot helps determine if a line is the best model for the data. Residual points that are randomly dispersed above and below the horizontal indicate that a linear model is appropriate, while a *u* shape or upside-down *u* shape indicate a nonlinear model would be more appropriate.

Once a best-fit line is established, it can be used to estimate output values given an input value within the domain of the data. For a short extension outside that domain, reasonable predictions may be possible. However, the further from the domain of the data the line is extended, the greater the reduction in the accuracy of the prediction.

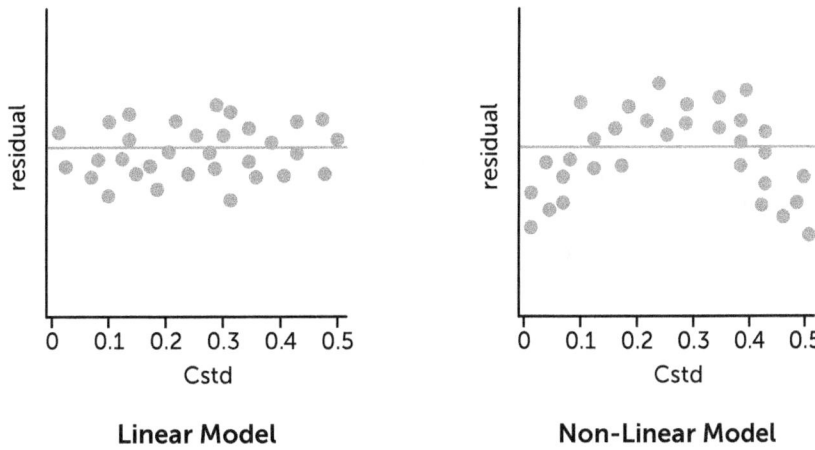

Figure 4.3. Residual Plots

It is important to note here that just because two variables have a strong positive or negative correlation, it cannot necessarily be inferred that those two quantities have a *causal* relationship—that is, that one variable changing *causes* the other quantity to change. There are often other factors that play into their relationship. For example, a positive correlation can be found between the number of ice cream sales and the number of shark attacks at a beach. It would be incorrect to say that selling more ice cream *causes* an increase in shark attacks. It is much more likely that on hot days more ice cream is sold, and many more people are swimming, so one of them is more likely to get attacked by a shark. Confusing correlation and causation is one of the most common statistical errors people make.

DID YOU KNOW?
A graphing calculator can provide the regression line, *r* value, and residuals list.

EXAMPLE

6. Based on the scatter plot on the following page, where the *x*-axis represents hours spent studying per week and the *y*-axis represents the average percent grade on exams during the school year, is there a correlation between the amount of studying for a test and test results?

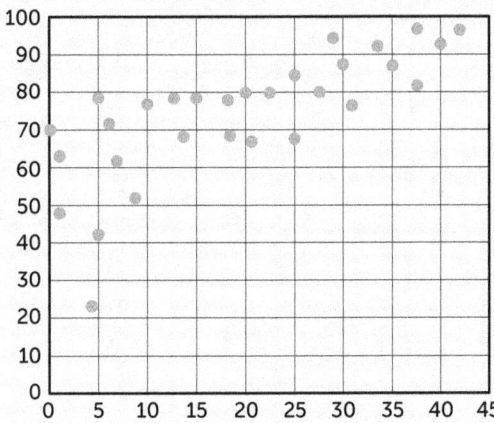

Statistics 83

LINE GRAPHS

Line graphs are used to display a relationship between two variables, such as change over time. Like scatter plots, line graphs exist in quadrant I of the xy-plane. Line graphs are constructed by graphing each point and connecting each point to the next consecutive point by a line. To create a line graph, it may be necessary to consolidate data into single bivariate data points. Thus, a line graph is a function, with each x-value having exactly one y-value, whereas a scatter plot may have multiple y-values for one x-value.

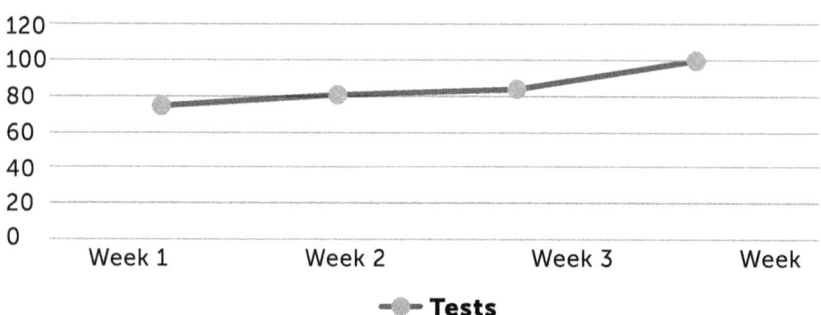

Figure 4.4. Line Graph

EXAMPLE

7. Create a line graph based on the following survey values, where the first column represents an individual's age and the other represents that individual's reported happiness level on a 20-point scale (0 being the least happy that person has been and 20 being the happiest). Then interpret the resulting graph to determine whether the following statement is true or false: *On average, middle-aged people are less happy than young or older people are.*

Age	Happiness	Age (continued)	Happiness (continued)
12	16	33	10
13	15	44	8
20	18	55	10
15	12	80	10
40	5	15	13
17	17	40	8
18	18	17	15
19	15	18	17
42	7	19	20
70	17	22	16
45	10	27	15
60	12	36	9
63	15	33	10
22	14	44	6
27	15		

BAR GRAPHS

Bar graphs compare differences between categories or changes over a time. The data is grouped into categories or ranges and represented by rectangles. A bar graph's rectangles can be vertical or horizontal, depending on whether the dependent variable is placed on the *x*- or *y*-axis. Instead of the *xy*-plane, however, one axis is made up of categories (or ranges) instead of a numeric scale. Bar graphs are useful because the differences between categories are easy to see: the height or length of each bar shows the value for each category.

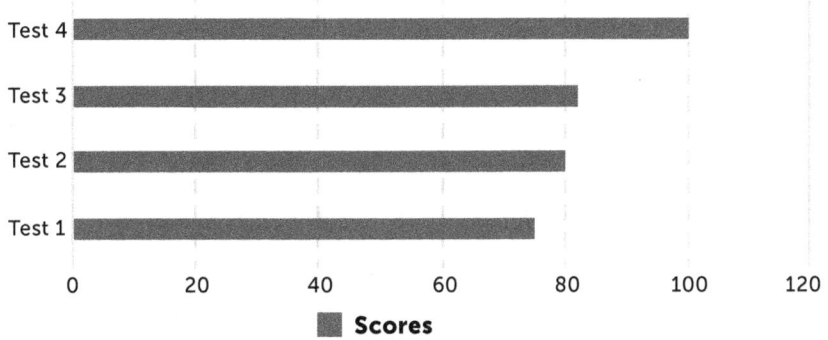

Figure 4.5. Bar Graph

EXAMPLE

8. A company X had a profit of $10,000 in 2010, $12,000 in 2011, $15,600 in 2012, and $20,280 in 2013. Create a bar graph displaying the profit from each of these four years.

STEM-and-LEAF PLOTS

Stem-and-leaf plots are ways of organizing large amounts of data by grouping it into classes. All data points are broken into two parts: a stem and a leaf. For instance, the number 512 might be broken into a stem of 5 and a leaf of 12. All data in the 500 range would appear in the same row (this group of data is a class). Usually a simple key is provided to explain how the data is being represented. For instance, 5|12 = 512 would show that the stems are representing hundreds. The advantage of this display is that it shows general density and shape of the data in a compact display, yet all original data points are preserved and available. It is also easy to find medians and quartiles from this display.

Stem	Leaf
0	5
1	6, 7
2	8, 3, 6
3	4, 5, 9, 5, 5, 8, 5
4	7, 7, 7, 8
5	5, 4
6	0

Figure 4.6. Stem-and-Leaf Plot

EXAMPLE

9. The table gives the weights of wrestlers (in pounds) for a certain competition. What is the mean, median, and IQR of the data?

2	05, 22, 53, 40
3	07, 22, 29, 45, 89, 96, 98
4	10, 25, 34
6	21

Key: 2|05 = 205 pounds

FREQUENCY TABLES and HISTOGRAMS

The frequency of a particular data point is the number of times that data point occurs. Constructing a frequency table requires that the data or data classes be arranged in ascending order in one column and the frequency in another column.

A histogram is a graphical representation of a frequency table used to compare frequencies. A histogram is constructed in quadrant I of the xy-plane, with data in each equal-width class presented as a bar and the height of each bar representing the frequency of that class. Unlike bar graphs, histograms cannot have gaps between bars. A histogram is used to determine the distribution of data among the classes.

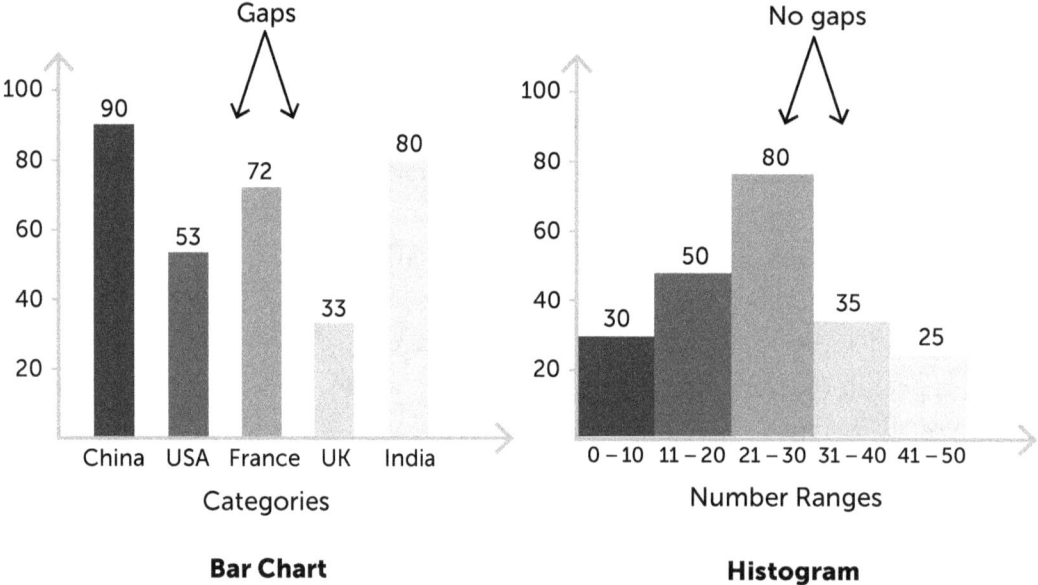

Figure 4.7. Bar Chart vs. Histogram

Histograms can be symmetrical, skewed left or right, or multimodal (data spread around). Note that SKEWED LEFT means the peak of the data is on the *right*, with a tail to the left, while SKEWED RIGHT means the peak is on the *left*, with a tail to the right. This seems counterintuitive to many; the "left" or "right" always refers to the tail of the data. This is because a long tail to the right, for example, means there are high outlier values that are skewing the data to the right.

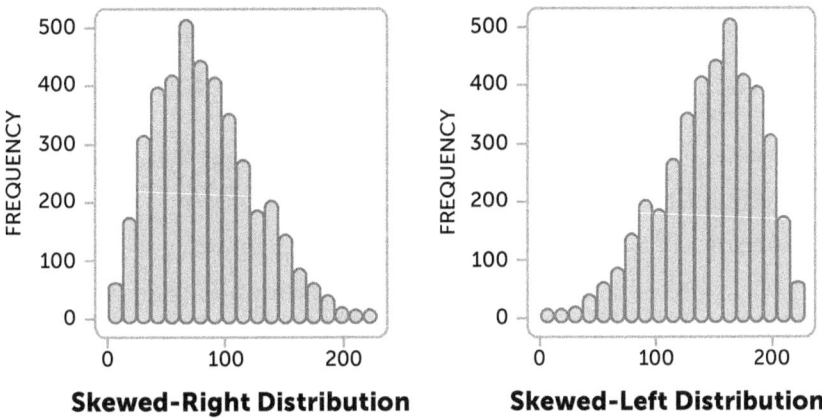

Figure 4.8. Histrograms

A TWO-WAY FREQUENCY TABLE compares CATEGORICAL DATA (data in more than one category) of two related variables (bivariate data). Two-way frequency tables are also called CONTINGENCY TABLES and are often used to analyze survey results. One category is displayed along the top of the table and the other category down along the side. Rows and columns are added and the sums appear at the end of the row or column. The sum of all the row data must equal the sum of all the column data.

From a two-way frequency table, the JOINT RELATIVE FREQUENCY of a particular category can be calculated by taking the number in the row and column of the categories in question and dividing by the total number surveyed. This gives the percent of the total in that particular category. Sometimes the CONDITIONAL RELATIVE FREQUENCY is of interest. In this case, calculate the relative frequency confined to a single row or column.

	Students by Grade and Gender				
	9TH GRADE	10TH GRADE	11TH GRADE	12TH GRADE	TOTAL
Male	57	63	75	61	256
Female	54	42	71	60	227
Total	111	105	146	121	483

Figure 4.9. Two-Way Frequency Table

EXAMPLES

10. Cineflix movie theater polled its moviegoers on a weeknight to determine their favorite type of movie. The results are in the two-way frequency table below.

Moviegoers	Comedy	Action	Horror	Totals
Male	15	24	21	60
Female	8	18	17	43
Totals	23	42	38	103

Determine whether each of the following statements is true or false.

A) Action films are the most popular type of movie

B) About 1 in 5 moviegoers prefers comedy films

C) Men choose the horror genre more frequently than women do

11. A café owner tracked the number of customers he had over a twelve-hour period in the following frequency table. Display the data in a histogram and determine what kind of distribution there is in the data.

Time	Number of Customers
6 a.m. – 8 a.m.	5
8 a.m. – 9 a.m.	6
9 a.m. – 10 a.m.	5
10 a.m. – 12 p.m.	23
12 p.m. – 2 p.m.	24
2 p.m. – 4 p.m.	9
4 p.m. – 6 p.m.	4

BOX PLOTS

A box plot depicts the median and quartiles along a scaled number line. It is meant to summarize the data in a visual manner and emphasize central trends while decreasing the pull of outlier data. To construct a box plot:

1. Create a number line that begins at the lowest data point and terminates at the highest data point.

2. Find the quartiles of the data. Create a horizontal rectangle (the "box") whose left border is Q_1 and right border is Q_3.

3. Draw a vertical line within the box to mark the median.

4. Draw a horizontal line going from the left edge of the box to the smallest data value.

5. Draw a horizontal line going from the right edge of the box to the largest data value.

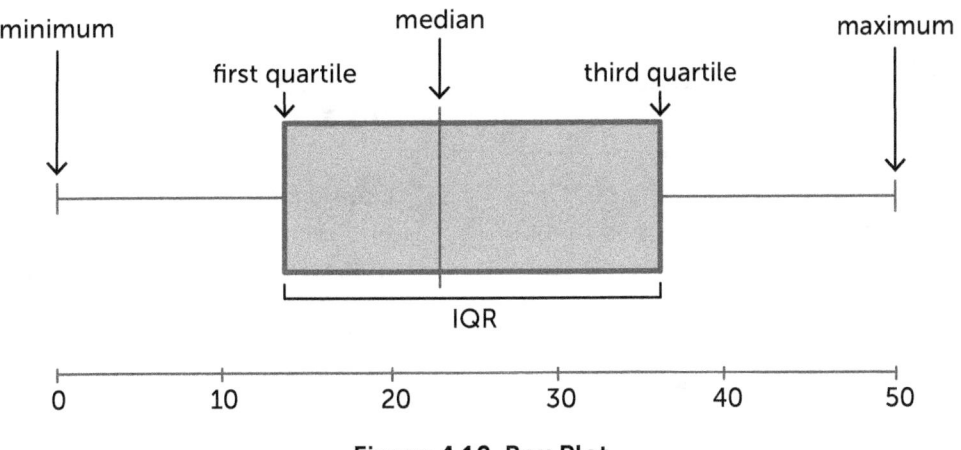

Figure 4.10. Box Plot

When reading a box plot, the following stands out:

▶ Reading from left to right: the horizontal line (whisker) shows the spread of the first quarter; the box's left compartment shows the spread of the second quarter; the box's right compartment shows the spread of the third quarter; and the right horizontal line shows the spread of the fourth quarter.

▶ The length of the box is the IQR, or the middle 50% of the data.

▶ Each of the four pieces (the whiskers and two pieces in the box) represent 25% of the data.

▶ The horizontal lines show by their length whether the data higher or lower than the middle 50% is prominent.

DID YOU KNOW?
Box plots are also known as **box-and-whisker plots**, because if they are drawn correctly the two horizontal lines look like whiskers.

EXAMPLE

12. A recent survey asked 8 people how many pairs of shoes they wear per week. Their answers are in the following data set: {1, 3, 5, 5, 7, 8, 12}. Construct a box plot from this data.

Answer Key

1. Use the equation to find the mean of a sample:
$$\frac{1000 + 0.1 + 10 + 1}{4} = \mathbf{252.78}$$

2. Since there are an even number of data points in the set, the median will be the mean of the two middle numbers. Order the numbers from least to greatest: 0.1, 1, 10, and 1000. The two middle numbers are 1 and 10, and their mean is:
$$\frac{1 + 10}{2} = \mathbf{5.5}$$

3. Even though Josey does not know her test scores, she knows her average. Therefore it can be assumed that each test score was 81, since four scores of 81 would average to 81. To find the score, x, that she needs use the equation for the mean of a sample:
$$\frac{4(81) + x}{5} = 83$$
$$324 + x = 415$$
$$\mathbf{x = 91}$$

4. Use the equation for range.
R = largest point – smallest point = 169 – 3 = **166**

Place the terms in numerical order and identify Q1, Q2, and Q3.

3
9
→ Q1 = $\frac{49 + 9}{2}$ = 29
49
64
81 → Q2
100
121
→ Q3 = $\frac{121 + 144}{2}$ =132.5
144
169

Find the IQR by subtracting Q1 from Q3.
IQR = Q3 – Q1 = 132.5 – 29 = **103.5**

5. Create a frequency table to find the percentages and angle measurement for each category.

Category	Frequency	Percent	Angle Measure
High School	30	24%	86.4
Associate	30	24%	86.4
Bachelor's	40	32%	115.2
Master's	20	16%	57.6
Doctorate	5	4%	14.4

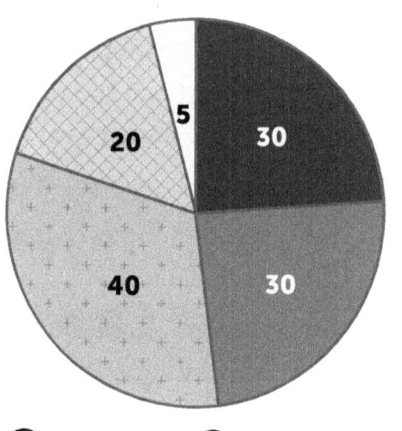

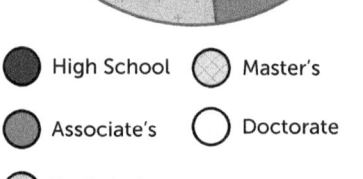

6. There is a somewhat weak positive correlation. As the number of hours spent studying increases, the average percent grade also generally increases.

7. To construct a line graph, the data must be ordered into consolidated categories by averaging the data

of people who have the same age so that the data is one-to-one. For example, there are 2 twenty-two-year-olds who are reporting. Their average happiness level is 15. When all the data has been consolidated and ordered from least to greatest, the table and graph below can be presented.

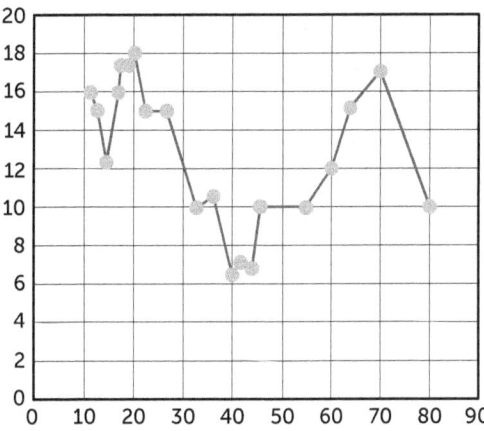

Age	Happiness
12	16
13	15
15	12.5
17	16
18	17.5
19	17.5
20	18
22	15
27	15
33	10
36	10.5
40	6.5
42	7
44	7
45	10
55	10
60	12
63	15
70	17
80	10

The statement that, on average, middle-aged people are less happy than young or older people appears to be true. According to the graph, people in their thirties, forties, and fifties are less happy than people in their teens, twenties, sixties, and seventies.

8. Place years on the independent axis, and profit on the dependent axis, and then draw a box showing the profit for each year.

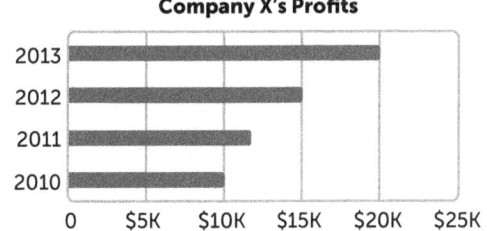

9. Find the mean using the equation for the population mean.

$\mu = \frac{\Sigma x}{N} = \frac{5281}{15} =$ **353.1 lbs.**

Find the median and IQR by counting the leaves and identifying Q1, Q2, and Q3.

Q1 = 253

Q2 = 345

Q3 = 410

IQR = 410 − 253 = 157

The median is 345 lbs. The IQR is 157 lbs.

10. **A) True.** More people (42) chose action movies than comedy (23) or horror (38).

    B) True. Find the ratio of total number of people who prefer comedy to total number of people. $\frac{23}{103}$ = 0.22; 1 in 5 is 20%, so 22% is about the same.

    C) False. The percentage of men who choose horror is less than the percentage of women who do.

    part = number of men who prefer horror = 21

    whole = number of men surveyed = 60

    percent = $\frac{part}{whole}$ = $\frac{21}{60}$
    = 0.35 = 35%

    part = number of women who prefer horror = 17

    whole = number of women surveyed = 43

    percent = $\frac{part}{whole}$ = $\frac{17}{43}$
    = 0.40 = 40%

11. Since time is the independent variable, it is on the *x*-axis and the number of customers is on the *y*-axis. For the histogram to correctly display data continuously, categories on the *x*-axis must be equal 2-hour segments. The 8 a.m. – 9 a.m. and 9 a.m. – 10 a.m. categories must be combined for a total of 11 customers in that time period. Although not perfectly symmetrical, the amount of customers peaks in the middle and is therefore considered symmetrical.

    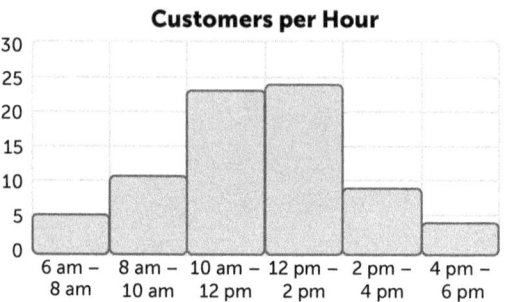

12. Create a number line that begins at 1 and ends at 12. Q_1 is 3, the median (Q_2) is 5, and Q_3 is 8. A rectangle must be drawn whose length is 5 and that borders on Q_1 and Q_3. Mark the median of 5 within the rectangle. Draw a horizontal line going left to 1. Draw a horizontal line going right to 12.

    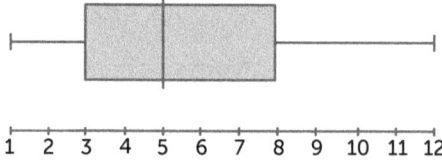

CHAPTER FIVE
Probability

Logic and Set Theory
LOGIC

Mathematical logic is a systematic method of determining the truth of a **PROPOSITION**, or statement. A proposition can be true or false, a label called the proposition's **TRUTH VALUE**. In the context of logical arguments, a statement cannot be both true and false; it also cannot be neither true nor false. Propositions are represented by variables, usually p, q, or r.

A **NEGATION** has the opposite truth value of the original statement, and is often denoted by the symbol tilde (~). The statement $\sim p$ is read as "not p." Examples of statements and their negations are below. Note that $\sim p$ is not necessarily false; it is simply the opposite of p.

- ▶ p: 4 is an even number (true)
  $\sim p$: 4 is not an even number (false)
- ▶ p: Dogs lay eggs (false)
  $\sim p$: Dogs do not lay eggs (true)

A **TRUTH TABLE** shows all the possible inputs and truth output values of a statement or proposition. These tables are constructed by writing the variables for each statement and operation across the top row, and then listing all possible true/false values in the columns. In the table below, the statement p and its negation are in the top row, and the possible true/false values for p are in the left column. The right column ($\sim p$) can then be filled in.

p	$\sim p$
T	F
F	T

Figure 5.1. Truth Table

A **CONJUNCTION** between two variables or statements is an *and* statement. It is true only when both variables or statements are true. For all other situations, the result is false. A conjunction between statements p and q is written $p \wedge q$.

p	q	p∧q
T	T	T
T	F	F
F	T	F
F	F	F

Figure 5.2. Conjunction

A **DISJUNCTION** between two variables or statements is an inclusive *or* statement, and is denoted $p \vee q$. This statement is true whenever p is true, q is true, or both are true.

An **IMPLICATION** statement is an *if... then* statement. The statement "if p, then q" is also written as $p \rightarrow q$. The implication statement is false only when the first proposition is true and the second is false:

The **BICONDITIONAL** or **EQUIVALENCE** statement is true whenever both p and q have the same truth value:

p	q	p∨q
T	T	T
T	F	T
F	T	T
F	F	F

Figure 5.3. Disjunction

p	q	p→q
T	T	T
T	F	F
F	T	T
F	F	T

Figure 5.4. Implication

p	q	p↔q
T	T	T
T	F	F
F	T	F
F	F	T

Figure 5.5. Biconditional

Truth tables can be used to show that two statements are logically equivalent by showing that they have the same truth values under all circumstances. For example, a truth table can prove that the implication statement $p \rightarrow q$ and the contrapositive of that statement $\sim q \rightarrow \sim p$ are equivalent. To construct the table, create columns for p and q, and fill these with all possible true/false combinations. Next, create columns for each operation and find its truth value. Because the columns for $p \rightarrow q$ and $\sim q \rightarrow \sim p$ are identical, the statements are equivalent.

p	q	~p	~q	p→q	~q→~p
T	T	F	F	T	T
T	F	F	T	F	F
F	T	T	F	T	T
F	F	T	T	T	T

Figure 5.6. Truth Table with Two Statements

EXAMPLE

1. Prove De Morgan's theorem $\sim(p \vee q) = \sim p \wedge \sim q$ using a truth table.

SET THEORY

A **SET** is any collection of items. In mathematics, a set is represented by a capital letter and described inside curly brackets. For example, if S is the set of all integers less than 10, then $S = \{x | x$ is an integer and $x < 10\}$. The vertical bar | is read *such that*. The set that contains no elements is called the **EMPTY SET** or the **NULL SET** and is denoted by empty brackets { } or the symbol $\emptyset$.

DID YOU KNOW?
The notation $x \in A$ is read as "x is an element of A."

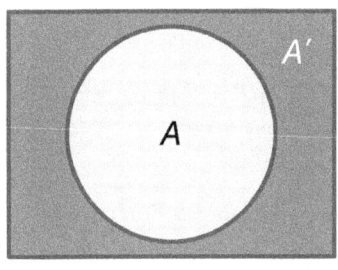
Figure 5.7. Venn Diagram

Usually there is a larger set that any specific problem is based in, called the **UNIVERSAL SET** or **U**. For example, in the set S described above, the universal set might be the set of all real numbers. The **COMPLEMENT** of set A, denoted by $\overline{A}$ or A', is the set of all items in the universal set, but NOT in A. It can be helpful when working with sets to represent them with a **VENN DIAGRAM**.

Oftentimes, the task will be working with multiple sets: A, B, C, etc. A **UNION** between two sets means that the data in both sets is combined into a single, larger set. The union of two sets, denoted $A \cup B$ contains all the data that is in either set A or set B or both (called an **INCLUSIVE OR**). If $A = \{1, 4, 7\}$ and $B = \{2, 4, 5, 8\}$, then $A \cup B = \{1, 2, 4, 5, 7, 8\}$ (notice 4 is included only once). The **INTERSECTION** of two sets, denoted $A \cap B$ includes only elements that are in both A and B. Thus, $A \cap B = \{4\}$ for the sets given above.

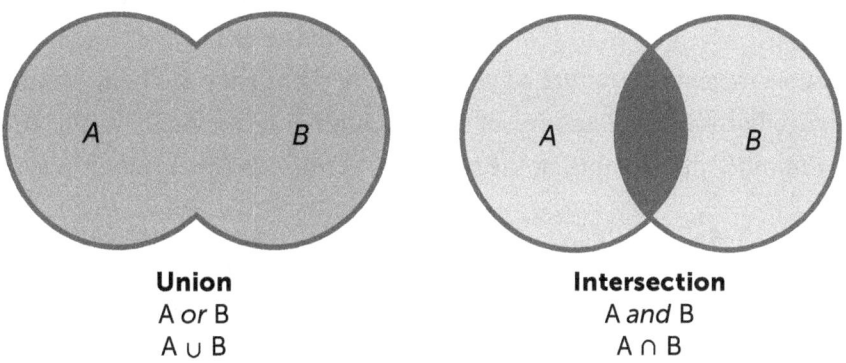

Figure 5.8. Unions and Intersections

If there is no common data in the sets in question, then the intersection is the null set. Two sets that have no elements in common (and thus have a null in the intersection set) are said to be **DISJOINT**. The **DIFFERENCE** $B - A$ or **RELATIVE COMPLEMENT** between two sets is the set of all the values that are in B, but not in A. For the sets defined above, $B - A = \{2, 5, 8\}$ and $A - B = \{1, 7\}$. The relative complement is sometimes denoted as $B \backslash A$.

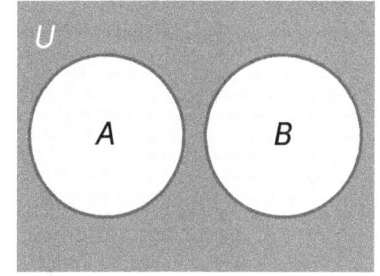
Figure 5.9. Disjoint Sets

Logic and Probability

Mathematical tasks often involve working with multiple sets. Just like numbers, sets and set operations have identities and properties.

Set Identities

$A \cup \emptyset = A$	$A \cup U = U$	$A \cup \bar{A} = U$
$A \cap \emptyset = A$	$A \cap U = A$	$A \cap \bar{A} = \emptyset$

Set Properties

Commutative Property	$A \cup B = B \cup A$	$A \cap B = B \cap A$
Associative Property	$A \cup (B \cup C) = (A \cup B) \cup C$	$A \cap (B \cap C) = (A \cap B) \cap C$
Distributive Property	$A \cup (B \cap C) = (A \cup B) \cap (A \cup C)$	$A \cap (B \cup C) = (A \cap B) \cup (A \cap C)$

De Morgan's Laws

$\overline{(A \cup B)} = \bar{A} \cap \bar{B}$	$\overline{(A \cap B)} = \overline{(A \cup B)}$

The number of elements in a set A is denoted $n(A)$. For the set A above, $n(A) = 3$, since there are three elements in that set. The number of elements in the union of two sets is $n(A \cup B) = n(A) + n(B) - n(A \cap B)$. Note that the number of elements in the intersection of the two sets must be subtracted because they are being counted twice, since they are both in set A and in set B. The number of elements in the complement of A is the number of elements in the universal set minus the number in set A: $n(\bar{A}) = n(U) - n(A)$.

It is helpful to note here how similar set theory is to the logic operators of the previous section: negation corresponds to complements, the "and" (∧) operator to intersection (∩), and the "or" (∨) operator to unions (∪); notice even the symbols are similar.

EXAMPLES

2. Suppose the universal set U is the set of all integers between −10 and 10 inclusive. If $A = \{x \in U | x$ is a multiple of 5$\}$ and $B = \{x \in U | x$ is a multiple of 2$\}$ are subsets within the universal set, find $\bar{A}$, $A \cup B$ and $A \cap B$, and $\bar{A}$, $A \cap B$.

   A. $\bar{A}$
   B. $A \cup B$
   C. $A \cap B$
   D. $\bar{A} \cap \bar{B}$

3. Construct a Venn diagram depicting the intersection, if any, of Y={x | x is an integer and 0 < x < 9} and Z = {−4, 0, 4, 8, 12, 16}.

Probability

Probability describes how likely something is to happen. In probability, an **EVENT** is the single result of a trial, and an **OUTCOME** is a possible event that results from a trial. The collection of all possible outcomes for a particular trial is called the **SAMPLE SPACE**. For example, when rolling a die, the sample space is the numbers 1 – 6. Rolling a single number, such as 4, would be a single event.

COUNTING PRINCIPLES

Counting principles are methods used to find the number of possible outcomes for a given situation. The **FUNDAMENTAL COUNTING PRINCIPLE** states that, for a series of independent events, the number of outcomes can be found by multiplying the number of possible outcomes for each event. For example, if a die is rolled (6 possible outcomes) and a coin is tossed (2 possible outcomes), there are 6 × 2 = 12 total possible outcomes.

Combinations and permutations describe how many ways a number of objects taken from a group can be arranged. The number of objects in the group is written n, and the number of objects to be arranged is represented by r (or k). In a **COMBINATION**, the order of the selections does not matter because every available slot to be filled is the same. Examples of combinations include:

- picking 3 people from a group of 12 to form a committee (220 possible committees)
- picking 3 pizza toppings from 10 options (120 possible pizzas)

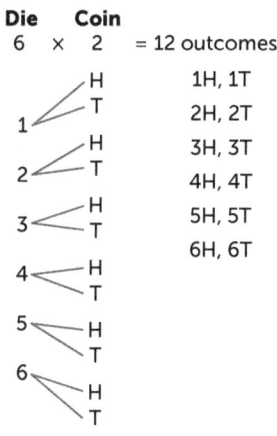

Figure 5.10. Fundamental Counting Principle

In a **PERMUTATION**, the order of the selection matters, meaning each available slot is different. Examples of permutations include:

- handing out gold, silver, and bronze medals in a race with 100 participants (970,200 possible combinations)
- selecting a president, vice-president, secretary, and treasurer from among a committee of 12 people (11,880 possible combinations)

The formulas for the both calculations are similar. The only difference—the $r!$ in the denominator of a combination—accounts for redundant outcomes. Note that both permutations and combinations can be written in several different shortened notations.

$$\text{Permutation: } P(n, r) = {_nP_r} = \frac{n!}{(n-r)!}$$

$$\text{Combination: } C(n, r) = nCr = \binom{n}{r} = \frac{n!}{(n-r)!r!}$$

EXAMPLES

4. A personal assistant is struggling to pick a shirt, tie, and cufflink set that go together. If his client has 70 shirts, 2 ties, and 5 cufflinks, how many possible combinations does he have to consider?

5. If there are 20 applicants for 3 open positions, in how many different ways can a team of 3 be hired?

6. Calculate the number of unique permutations that can be made with five of the letters in the word *pickle*.

7. Find the number of permutations that can be made out of all the letters in the word *cheese*.

PROBABILITY of a SINGLE EVENT

The probability of a single event occurring is the number of outcomes in which that event occurs (called **FAVORABLE EVENTS**) divided by the number of items in the sample space (total possible outcomes):

$$P(\text{an event}) = \frac{\text{number of favorable outcomes}}{\text{total number of possible outcomes}}$$

The probability of any event occurring will always be a fraction or decimal between 0 and 1. It may also be expressed as a percent. An event with 0 probability will never occur and an event with a probability of 1 is certain to occur. The probability of an event not occurring is referred to as that event's **COMPLEMENT**. The sum of an event's probability and the probability of that event's complement will always be 1.

EXAMPLES

8. What is the probability that an even number results when a six-sided die is rolled? What is the probability the die lands on 5?

9. Only 20 tickets were issued in a raffle. If someone were to buy 6 tickets, what is the probability that person would not win the raffle?

10. A bag contains 26 tiles representing the 26 letters of the English alphabet. If 3 tiles are drawn from the bag without replacement, what is the probability that all 3 will be consonants?

PROBABILITY of MULTIPLE EVENTS

If events are **INDEPENDENT**, the probability of one occurring does not affect the probability of the other event occurring. Rolling a die and getting one number does not change the probability of getting any particular number on the next roll. The number of faces has not changed, so these are independent events.

If events are **DEPENDENT**, the probability of one occurring changes the probability of the other event occurring. Drawing a card from a deck without replacing it will affect the probability of the next card drawn because the number of available cards has changed.

DID YOU KNOW?
When drawing objects, the phrase *with replacement* describes independent events, and *without replacement* describes dependent events.

To find the probability that two or more independent events will occur (*A* and *B*), simply multiply the probabilities of each individual event together. To find the probability that one, the other, or both will occur (*A* or *B*), it's necessary to add their probabilities and then subtract their overlap (which prevents the same values from being counted twice).

CONDITIONAL PROBABILITY is the probability of an event occurring given that another event has occurred. The notation $P(B|A)$ represents the probability that event *B* occurs, given that event *A* has already occurred (it is read "probability of *B*, given *A*").

Table 5.1. Probability Formulas

INDEPENDENT EVENTS		DEPENDENT EVENTS
Intersection and	Union or	Conditional
$P(A \cap B) = P(A) \times P(B)$	$P(A \cup B) = P(A) + P(B) - P(A \cap B)$	$P(B|A) = P(A \cap B)/P(A)$

Two events that are **MUTUALLY EXCLUSIVE** CANNOT happen at the same time. This is similar to disjoint sets in set theory. The probability that two mutually exclusive events will occur is zero. **MUTUALLY INCLUSIVE** events share common outcomes.

EXAMPLES

11. A card is drawn from a standard 52 card deck. What is the probability that it is either a queen or a heart?

12. A group of ten individuals is drawing straws from a group of 28 long straws and 2 short straws. If the straws are not replaced, what is the probability, as a percentage, that neither of the first two individuals will draw a short straw?

BINOMIAL PROBABILITY

A binomial (or Bernoulli) trial is an experiment with exactly two mutually exclusive outcomes (often labeled success and failure) where the probability of each outcome is constant. The probability of success is given as p, and the probability of failure is $q = 1 - p$. The **BINOMIAL PROBABILITY** formula can be used to determine the probability of getting a certain number of successes (r) within a given number of trials (n). These values can also be used to find the expected value (μ), or mean, of the trial, and its standard deviation (σ).

$$P = {}_nC_r(p^r)(q^{n-r}) \qquad \mu = np \qquad \sigma = \sqrt{np(1-p)}$$

EXAMPLE

13. What is the probability of rolling a five on a standard 6-sided die 4 times in 10 tries?

Answer Key

1. Begin by making a table with columns for *p*, *q*, ~*p*, and ~*q*. Then create and fill in columns for the left statement and the right statement.

p	q	~p	~q	p ∨ q	~(p ∨ q)	~p ∧ ~q
T	T	F	F	T	F	F
T	F	F	T	T	F	F
F	T	T	F	T	F	F
F	F	T	T	F	T	T

The last two columns have the exact same truth values, which means the statements are logically equivalent. Thus, **the proposition is a true statement.**

2. A. $\overline{A}$ includes all elements of the universal set that are not in set *A*:

   $\overline{A}$ = **{−9, −8, −7, −6, −4, −3, −2, −1, 1, 2, 3, 4, 6, 7, 8, 9}**.

   B. *A* ∪ *B* is all elements in either *A* or *B*:

   A ∪ *B* = **{ −10, −5, 0, 5, 10, −8, −6, −4, −2, 2, 4, 6, 8}**

   C. *A* ∩ *B* is all elements in both *A* and *B*:

   A ∩ *B* = **{−10, 0, 10}**

   D. $\overline{A}$ ∩ $\overline{B}$ is all the elements of the universal set that are not in either *A* or *B*:

   $\overline{A}$ ∩ $\overline{B}$ = **{−9, −7, −3, −1, 1, 3, 7, 9}**

3.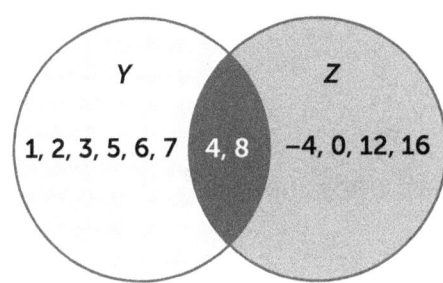

4. Multiply the number of outcomes for each individual event:

   (70)(2)(5) = **700 outfits**

5. The order of the items doesn't matter, so use the formula for combinations:

   $C(n,r) = \dfrac{n!}{(n-r)!r!}$

   $C(20,3) = \dfrac{20!}{(20-3)!3!}$

   $= \dfrac{20!}{(17!\,3!)} = \dfrac{(20)(19)(18)}{3!}$

   = **1140 possible teams**

6. To find the number of unique permutations of 5 letters in pickle, use the permutation formula:

$$P(n,r) = \frac{n!}{(n-r)!}$$

$$P(6,5) = \frac{6!}{(6-5)!} = \frac{720}{1} = \mathbf{720}$$

7. The letter *e* repeats 3 times in the word *cheese*, meaning some permutations of the 6 letters will be indistinguishable from others. The number of permutations must be divided by the number of ways the three *e*'s can be arranged to account for these redundant outcomes:

   total number of permutations

   $= \frac{\text{number of ways of arranging 6 letters}}{\text{number of ways of arranging 3 letters}}$

   $= \frac{6!}{3!} = 6 \times 5 \times 4 = \mathbf{120}$

8. $P(\text{rolling even}) = \frac{\text{number of favorable outcomes}}{\text{total number of possible outcomes}} = \frac{3}{6} = \mathbf{\frac{1}{2}}$

   $P(\text{rolling 5}) = \frac{\text{number of favorable outcomes}}{\text{total number of possible outcomes}} = \mathbf{\frac{1}{6}}$

9. $P(\text{not winning}) = \frac{\text{number of favorable outcomes}}{\text{total number of possible outcomes}} = \frac{14}{20} = \mathbf{\frac{7}{10}}$ or

   $P(\text{not winning}) = 1 - P(\text{winning}) = 1 - \frac{6}{20} = \frac{14}{20} = \mathbf{\frac{7}{10}}$

10. $P = \frac{\text{number of favorable outcomes}}{\text{total number of possible outcomes}} = \frac{\text{number of 3-consonant combinations}}{\text{number of 3-tile combinations}} = \frac{_{21}C_3}{_{26}C_3}$

    $= \frac{1330}{2600} = 0.51 = \mathbf{51\%}$

11. This is a union (*or*) problem.

    $P(A)$ = the probability of drawing a queen = $\frac{1}{13}$

    $P(B)$ = the probability of drawing a heart = $\frac{1}{4}$

    $P(A \cap B)$ = the probability of drawing a heart and a queen = $\frac{1}{52}$

    $P(A \cup B) = P(A) + P(B) - P(A \cap B)$

    $= \frac{1}{13} + \frac{1}{4} - \frac{1}{52}$

    $= \mathbf{0.31}$

12. This scenario includes two events, *A* and *B*.

    The probability of the first person drawing a long straw is an independent event:

    $P(A) = \frac{28}{30}$

    The probability the second person draws a long straw changes because one long straw has already been drawn. In other words, it is the probability of event *B* given that event *A* has already happened:

    $P(B|A) = \frac{27}{29}$

    The conditional probability formula can be used to determine the probability of both people drawing long straws:

$P(A \cap B) = P(A)P(B|A)$

$= (\frac{28}{30})(\frac{27}{29})$

$= 0.87$

There is an **87% chance** that neither of the first two individuals will draw short straws.

13. Identify the variables given in the problem.

    $p = \frac{1}{6}$

    $q = \frac{5}{6}$

    $n = 10$

    $r = 4$

    Plug these values into the binomial probability formula.

    $P = {}_nC_r(p^r)(q^{n-r})$

    $= (\frac{10!}{(10-4)!4!})(\frac{1}{6})^4(\frac{5}{6})^{10-4}$

    $= 0.054$

    There is a **5.4% chance**.

CHAPTER SIX
Reading

To do well on reading comprehension questions on the TSI, you should be able to identify explicit details in a text, draw inferences about the text, grasp the author's intent, and understand the main idea of a text.

The Main Idea

The main idea of a text describes the author's main topic and general concept; it also generalizes the author's point of view about a subject. It is contained within and throughout the text. The reader can find the main idea by considering how the main topic is addressed throughout a passage. On reading questions, you are expected not only to identify the main idea but also to be able to differentiate it from a text's theme and to summarize the main idea clearly and concisely. For instance, you might be asked to pick an answer choice that best summarizes the main idea of a passage.

The main idea is closely connected to topic sentences and how they are supported in a text. Questions may deal with finding topic sentences, summarizing a text's ideas, or locating supporting details. The sections and practice examples that follow detail the distinctions between these aspects of text.

> **DID YOU KNOW?**
> The author's perspective on the subject of the text and how he or she has framed the argument or story hints at the main idea. For example, if the author framed the story with a description, image, or short anecdote, he or she is hinting at a particular idea or point of view.

IDENTIFYING the MAIN IDEA

To identify the main idea, first identify the topic. The difference between these two things is simple: the **TOPIC** is the overall subject matter of a passage; the **MAIN IDEA** is what the author wants to say about that topic. The main idea covers the author's direct perspective about a topic, as distinct from the **THEME**, which is a generally true idea that the reader might derive from a text. Most of the time, fiction has a theme, whereas nonfiction has a main idea. This is the case because in a nonfiction text, the author speaks more directly to the audience about a topic—his or her perspective is more visible. For example, the following passage conveys the topic as well as what the author wants to communicate about that topic.

> The "shark mania" of recent years can be largely pinned on the sensationalistic media surrounding the animals: from the release of *Jaws* in 1975 to the week of ultra-hyped shark feeding frenzies and "worst shark attacks" countdowns known as *Shark Week*, popular culture both demonizes and fetishizes sharks until the public cannot get enough. Swimmers and beachgoers may look nervously for the telltale fin skimming the surface, but the reality is that shark bites are extremely rare and they are almost never unprovoked. Sharks attack people at very predictable times and for very predictable reasons. Rough surf, poor visibility, or a swimmer sending visual and physical signals that mimic a shark's normal prey are just a few examples.
>
> Of course, some places are just more dangerous to swim. Shark attack "hot spots," such as the coasts of Florida, South Africa, and New Zealand try a variety of solutions to protect tourists and surfers. Some beaches employ "shark nets," meant to keep sharks away from the beach, though these are controversial because they frequently trap other forms of marine life as well. Other beaches use spotters in helicopters and boats to alert beach officials when there are sharks in the area. In addition, there is an array of products that claim to offer personal protection from sharks, ranging from wetsuits in different colors to devices that broadcast electrical signals in an attempt to confuse the sharks' sensory organs. At the end of the day, though, beaches like these remain dangerous, and swimmers must assume the risk every time they paddle out from shore.

The author of this passage has a clear topic: sharks and their relationship with humans. In order to identify the main idea of the passage, the reader must ask, What does the author want to say about this topic? What is the reader meant to think or understand?

DID YOU KNOW?
Readers should identify the topic of a text and pay attention to how the details about it relate to one another. A passage may discuss, for example, topic similarities, characteristics, causes, and/ or effects.

The author makes sure to provide information about several different aspects of the relationship between sharks and humans, and points out that humans must respect sharks as dangerous marine animals, without sensationalizing the risk of attack. The reader can figure this out by looking at the various pieces of information the author includes as well as the similarities between them. The passage describes sensationalistic media, then talks about how officials and governments try to protect beaches, and ends with the observation that people must take personal responsibility. These details clarify what the author's main idea is: thanks to safety precautions and their natural behavior, sharks are not as dangerous as they are portrayed to be. Summarizing that main idea by focusing on the connection between the different details helps the reader draw a conclusion.

EXAMPLES

The art of the twentieth and twenty-first centuries demonstrates several aspects of modern social advancement. A primary example is the advent of technology: new technologies have developed new avenues for art making, and the globalization brought about by the internet has both diversified the art world and brought it together simultaneously. Even as artists are able to engage in a global conversation about the categories and characteristics of art, creating a more uniform understanding, they can now express themselves in a diversity of ways for a diversity of audiences. The result has been a rapid change in how art is made and consumed.

1. This passage is primarily concerned with
   A) the importance of art in the twenty-first century.
   B) the use of art to communicate overarching ideals to diverse communities.
   C) the importance of technology to art criticism.
   D) the change in understanding and creation of art in the modern period.

2. Which of the following best describes the main idea of the passage?
   A) Modern advances in technology have diversified art making and connected artists to distant places and ideas.
   B) Diversity in modern art is making it harder for art viewers to understand and talk about that art.
   C) The use of technology to discuss art allows us to create standards for what art should be.
   D) Art-making before the invention of technology such as the internet was disorganized and poorly understood.

TOPIC and SUMMARY SENTENCES

Identifying the main idea requires understanding the structure of a piece of writing. In a short passage of one or two paragraphs, the topic and summary sentences quickly relate what the paragraphs are about and what conclusions the author wants the reader to draw. These sentences function as bookends to a paragraph or passage, telling readers what to think and keeping the passage tied tightly together.

Generally, the TOPIC SENTENCE is the first, or very near the first, sentence in a paragraph. It is a general statement that introduces the topic, clearly and specifically directing the reader to access any previous experience with that topic.

> **DID YOU KNOW?**
> A summary is a very brief restatement of the most important parts of an argument or text. Building a summary begins with the most important idea in a text. A longer summary also includes supporting details. The text of a summary should be much shorter than the original.

The SUMMARY SENTENCE, on the other hand, frequently—but not always!—comes at the end of a paragraph or passage, because it wraps up all the ideas presented. This sentence provides an understanding of what the author wants to say about the topic and what conclusions to draw about it. While a topic sentence acts as an introduction to a topic, allowing the reader to activate his or her own ideas and experiences, the summary statement asks the reader to accept the author's ideas about that topic. Because of this, a summary sentence helps the reader quickly identify a piece's main idea.

EXAMPLES

There is nowhere more beautiful and interesting than California. With glimmering azure seas, fertile green plains, endless deserts, and majestic mountains, California offers every landscape. Hikers can explore the wilderness in Yosemite National Park, where a variety of plants and animals make their home. Farmers grow almonds, apricots, cotton, tomatoes, and more in the Central Valley that winds through the middle of the state. Skiers enjoy the slopes and backcountry of the Sierra Nevada and Lake Tahoe area. In the desert of Death Valley, temperatures rise well over one hundred degrees Fahrenheit. And of course, California's famous beaches stretch from the Mexican border to Oregon. Furthermore, California features some of America's most important cities. In the south, Los Angeles is home to the movie industry and Hollywood. Farther north, the San Francisco Bay Area includes Silicon Valley, where the US tech industry is based. Both places are centers of commercial activity. In fact, California is the most populous state in the country. There is no shortage of things to do or sights to see!

3. Which of the following best explains the general idea and focus indicated by the topic sentence?

   A) The diversity of California's landscape allows agriculture to flourish, and the most important crops will be detailed.

   B) California is beautiful and diverse; the reader will read on to find out what makes it so interesting.

   C) California is a peaceful place; its people live with a sense of predictability and the state is prosperous.

   D) The incredible geography of California is the reason it is a rural state, and the reader can expect a discussion of the countryside.

4. Which of the following best states what the author wants the reader to understand after reading the summary sentence?

- **A)** Tourists should see everything in California when they visit.
- **B)** The cities of California are interesting, but the rural parts are better.
- **C)** The resources of California are nearly exhausted.
- **D)** California is an inspiring and exciting place.

Supporting Details

Between a topic sentence and a summary sentence, the rest of a paragraph is built with **SUPPORTING DETAILS**. Supporting details come in many forms; the purpose of the passage dictates the type of details that will support the main idea. A persuasive passage may use facts and data or detail specific reasons for the author's opinion. An informative passage will primarily use facts about the topic to support the main idea. Even a narrative passage will have supporting details—specific things the author says to develop the story and characters.

The most important aspect of supporting details is exactly what it sounds like: they support the main idea. Examining the various supporting details and how they work with one another will reveal how the author views a topic and what the main idea of the passage is. Supporting details are key to understanding a passage.

Supporting details can often be found in texts by looking for **SIGNAL WORDS**—transitions that explain to the reader how one sentence or idea is connected to another. Signal words can add information, provide counterarguments, create organization in a passage, or draw conclusions. Some common signal words and phrases include *in particular*, *in addition*, *besides*, *contrastingly*, *therefore*, and *because*.

EXAMPLE

Increasingly, companies are turning to subcontracting services rather than hiring full-time employees. This provides companies with advantages like greater flexibility, reduced legal responsibility to employees, and lower possibility of unionization within the company. However, this has led to increasing confusion and uncertainty over the legal definition of employment. Courts have grappled with questions about the hiring company's responsibility in maintaining fair labor practices. Companies argue that they delegate that authority to subcontractors, while unions and other worker advocate groups argue that companies still have a legal obligation to the workers who contribute to their business.

5. According to the passage, why do companies use subcontractors?
Hiring subcontractors

A) costs less money than hiring full-time employees.
B) increases the need for unionization of employees.
C) reduces the company's legal responsibilities.
D) gives the company greater control over worker's hours.

The Author's Purpose

The author of a passage sets out with a specific goal in mind: to communicate a particular idea to an audience. The **AUTHOR'S PURPOSE** is determined by asking why the author wants the reader to understand the passage's main idea. There are four basic purposes to which an author can write: narrative, expository, technical, and persuasive. Within each of these general purposes, the author may direct the audience to take a clear action or respond in a certain way.

The purpose for which an author writes a passage is also connected to the structure of that text. In a **NARRATIVE**, the author seeks to tell a story, often to illustrate a theme or idea the reader needs to consider. In a narrative, the author uses characteristics of storytelling, such as chronological order, characters, and a defined setting, and these characteristics communicate the author's theme or main idea.

In an **EXPOSITORY** passage, on the other hand, the author simply seeks to explain an idea or topic to the reader. The main idea will probably be a factual statement or a direct assertion of a broadly held opinion. Expository writing can come in many forms, but one essential feature is a fair and balanced representation of a topic. The author may explore one detailed aspect or a broad range of characteristics, but he or she mainly seeks to prompt a decision from the reader.

Similarly, in **TECHNICAL** writing, the author's purpose is to explain specific processes, techniques, or equipment in order for the reader to use that process or equipment to obtain a desired result. Writing like this employs chronological or spatial structures, specialized vocabulary, and imperative or directive language.

DID YOU KNOW?
Reading persuasive text requires an awareness of what the author believes about the topic.

In **PERSUASIVE** writing, the author actively seeks to convince the reader to accept an opinion or belief. Much like expository writing, persuasive writing is presented in many organizational forms.

EXAMPLE

University of California, Berkeley, researchers decided to tackle an age-old problem: why shoelaces come untied. They recorded the shoelaces of a volunteer walking on a treadmill by attaching devices to record the acceleration, or g-force, experienced by the knot. The results were surprising. A shoelace knot experiences more g-force from a person walking than any rollercoaster can generate. However, if the person simply stomped or swung their feet—the two movements that make up a walker's stride—the g-force was not enough to undo the knots.

6. What is the purpose of this passage?
- **A)** to confirm if shoelaces always come undone
- **B)** to compare the force of treadmills and rollercoasters
- **C)** to persuade readers to tie their shoes tighter
- **D)** to describe the results of an experiment on shoelaces

Organization and Text Structures

It's important to analyze the organization and structure of informational texts, as these details can provide valuable insight into the author's purpose and the overall meaning of a text. Several common structures are used in informative texts, and understanding these structures will help readers quickly make sense of new texts. Texts may be organized in one of the following ways:

- ▶ **CHRONOLOGICAL** texts describe events in the order they occurred.
- ▶ **PROBLEM-SOLUTION** texts begin by describing a problem and then offer a possible solution to the issue.
- ▶ **CAUSE-EFFECT** is a text structure that shows a causal chain of events or ideas.
- ▶ **GENERAL-TO-SPECIFIC** is a text structure that describes a general topic then provides details about a specific aspect of that topic.
- ▶ **COMPARE-CONTRAST** texts give the similarities and differences between two things.

Authors choose the organizational structure of their text according to their purpose. For example, an author who hopes to convince people to begin recycling might begin by talking about the problems that are caused by excessive waste and end by offering recycling as a reasonable solution. On the other hand, the author might choose to use a chronological structure for an article whose purpose is to give an impartial history of recycling.

EXAMPLE

For thirteen years, a spacecraft called *Cassini* was on an exploratory mission to Saturn. The spacecraft was designed not to return but to end its journey by diving into Saturn's atmosphere. This dramatic ending provided scientists with unprecedented information about Saturn's atmosphere and its magnetic and gravitational fields. First, however, *Cassini* passed Saturn's largest moon, Titan, where it recorded data on Titan's curious methane lakes, gathering information about potential seasons on the planet-sized moon. Then it passed through the unexplored region between Saturn itself and its famous rings. Scientists hope to learn how old the rings are and to directly examine the particles that make them up. *Cassini*'s mission ended in 2017, but researchers have new questions for future exploration.

7. Which of the following best describes the organization of this passage?
   A) general-to-specific
   B) compare-contrast
   C) chronological
   D) problem-solution

The Audience

The structure, purpose, main idea, and language of a text all converge on one target: the intended AUDIENCE. An author makes decisions about every aspect of a piece of writing based on that audience, and readers can evaluate the writing by considering who the author is writing for. By considering the probable reactions of an intended audience, readers can determine many things:

- whether they are part of that intended audience
- the author's purpose for using specific techniques or devices
- the biases of the author and how they appear in the writing
- how the author uses rhetorical strategies.

DID YOU KNOW?
When reading a persuasive text, students should maintain awareness of what the author believes about the topic.

The audience for a text can be identified by careful analysis of the text. First, the reader considers who most likely cares about the topic and main idea of the text: who would want or need to know about this topic? The audience may be SPECIFIC (e.g., biologists who study sharks) or more GENERAL (e.g., people with an interest in marine life).

Next, consider the language of the text. The author tailors language to appeal to the intended audience, so the reader can determine from the language who the author is speaking to. A FORMAL style is used in business and academic settings and can make the author seem more credible. Characteristics of a formal style include:

- third person perspective (i.e., no use of *I* or *you*)
- no use of slang or clichés
- follows a clear structure (e.g., an introduction, a body, and a conclusion)
- technically correct grammar and sentence structure
- objective language

An **INFORMAL** style is used to appeal to readers in a more casual setting, such as a magazine or blog. Using an informal style may make the author seem less credible, but it can help create an emotional connection with the audience. Characteristics of informal writing include:

- use of first or second person (e.g., *I* or *you*)
- use of slang or casual language
- follows an unusual or flexible structure
- bends the rules of grammar
- appeals to audience's emotions

EXAMPLE

What do you do with plastic bottles? Do you throw them away, or do you recycle or reuse them? As landfills continue to fill up, there will eventually be no place to put our trash. If you recycle or reuse bottles, you will help reduce waste and turn something old into a creative masterpiece!

8. Which of the following BEST describes the intended audience for this passage?
  - **A)** a formal audience of engineering professionals
  - **B)** an audience of English language learners
  - **C)** a general audience that includes children
  - **D)** a group of scientists at an environmental conference

Evaluating Arguments

An author selects details to help support the main idea. The reader must then evaluate these details for relevance and consistency. Though the author generally includes details that support the text's main idea, it's up to the reader to decide whether those details are convincing.

Readers should be able to differentiate between facts and opinions in order to more effectively analyze supporting details. **FACTS** are based in truth and can usually be proven. They are pieces of information that have been confirmed or validated. An opinion is a judgment, belief, or viewpoint that is not based on evidence. **OPINIONS** are often stated in descriptive, subjective language that is difficult to define or prove. While opinions can be included in informative texts, they are often of little impact unless they are supported by some kind of evidence.

Sometimes, the author's **BIAS**—an inclination towards a particular belief—causes the author to leave out details that do not directly support the main idea or that support

> **QUICK REVIEW**
> Which of the following phrases would be associated with opinions? *for example, studies have shown, I believe, in fact, it's possible that*

an opposite idea. The reader has to be able to notice not only what the author says but also what the author leaves out. Discovering the author's bias and how the supporting details reveal that bias is also key to understanding a text.

Writers will often use specific techniques, or **RHETORICAL STRATEGIES**, to build an argument. Readers can identify these strategies in order to clearly understand what an author wants them to believe, how the author's perspective and purpose may lead to bias, and whether the passage includes any logical fallacies.

Common rhetorical strategies include the appeals to ethos, logos, and pathos. An author uses these to build trust with the reader, explain the logical points of his or her argument, and convince the reader that his or her opinion is the best option.

An **ETHOS (ETHICAL) APPEAL** uses balanced, fair language and seeks to build a trusting relationship between the author and the reader. An author might explain her or his credentials, include the reader in an argument, or offer concessions to an opposing argument.

QUICK REVIEW
Consider how different audiences would react to the same text.

A **LOGOS (LOGICAL) APPEAL** builds on that trust by providing facts and support for the author's opinion, explaining the argument with clear connections and reasoning. At this point, the reader should beware of logical fallacies that connect unconnected ideas and build arguments on incorrect premises. With a logical appeal, an author strives to convince the reader to accept an opinion or belief by demonstrating that not only is it the most logical option but that it also satisfies her or his emotional reaction to a topic.

A **PATHOS (EMOTIONAL) APPEAL** does not depend on reasonable connections between ideas; rather, it seeks to remind the reader, through imagery, strong language, and personal connections, that the author's argument aligns with her or his best interests.

EXAMPLE

Exercise is critical for healthy development in children. Today in the United States, there is an epidemic of poor childhood health; many of these children will face further illnesses in adulthood that are due to poor diet and lack of exercise now. This is a problem for all Americans, especially with the rising cost of health care.

It is vital that school systems and parents encourage children to engage in a minimum of thirty minutes of cardiovascular exercise each day, mildly increasing their heart rate for a sustained period. This is proven to decrease the likelihood of developmental diabetes, obesity, and a multitude of other health problems. Also, children need a proper diet, rich in fruits and vegetables, so they can develop physically and learn healthy eating habits early on.

9. Which of the following statements from the passage is a fact, not an opinion?
   A) Fruits and vegetables are the best way to help children be healthy.
   B) Children today are lazier than they were in previous generations.
   C) The risk of diabetes in children is reduced by physical activity.
   D) Children should engage in thirty minutes of exercise a day.

Drawing Conclusions

Reading text begins with making sense of the explicit meanings of information or a narrative. Understanding occurs as the reader draws conclusions and makes logical inferences. First, the reader considers the details or facts. He or she then comes to a CONCLUSION—the next logical point in the thought sequence. For example, in a Hemingway story, an old man sits alone in a cafe. A young waiter says that the cafe is closing, but the old man continues to drink. The waiter starts closing up, and the old man signals for a refill. Based on these details, the reader might conclude that the old man has not understood the young waiter's desire for him to leave.

> **DID YOU KNOW?**
> When considering a character's motivations, the reader should ask what the character wants to achieve, what the character will get by accomplishing this, and what the character seems to value the most.

An inference is distinguished from a conclusion drawn. An INFERENCE is an assumption the reader makes based on details in the text as well as his or her own knowledge. It is more of an educated guess that extends the literal meaning of a text. Inferences begin with the given details; however, the reader uses the facts to determine additional information. What the reader already knows informs what is being suggested by the details of decisions or situations in the text. Returning to the example of the Hemingway story, the reader might *infer* that the old man is lonely, enjoys being in the cafe, and therefore is reluctant to leave.

When reading fictional text, inferring character motivations is essential. The actions of the characters move the plot forward; a series of events is understood by making sense of why the characters did what they did. Hemingway includes contrasting details as the young waiter and an older waiter discuss the old man. The older waiter sympathizes with the old man; both men have no one at home and experience a sense of emptiness in life, which motivates them to seek the cafe.

> **DID YOU KNOW?**
> Conclusions are drawn by thinking about how the author wants the reader to feel. A group of carefully selected facts can cause the reader to feel a certain way.

Another aspect of understanding text is connecting it to other texts. Readers may connect the Hemingway story about the old man in the cafe to other Hemingway stories about individuals struggling to deal with loss and loneliness in a dignified way.

They can extend their initial connections to people they know or their personal experiences. When readers read a persuasive text, they often connect the arguments made to counterarguments and opposing evidence of which they are aware. They use these connections to infer meaning.

> **EXAMPLE**
>
> After World War I, political and social forces pushed for a return to normalcy in the United States. The result was disengagement from the larger world and increased focus on American economic growth and personal enjoyment. Caught in the middle were American writers, raised on the values of the prewar world and frustrated with what they viewed as the superficiality and materialism of postwar American culture. Many of them fled to Paris, where they became known as the "lost generation," creating a trove of literary works criticizing their home culture and delving into their own feelings of alienation.
>
> 10. Which conclusion about the effects of war is most likely true, according to the passage?
>   A) War served as an inspiration for literary works.
>   B) It was difficult to stabilize countries after war occurred.
>   C) Writers were torn between supporting war and their own ideals.
>   D) Individual responsibility and global awareness declined after the war.

Tone and Mood

The **TONE** of a passage describes the author's attitude toward the topic. In general, the author's tone can be described as positive, negative, or neutral. The **MOOD** is the pervasive feeling or atmosphere in a passage that provokes specific emotions in the reader. Put simply, tone is how the author feels about the topic. Mood is how the reader feels about the text.

DICTION, or word choice, helps determine mood and tone in a passage. Many readers make the mistake using the author's ideas alone to determine tone; a much better practice is to look at specific words and try to identify a pattern in the emotion they evoke. Does the writer choose positive words like *ambitious* and *confident*? Or does he describe those concepts with negative words like *greedy* and *overbearing*? The first writer's tone might be described as admiring, while the more negative tone would be disapproving.

DID YOU KNOW?
To decide the connotation of a word, the reader examines whether the word conveys a positive or negative association in the mind. Adjectives are often used to influence the feelings of the reader, such as in the phrase *an ambitious attempt to achieve*.

When looking at tone, it's important to examine not just the literal definition of words. Every word has not only a literal meaning but also a **CONNOTATIVE MEANING**, which relies on the common emotions and experiences an audience might associate with that word. The following words are all synonyms: *dog, puppy, cur, mutt,* *canine*, *pet*. Two of these words—*dog* and *canine*—are neutral words, without strong associations or emotions. Two others—*pet* and *puppy*—have positive associations. The last two—*cur* and *mutt*—have negative associations. A passage that uses one pair of these words versus another pair activates the positive or negative reactions of the audience.

Table 6.1. Words That Describe Tone

Positive	Neutral	Negative
admiring	casual	angry
approving	detached	annoyed
celebratory	formal	belligerent
earnest	impartial	bitter
encouraging	informal	condescending
excited	objective	confused
funny	questioning	cynical
hopeful	unconcerned	depressed
humorous		disrespectful
nostalgic		embarrassed
optimistic		fearful
playful		gloomy
poignant		melancholy
proud		mournful
relaxed		pessimistic
respectful		skeptical
sentimental		solemn
silly		suspicious
sympathetic		unsympathetic

EXAMPLES

Day had broken cold and grey, exceedingly cold and grey, when the man turned aside from the main Yukon trail and climbed the high earth-bank, where a dim and little-travelled trail led eastward through the fat spruce timberland. It was a steep bank, and he paused for breath at the top, excusing the act to himself by looking at his watch. It was nine o'clock. There was no sun nor hint of sun, though there was not a cloud in the sky. It was a clear day, and yet there seemed an intangible pall over the face of things, a subtle gloom that made the day dark, and that was due to the absence of sun. This fact did not worry the man. He was used to the lack of sun. It had been days since he had seen the sun, and he knew that a few more days must pass before that cheerful orb, due south, would just peep above the sky-line and dip immediately from view.

—from "To Build a Fire" by Jack London

11. Which of the following best describes the mood of the passage?
- **A)** exciting and adventurous
- **B)** unhappy and anxious
- **C)** bleak but accepting
- **D)** grim yet hopeful

12. The connotation of the words *intangible pall* is
- **A)** a death-like covering.
- **B)** a sense of familiarity.
- **C)** a feeling of communal strength.
- **D)** an understanding of the struggle ahead.

Meaning of Words and Phrases

The TSI does not specifically ask you to define words, but it is good to know strategies to determine the meaning of unfamiliar words you may encounter when analyzing reading passages and improving paragraphs.

When confronted with unfamiliar words, the passage itself can help clarify their meaning. Often, identifying the tone or main idea of the passage can help eliminate answer choices. For example, if the tone of the passage is generally positive, try eliminating the answer choices with a negative connotation. Or, if the passage is about a particular occupation, rule out words unrelated to that topic.

Passages may also provide specific context clues that can help determine the meaning of a word. One type of context clue is a **DEFINITION**, or **DESCRIPTION, CLUE**. Sometimes, authors use a difficult word, then include *that is* or *which is* to signal that they are providing a definition. An author also may provide a synonym or restate the idea in more familiar words:

> Teachers often prefer teaching students with intrinsic motivation; these students have an internal desire to learn.

The meaning of *intrinsic* is restated as *an internal desire*.

Similarly, authors may include an **EXAMPLE CLUE**, providing an example phrase that clarifies the meaning of the word:

> Teachers may view extrinsic rewards as efficacious; however, an individual student may not be interested in what the teacher offers. For example, a student who does not like sweets may not feel any incentive to work when offered a sugary reward.

Efficacious is explained with an example that demonstrates how an extrinsic reward may not be effective.

Another commonly used context clue is the **CONTRAST**, or **ANTONYM**, **CLUE**. In this case, authors indicate that the unfamiliar word is the opposite of a familiar word:

> In contrast to intrinsic motivation, extrinsic motivation is contingent on teachers offering rewards that are appealing.

The phrase *in contrast* tells the reader that extrinsic is the opposite of intrinsic.

EXAMPLES

13. Which of the following is the meaning of *incentivize* as used in the sentence?

    One challenge of teaching is finding ways to incentivize, or to motivate, learning.

    A) encourage
    B) determine
    C) challenge
    D) improve

14. Which of the following is the meaning of *apprehensive* as used in the sentence?

    If an extrinsic reward is extremely desirable, a student may become so apprehensive he or she cannot focus. The student may experience such intense pressure to perform that the reward undermines its intent.

    A) uncertain
    B) distracted
    C) anxious
    D) forgetful

WORD STRUCTURE

In addition to the context of a sentence or passage, an unfamiliar word itself can give the reader clues about its meaning. Each word consists of discrete pieces that determine meaning; the most familiar of these pieces are word roots, prefixes, and suffixes.

WORD ROOTS are the bases from which many words take their form and meaning. The most common word roots are Greek and Latin, and a broad knowledge of these roots can greatly improve a reader's ability to determine the meaning of words in context. The root of a word does not always point to the word's exact meaning, but combined with an understanding of the word's place in a sentence and the context of a passage, it will often be enough to answer a question about meaning or relationships.

Table 6.2. Common Word Roots

Root	Meaning	Examples
alter	other	alternate, alter ego
ambi	both	ambidextrous
ami, amic	love	amiable
amphi	both ends, all sides	amphibian
anthrop	man, human, humanity	misanthrope, anthropologist
apert	open	aperture
aqua	water	aqueduct, aquarium
aud	to hear	audience
auto	self	autobiography
bell	war	belligerent, bellicose
bene	good	benevolent
bio	life	biology
ced	yield, go	secede, intercede
cent	one hundred	century
chron	time	chronological
circum	around	circumference
contra, counter	against	contradict
crac, crat	rule, ruler	autocrat, bureaucrat
crypt	hidden	cryptogram, cryptic
curr, curs, cours	to run	precursory
dict	to say	dictator, dictation
dyna	power	dynamic
dys	bad, hard, unlucky	dysfunctional
equ	equal, even	equanimity
fac	to make, to do	factory
form	shape	reform, conform
fort	strength	fortitude
fract	to break	fracture
grad, gress	step	progression
gram	thing written	epigram

Root	Meaning	Examples
graph	writing	graphic
hetero	different	heterogeneous
homo	same	homogenous
hypo	below, beneath	hypothermia
iso	identical	isolate
ject	throw	projection
logy	study of	biology
luc	light	elucidate
mal	bad	malevolent
meta, met	behind, between	metacognition (behind the thinking)
meter, metr	measure	thermometer
micro	small	microbe
mis, miso	hate	misanthrope
mit	to send	transmit
mono	one	monologue
morph	form, shape	morphology
mort	death	mortal
multi	many	multiple
phil	love	philanthropist
port	carry	transportation
pseudo	false	pseudonym
psycho	soul, spirit	psychic
rupt	to break	disruption
scope	viewing instrument	microscope
scrib, scribe	to write	inscription
sect, sec	to cut	section
sequ, secu	follow	consecutive
soph	wisdom, knowledge	philosophy
spect	to look	spectator
struct	to build	restructure
tele	far off	telephone

Table 6.2. Common Word Roots (continued)

Root	Meaning	Examples
terr	earth	terrestrial
therm	heat	thermal
vent, vene	to come	convene
vert	turn	vertigo
voc	voice, call	vocalize, evocative

In addition to understanding the base of a word, it is vital to recognize common affixes that change the meaning of words and demonstrate their relationships to other words. **Prefixes** are added to the beginning of words and frequently change their meaning, sometimes to an opposite meaning.

Table 6.3. Common Prefixes

Prefix	Meaning	Examples
a, an	without, not	anachronism, anhydrous
ab, abs, a	apart, away from	abscission, abnormal
ad	toward	adhere
agere	act	agent
amphi, ambi	round, both sides	ambivalent
ante	before	antedate, anterior
anti	against	antipathy
archos	leader, first, chief	oligarchy
bene	well, favorable	benevolent, beneficent
bi	two	binary, bivalve
caco	bad	cacophony
circum	around	circumnavigate
corpus	body	corporeal
credo	belief	credible
demos	people	demographic
di	two, double	dimorphism, diatomic
dia	across, through	dialectic
dis	not, apart	disenfranchise
dynasthai	be able	dynamo, dynasty

Prefix	Meaning	Examples
ego	I, self	egomaniac, egocentric
epi	upon, over	epigram, epiphyte
ex	out	extraneous, extemporaneous
geo	earth	geocentric, geomancy
ideo	idea	ideology, ideation
in	in	induction, indigenous
in, im	not	ignoble, immoral
inter	between	interstellar
lexis	word	lexicography
liber	free, book	liberal
locus	place	locality
macro	large	macrophage
micro	small	micron
mono	one, single	monocle, monovalent
mortis	death	moribund
olig	few	oligarchy
peri	around	peripatetic, perineum
poly	many	polygamy
pre	before	prescient
solus	alone	solitary
subter	under, secret	subterfuge
un	not	unsafe
utilis	useful	utilitarian

Suffixes, on the other hand, are added to the end of words, and they generally point out a word's relationship to other words in a sentence. Suffixes might change a part of speech or indicate if a word is plural or related to a plural.

Table 6.4. Common Suffixes

Suffix	Meaning	Examples
able, ible	able, capable	visible
age	act of, state of, result of	wreckage
al	relating to	gradual

Table 6.4. Common Suffixes (continued)

Suffix	Meaning	Examples
algia	pain	myalgia
an, ian	native of, relating to	riparian
ance, ancy	action, process, state	defiance
ary, ery, ory	relating to, quality, place	aviary
cian	processing a specific skill or art	physician
cule, ling	very small	sapling, animalcule
cy	action, function	normalcy
dom	quality, realm	wisdom
ee	one who receives the action	nominee
en	made of, to make	silken
ence, ency	action, state of, quality	urgency
er, or	one who, that which	professor
escent	in the process of	adolescent, senescence
esis, osis	action, process, condition	genesis, neurosis
et, ette	small one, group	baronet, lorgnette
fic	making, causing	specific
ful	full of	frightful
hood	order, condition, quality	adulthood
ice	condition, state, quality	malice
id, ide	connected with, belonging to	bromide
ile	relating to, suited for, capable of	puerile, juvenile
ine	nature of	feminine
ion, sion, tion	act, result, state of	contagion
ish	origin, nature, resembling	impish
ism	system, manner, condition, characteristic	capitalism
ist	one who, that which	artist, flautist
ite	nature of, quality of, mineral product	graphite
ity, ty	state of, quality	captivity
ive	causing, making	exhaustive
ize, ise	make	idolize, bowdlerize

Suffix	Meaning	Examples
ment	act of, state or, result	containment
nomy	law	autonomy, taxonomy
oid	resembling	asteroid, anthropoid
some	like, apt, tending to	gruesome
strat	cover	strata
tude	state of, condition of	aptitude
um	forms single nouns	spectrum
ure	state of, act, process, rank	rupture, rapture
ward	in the direction of	backward
y	inclined to, tend to	faulty

EXAMPLES

Width and intensity are leading characteristics of his writings—width both of subject-matter and of comprehension, intensity of self-absorption into what the poet contemplates and expresses. He scans and presents an enormous panorama, unrolled before him as from a mountain-top; and yet, whatever most large or most minute or casual thing his eye glances upon, that he enters into with a depth of affection which identifies him with it for a time, be the object what it may. There is a singular interchange also of actuality and of ideal substratum and suggestion. While he sees men, with even abnormal exactness and sympathy, as men, he sees them also "as trees walking," and admits us to perceive that the whole show is in a measure spectral and unsubstantial, and the mask of a larger and profounder reality beneath it, of which it is giving perpetual intimations and auguries.

—from "Prefatory Notice," in the first edition of Walt Whitman's *Leaves of Grass*, by W. M. Rossetti

15. Which of the following is the best definition of the word *substratum*?
- **A)** meaningful crest
- **B)** distracting idea
- **C)** reduction
- **D)** underlying foundation

16. The prefix *un* in a word like *unsubstantial* indicates the meaning of the word is
- **A)** not whatever the root word is.
- **B)** suggestive of an undercurrent of whatever the root word is.
- **C)** a lower value of the root word.
- **D)** in opposition to whatever the root word is.

Figurative Language

Figures of speech are expressions that are understood to have a nonliteral meaning. Rather than stating their ideas directly, authors use **FIGURATIVE LANGUAGE** to suggest meaning by speaking of a subject as if it were something else. For example, when Shakespeare says, "All the world's a stage,/ And all men and women merely players," he is speaking of the world as if it is a stage. Since the world is not literally a stage, the reader has to ask how the two are similar and what Shakespeare might be implying about the world through this comparison. Figures of speech extend the meaning of words by engaging the reader's imagination and adding emphasis to different aspects of their subject.

A **METAPHOR** is a type of figurative language that describes something that may be unfamiliar to the reader (the topic) by referring to it as though it were something else that is more familiar to the reader (the vehicle). A metaphor stands in as a synonym, interchangeable with its corresponding topic. As the reader reflects on the similarities between the topic and the vehicle, he or she forms a clearer understanding of the topic. For example, in Shakespeare's *Romeo and Juliet*, Romeo says that "Juliet is the sun." By making this comparison, Romeo is comparing Juliet's energy to the brightness of the sun, which is familiar to readers.

A **SIMILE** is a type of figurative language that directly points to similarities between two things. As with a metaphor, the author uses a familiar vehicle to express an idea about a less familiar topic. Unlike a metaphor, however, a simile does not replace the object with a figurative description; it compares the vehicle and topic using "like," "as," or similar words. For example, in his poem "The Rime of the Ancient Mariner," Coleridge describes his ship as "idle as a painted ship/ Upon a painted ocean." He speaks about the boat as if it were painted (unlike Romeo above, who says explicitly that Juliet is the sun itself). The reader understands that paintings do not move, so Coleridge uses this comparison to show the reader that the ship in the poem is completely motionless.

IMAGERY is vivid description that appeals to the reader's sense of sight, sound, smell, taste, or touch. This type of figurative language allows readers to experience through their senses what is being described; as readers use their imaginations to visualize or recall sensory experience, they are drawn into the scene of the story or poem.

HYPERBOLE is an overstatement, an exaggeration intended to achieve a particular effect. Hyperbole can create humor or add emphasis to a text by drawing the reader's attention to a particular idea. For example, a character might say he or she is "so hungry, [he or she] could eat a horse." Though the character probably cannot literally eat a horse, the reader understands that he or she is extremely hungry.

PERSONIFICATION is a type of figurative language in which human characteristics are attributed to objects, abstract ideas, natural forces, or animals. For example, if a writer refers to "murmuring pine trees," he or she is attributing to the pine trees the human ability of murmuring. The writer is using the familiar vehicle of the sound of murmuring to help the reader understand the sound pine trees make in the wind.

SYMBOLISM is a literary device in which the author uses a concrete object, action, or character to represent an abstract idea. The significance of the symbol reaches beyond the object's ordinary meaning. Familiar symbols are roses representing beauty, light representing truth, and darkness representing evil. As readers notice an author's use of symbolism, they begin to make connections and to formulate ideas about what the author is suggesting.

An **ALLUSION**, not to be confused with illusion, is a reference to a historical person or event, a fictional character or event, a mythological or religious character or event, or an artist or artistic work. When a reader recognizes an allusion, he or she may make associations that contribute to his or her understanding of the text. For example, if a character is described as having a "Mona Lisa smile," an instant image will arise in the minds of most readers. Because allusions can be difficult to recognize, especially for young readers whose experiences are limited, teachers must provide instruction in how to recognize, research, and interpret unfamiliar references.

CLICHÉS are common sayings that lack originality but are familiar and relatable to an audience. Though clichés are not necessarily beneficial to the author who is trying to write a wholly original work, they can be helpful for a writer who is attempting to show that he or she can relate to the audience.

DIALECT and **SLANG** are linguistic qualities that an author might incorporate into his or her writing in order to develop characters or setting. A character's dialect may reveal where he or she is from, while the slang he or she uses may be an indication of social, economic, and educational status.

IRONY comes in different forms. **VERBAL IRONY** is used when a character or narrator says something that is the opposite of what he or she means. **SITUATIONAL IRONY** occurs when something happens that contradicts what the audience expected to happen. **DRAMATIC IRONY** occurs when the audience knows about something of which a character or characters are not aware.

EXAMPLE

Alfie closed his eyes and took several deep breaths. He was trying to ignore the sounds of the crowd, but even he had to admit that it was hard not to notice the tension in the stadium. He could feel 50,000 sets of eyes burning through his skin—this crowd expected perfection from him. He took another breath and opened his eyes, setting his sights on the soccer ball resting peacefully in the grass. One shot, just one last shot, between his team and the championship. He didn't look up at the goalie, who was jumping nervously on the goal line just a few yards away. Afterward, he would swear he didn't remember anything between the referee's whistle and the thunderous roar of the crowd.

17. Which of the following best describes the meaning of the phrase "he could feel 50,000 sets of eyes burning through his skin"?
- **A)** The 50,000 people in the stadium were trying to hurt Alfie.
- **B)** Alfie felt uncomfortable and exposed in front of so many people.
- **C)** Alfie felt immense pressure from the 50,000 people watching him.
- **D)** The people in the stadium are warning Alfie that the field is on fire.

Graphic Sources of Information

Informational texts on the TSI may be accompanied by graphic sources of information, including graphs, diagrams, or photographs. There's no simple set of rules for handling these questions, but many of the same strategies that are used for other figures and for text passages are applicable.

Always start with the **TITLE** of a figure—it will provide information that is likely crucial to understanding the figure. An anatomical diagram might have a title such as *Lobes of the Brain* that tells the viewer that the diagram will likely show the names and locations of the brain's lobes. Similarly, a graph may have a title like *Number of Customers per Month*, which describes the information in the graph.

Also make sure to examine any **LABELS**, legends, or scales provided with the figure. Graphs, for example, should always include labels on the axes that describe what's shown on each axis, and a flowchart will have arrows indicating an ordered sequence.

Many of the strategies needed to interpret traditional reading passages can also be used for graphic representations of information, particularly those that may be text heavy. When looking at a photograph or advertisement, it will help to identify:

- the purpose of the author
- the intended audience
- rhetorical strategies designed to influence the viewer
- the main idea of the image

A flyer for a local bake sale, for example, may be designed to appeal to the viewer's emotions by including pictures of local schoolchildren. Similarly, a computer advertisement meant to appeal to corporate buyers would probably use more formal language than one aimed at teenagers.

EXAMPLE

As you can see from the graph, my babysitting business has been really successful. The year started with a busy couple of months—several snows combined with a large number of requests for Valentine's Day services boosted our sales quite a bit. The spring months have admittedly been a bit slow, but we're hoping for a big summer once school gets out. Several clients have already put in requests for our services!

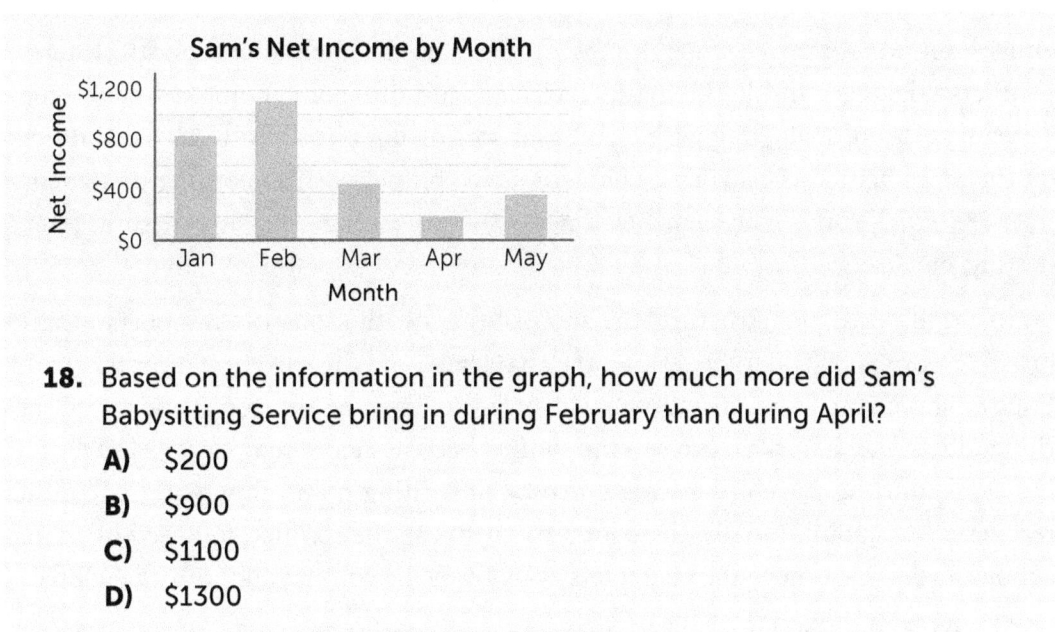

18. Based on the information in the graph, how much more did Sam's Babysitting Service bring in during February than during April?

- **A)** $200
- **B)** $900
- **C)** $1100
- **D)** $1300

Elements of Fiction

FICTION is a prose genre, made up of narratives whose details are not based in truth but are instead the creation of the author. Just as artists have the tools of color and shape to communicate ideas, so have writers their literary tools. These tools include point of view, plot, setting, character, tone, and figurative language. Each of these elements contributes to the overall idea that is developed in the text and, as such, can provide valuable insight into the theme of the work.

POINT OF VIEW is the perspective from which the action in a story is told. By carefully selecting a particular point of view, writers are able to control what their readers know. Most literature is written in either first person or third person point of view. With the FIRST PERSON POINT OF VIEW, the action is narrated by a character within the story, which can make it feel more believable and authentic to the reader. However, as a result of the first person point of view, the reader's knowledge and understanding are constrained by what the narrator notices and influenced by what the narrator thinks and values.

An author may, on the other hand, choose to tell the story from the THIRD PERSON POINT OF VIEW. A third person narrator is a voice outside the action of the story, an observer who shares what he or she knows, sees, or hears with the reader. A third person narrator might be FULLY OMNISCIENT (able to see into the minds of the characters and share what they are thinking and feeling), PARTIALLY OMNISCIENT (able to see into the minds of just one or a few characters), or LIMITED (unable to see into the minds of any of the characters and only able to share what can be seen and heard).

PLOT STRUCTURE is the way the author arranges the events of a narrative. In a conventional plot line, the story is structured around a central conflict, a struggle between two opposing forces. Conflicts in literature can be categorized in general terms as

Reading 129

either internal or external, though most stories have a combination of both. Internal conflicts take place inside the main character's mind; he or she might be making a difficult decision, struggling with change, or sorting out priorities. External conflicts, on the other hand, occur when a character is in conflict with something or someone in the external world—the elements of nature, another character, supernatural forces, destiny, or society.

In a traditional plot structure, the author begins with **EXPOSITION:** important background information about the setting, the characters, and the current state of the world. Following the exposition, an **INCITING INCIDENT** introduces the antagonist and establishes the conflict. As the story progresses, the conflict becomes more complicated and tension increases, moving the story toward a **CLIMAX** or turning point, in which the conflict reaches a crisis point. Finally, there is a **RESOLUTION** to the conflict, followed by falling actions, events that move the characters away from the conflict and into a new life.

SETTING is the geographical and chronological location of events in a story. When considering setting, readers should examine how characters interact with their surroundings, how they are influenced by the societal expectations of that time and place, and how the location and time period impact the development of the story. Often, setting can seem inseparable from plot; therefore, a helpful question for beginning the discussion of setting is, How would this story change if it were set in a different time or place?

CHARACTER DEVELOPMENT is the process an author uses to create characters that are complex and, to some degree, believable. One way authors develop their characters is directly: they tell the reader explicitly what the character is like by describing traits and assigning values. Sometimes, authors might include the thoughts and feelings of the characters themselves, offering readers even more insight. Authors can also develop their characters indirectly by revealing their actions and interactions with others, sometimes including what one character says or thinks about another and allowing the reader to draw his or her own conclusions. Most authors use a combination of direct and indirect characterization; this ensures that readers know what they need to know while also providing opportunities for reflection and interpretation.

EXAMPLE

19. Which passage below from *A Mystery of Heroism* by Stephen Crane best demonstrates the third person omniscient point of view?

- **A)** In the midst of it all Smith and Ferguson, two privates of A Company, were engaged in a heated discussion, which involved the greatest questions of the national existence.

- **B)** An officer screamed out an order so violently that his voice broke and ended the sentence in a falsetto shriek.

- **C)** The officer's face was grimy and perspiring, and his uniform was tousled as if he had been in direct grapple with an enemy. He smiled grimly when the men stared at him.

- **D)** No, it could not be true. He was not a hero. Heroes had no shames in their lives, and, as for him, he remembered borrowing fifteen dollars from a friend and promising to pay it back the next day, and then avoiding that friend for ten months.

Answer Key

1. **D) is correct.** The art of the modern period reflects the new technologies and globalization possible through the internet.

2. **A) is correct.** According to the text, technology and the internet have "diversified the art world and brought it together simultaneously."

3. **B) is correct.** This option indicates both the main idea and what the reader will focus on while reading.

4. **D) is correct.** The phrase "no shortage of things to do or sights to see" suggests the writer is enthusiastic about the many interesting activities possible in California. There is no indication that the writer should do everything, though, or that one part is better than another.

5. **C) is correct.** The passage states that hiring subcontractors provides the advantage of "reduced legal responsibility to employees."

6. **D) is correct.** The text provides details on the experiment as well as its results.

7. **C) is correct.** The passage describes the journey of Cassini in chronological order: it passed by Titan, went through the region between Saturn and its rings, and ended its mission in 2017.

8. **C) is correct.** The informal tone and direct address of this passage suggest that the author is writing for a general audience that may include children. For instance, turning bottles into an art project could be a good activity for children.

9. **C) is correct.** Choice C is a simple fact stated by the author. It is introduced by the word *proven* to indicate that it is supported by evidence.

10. **D) is correct.** After the war, in the US there was a lack of focus on the world and greater focus on personal comforts, which writers viewed as superficiality and materialism.

11. **C) is correct.** The day is described as "cold and grey" with an "intangible pall," which creates a bleak mood. However, the man himself "did not worry" and knew that only "a few more days must pass" before he would see the sun again, suggesting he has accepted his circumstances.

12. **A) is correct.** Within the context of the sentence "It was a clear day, and yet there seemed an intangible pall over the face of things, a subtle gloom that made the day dark," the words *gloom* and *dark* are suggestive of death; the phrase *over the face* suggests a covering.

13. **A) is correct.** The word *incentivize* is defined immediately with the synonym *motivate*, or *encourage*.

14. **C) is correct.** The reader can infer that the *pressure to perform* is making the student anxious.

15. D) is correct. Combining the prefix *sub* (under) and the root *strata* (cover) with the singular suffix *um*, the word *substratum* means underlying layer or substance. An "ideal underlying foundation" makes sense.

16. A) is correct. The prefix *un* means not, and the root word *substantial* means real. *Unsubstantial* means not of physical reality.

17. C) is correct. The metaphor implies that Alfie felt pressure from the people watching him to perform well. There is no indication that he is threatened physically.

18. B) is correct. In February the service earned $1100, and in April it earned $200. The difference between the two months is $900.

19. D) is correct. The narrator is reporting the thoughts of the character, as the character's memory about not acting heroic in the past is revealed. The other choices only include descriptions of the characters words or actions.

CHAPTER SEVEN
Language Skills

Parts of Speech

The **PARTS OF SPEECH** are the building blocks of sentences, paragraphs, and entire texts. Grammarians have typically defined eight parts of speech—nouns, pronouns, verbs, adverbs, adjectives, conjunctions, prepositions, and interjections—all of which play unique roles in the context of a sentence. Thus, a fundamental understanding of the parts of speech is necessary for comprehending basic sentence construction.

Though some words fall easily into one category or another, many words can function as different parts of speech based on their usage within a sentence.

NOUNS and PRONOUNS

NOUNS are the words that describe people, places, things, and ideas. Most often, nouns fill the position of subject or object within a sentence. Nouns have several subcategories: common nouns (*chair, car, house*), proper nouns (*Julie, David*), noncountable nouns (*money, water*), and countable nouns (*dollars, cubes*), among others. There is much crossover among these subcategories (for example, *chair* is common and countable), and other subcategories do exist.

PRONOUNS replace nouns in a sentence or paragraph, allowing a writer to achieve a smooth flow throughout a text by avoiding unnecessary repetition. While there are countless nouns in the English language, there are only a few types of pronouns. The ones important for the TSI follow:

PERSONAL PRONOUNS act as subjects or objects in a sentence.

> She received a letter; I gave the letter to her.

Possessive pronouns indicate possession.

> The apartment is <u>hers</u>, but the furniture is <u>mine</u>.

Reflexive or **intensive pronouns** intensify a noun or reflect back on a noun.

> I made the dessert <u>myself.</u>

Indefinite pronouns simply replace nouns to avoid unnecessary repetition.

> <u>Several</u> came to the party to see <u>both</u>.

Table 7.1. Personal, Possessive, and Reflexive Pronouns

Case	First Person		Second Person		Third Person	
	Singular	Plural	Singular	Plural	Singular	Plural
Subject	I	we	you	you (all)	he, she, it	they
Object	me	us	you	you (all)	him, her, it	them
Possessive	mine	ours	yours	yours	his, hers, its	theirs
Reflexive/intensive	myself	ourselves	yourself	yourselves	himself, herself, itself	themselves

EXAMPLES

1. What purpose do nouns usually serve in a sentence?
   A) They indicate possession.
   B) They act as subject or object.
   C) They intensify other nouns.
   D) They clarify when an action occurs.

2. Which pronoun best completes the sentence?
   _____ baked the cookies ourselves and ate most of them.
   A) She
   B) Her
   C) I
   D) We

VERBS

Verbs express action (*run, jump, play*) or state of being (*is, seems*). Verbs that describe action are **action verbs**, and those that describe being are **linking verbs**.

> ACTION: My brother <u>plays</u> tennis.
> LINKING: He <u>is</u> the best player on the team.

Verbs are conjugated to indicate **PERSON**, which refers to the point of view of the sentence. First person is the speaker (*I, we*); second person is the person being addressed (*you*); and third person is outside the conversation (*they, them*). Verbs are also conjugated to match the **NUMBER** (singular or plural) of their subject. **HELPING VERBS** (*to be, to have, to do*) are used to conjugate verbs. An unconjugated verb is called an **INFINITIVE** and includes the word *to* in front (*to be, to break*).

PARTICIPLES are verb forms lacking number and person. The **PAST PARTICIPLE** is usually formed by adding the suffix *–ed* to the verb stem (*type* becomes *typed*; *drop* becomes *dropped*). The **PRESENT PARTICIPLE** is always formed by adding the suffix *–ing* to the verb stem (*typing, dropping*). Participles are used in verb conjugation to indicate the state of an action (*she is going; we had waited*).

Participles also act in *participial phrases* that act as descriptors in sentences:

> <u>Seated</u> politely, Ron listened to his friend's boring story.
> Maya petted the <u>sleeping</u> cat.

When a present participle acts as a noun, it is called a **GERUND**. In the following sentence, *running* is a noun and serving as the subject of the sentence:

> <u>Running</u> is my favorite form of exercise.

A common error in sentence structure is the *dangling participle*: when a participial phrase is disconnected from the word or phrase it modifies.

> **INCORRECT:** <u>Discussing the state of the nation</u>, I listened to the president's speech.

Here, the president, not the narrator, is discussing the state of the nation; the narrator is simply *listening*. However, the participial phrase "Discussing the state of the nation" is disconnected from the word it modifies, *president*. Thus it is *dangling* in the sentence—a dangling participle.

To fix a dangling particle, rearrange the sentence so that the modifying phrase is next to the word it modifies.

> **CORRECT:** I listened to the president's speech <u>discussing the state of the nation</u>.

Verbs are also conjugated to indicate **TENSE**, or when the action has happened. Actions can happen in the past, present, or future. Tense also describes over how long a period the action took place:

- ▶ **SIMPLE** verbs describe something that happened once or general truths.
- ▶ **CONTINUOUS** verbs describe an ongoing action.

- **PERFECT** verbs describe repeated actions or actions that started in the past and have been completed.
- **PERFECT CONTINUOUS** verbs describe actions that started in the past and are continuing.

Table 7.2. Verb Conjugation (Present Tense)

Person	Singular	Plural
First person	I give	we give
Second person	you give	you (all) give
Third person	he/she/it/ gives	they give

Table 7.3. Verb Tenses

Tense	Past	Present	Future
Simple	I gave her a gift yesterday.	I give her a gift every day.	I will give her a gift on her birthday.
Continuous	I was giving her a gift when you got here.	I am giving her a gift; come in!	I will be giving her a gift at dinner.
Perfect	I had given her a gift before you got there.	I have given her a gift already.	I will have given her a gift by midnight.
Perfect continuous	Her friends had been giving her gifts all night when I arrived.	I have been giving her gifts every year for nine years.	I will have been giving her gifts on holidays for ten years next year.

Verbs that follow the standard rules of conjugation are called **REGULAR** verbs. **IRREGULAR** verbs do not follow these rules, and their conjugations must be memorized. Some examples of irregular verbs are given in Table 7.4.

Table 7.4. Irregular Verbs

Present	Past	Has/Have/Had
am	was	been
do	did	done
see	saw	seen
write	wrote	written
break	broke	broken
grow	grew	grown
speak	spoke	spoken
begin	began	begun

Present	Past	Has/Have/Had
run	ran	run
buy	bought	bought

Transitive verbs take a **direct object**, which receives the action of the verb. Intransitive verbs have no object. The person or thing that receives the direct object is the **indirect object**.

> **Transitive:** Alex gave the ball to his brother.
> (The *ball* is the direct object; *his* brother is the indirect object.)
> **Intransitive:** She jumped over the fence.

EXAMPLES

3. Which verb phrase best completes the sentence?

    By this time tomorrow, we _____ in New York.

    A) will have arrived
    B) have arrived
    C) arrive
    D) was arriving

4. Identify the direct object in the following sentence:

    My friends brought me a package of souvenirs from their trip to Spain.

    A) friends
    B) me
    C) package
    D) trip

ADJECTIVES and ADVERBS

Adjectives modify or describe nouns and pronouns. In English, adjectives are usually placed before the word being modified, although they can also appear after a linking verb such as *is* or *smells*.

> The beautiful blue jade necklace will go perfectly with my dress.
> I think that lasagna smells delicious.

When multiple adjectives are used, they should be listed in the following order:

1. Determiners: articles (*a*, *an*, and *the*), possessive adjectives (e.g., *my*, *her*), and descriptors of quantity (e.g., *three*, *several*)
2. Opinions: modifiers that imply a value (e.g., *beautiful*, *perfect*, *ugly*)

3. Size: descriptions of size (e.g., *small, massive*)
4. Age: descriptions of age (e.g., *young, five-year-old*)
5. Shape: descriptions of appearance or character (e.g., *smooth, loud*)
6. Color: descriptions of color (e.g., *blue, dark*)
7. Origin: modifiers that describe where something came from (e.g., *American, homemade*)
8. Material: modifiers that describe what something is made from (e.g., *cotton, metallic*)
9. Purpose: adjectives that function as part of the noun to describe its purpose (e.g., <u>sewing</u> *machine*, <u>rocking</u> *chair*)

ADVERBS, which are often formed by adding the suffix *–ly*, modify any word or set of words that is not a noun or pronoun. They can modify verbs, adjectives, other adverbs, phrases, or clauses.

> He <u>quickly</u> ran to the house next door. (*Quickly* modifies the verb *ran*.)
> Her <u>very</u> effective speech earned her a promotion. (*Very* modifies the adjective *effective*.)
> <u>Finally</u>, the table was set and dinner was ready. (*Finally* modifies the clause *the table was set and dinner was ready*.)

DID YOU KNOW?
Adjectives answer the questions *what kind, how many,* or *which one?*
Adverbs answer the questions *how, when, where, why,* or *to what extent?*

COMPARATIVE adjectives and adverbs compare two items. For most one- or two-syllable words, the suffix *–er* is added to make it comparative; the word may be followed by *than*.

SUPERLATIVE adjectives and adverbs compare three or more items. Most one- or two-syllable words are made superlative by adding a suffix, *–est*.

> Comparative: My brother is <u>taller</u> than my sister.
> Superlative: My brother is the <u>tallest</u> of my five siblings.

Longer adjectives and adverbs must be preceded by *more* to form the comparative and *most* to form the superlative.

> Comparative: My bed at home is <u>more comfortable</u> than the one at the hotel.
> Superlative: The bed in your guestroom is the <u>most comfortable</u> bed I've ever slept in!

Some adjectives and adverbs form irregular comparatives and superlatives (see Table 7.5.).

> Comparative: The weather is bad today, but it was <u>worse</u> yesterday.
> Superlative: The <u>worst</u> day this week was Monday, when it rained.

Table 7.5. Irregular Comparative and Superlative Adjectives and Adverbs

ADJECTIVE/ADVERB	COMPARATIVE	SUPERLATIVE
much	more	most
bad	worse	worst
good	better	best
little	less	least
far	further/farther	furthest/farthest

EXAMPLES

5. Which of the following sentences is CORRECTLY constructed?
    A) Between my mom and dad, my father is the oldest.
    B) I ran less than usual today.
    C) Henry's cat is more fatter than mine.
    D) After taking medicine, she felt worser.

6. Which is the adverb in the following sentence?
   He carelessly sped around the flashing yellow light.
    A) flashing
    B) yellow
    C) around
    D) carelessly

CONJUNCTIONS

CONJUNCTIONS join words into phrases, clauses, and sentences. The *coordinating conjunctions* (FANBOYS) join two independent clauses: **F**or, **A**nd, **N**or, **B**ut, **O**r, **Y**et, **S**o.

> Marta went to the pool, <u>and</u> Alex decided to go shopping.
> Aisha didn't want to eat tacos for dinner, <u>so</u> she picked up a pizza on her way home.

Subordinating conjunctions join dependent clauses to the independent clauses to which they are related.

> We chose that restaurant <u>because</u> Juan loves pizza.

	Table 7.6. Subordinating Conjunctions
Time	after, as, as long as, as soon as, before, since, until, when, whenever, while
Manner	as, as if, as though
Cause	because
Condition	although, as long as, even if, even though, if, provided that, though, unless, while
Purpose	in order that, so that, that
Comparison	as, than

EXAMPLES

7. The following sentence contains an error. How should it be rewritten?

    He liked to cook and baking was his specialty.

    A) He liked to cook, and baking was his specialty.

    B) He liked to cook so baking was his specialty.

    C) He liked to cook; and baking was his specialty.

    D) He liked to cook, baking was his specialty.

8. Identify the underlined part of speech in the following sentence:

    Anne and Peter drank their coffee languidly <u>while</u> they read the paper.

    A) subordinating conjunction

    B) coordinating conjunction

    C) irregular verb

    D) adverb

PREPOSITIONS

PREPOSITIONS set up relationships in time (*after the party*) or space (*under the cushions*) within a sentence. A preposition will always function as part of a prepositional phrase—the preposition along with the object of the preposition.

Table 7.7. Common Prepositions			
PREPOSITIONS			
about	by	off	toward
among	despite	on	under

PREPOSITIONS (CONTINUED)			
around	down	onto	underneath
at	during	out	until
before	except	outside	up
behind	for	over	upon
below	from	past	with
beneath	in	since	within
beside	into	through	
between	near	till	
beyond	of	to	

COMPOUND PREPOSITIONS			
according to	because of	in place of	on account of
as of	by means of	in respect to	out of
as well as	in addition to	in spite of	prior to
aside from	in front of	instead of	with regard to

EXAMPLE

9. Identify the prepositional phrase in the following sentence.

    John and Carol must drive through the tunnel, but Carol is claustrophobic.

    A) must drive
    B) through the tunnel
    C) drive through
    D) but Carol is

INTERJECTIONS

INTERJECTIONS have no grammatical attachment to the sentence itself other than to add expressions of emotion. These parts of speech may be punctuated with commas or exclamation points and may fall anywhere within the sentence.

> Ouch! He stepped on my toe.

Language Skills 143

EXAMPLE

10. Identify the interjection in the following sentence.

"Come here! Look! Our team won the Super Bowl! Yay!"

- **A)** Come here!
- **B)** Our team won
- **C)** Look!
- **D)** Yay!

Constructing Sentences
PHRASES

A **PHRASE** is a group of words that communicates a partial idea and lacks either a subject or a predicate. Several phrases may be strung together, one after another, to add detail and interest to a sentence.

Phrases are categorized based on the main word in the phrase. A **PREPOSITIONAL PHRASE** begins with a preposition and ends with an object of the preposition; a **VERB PHRASE** is composed of the main verb along with its helping verbs; and a **NOUN PHRASE** consists of a noun and its modifiers.

> **PREPOSITIONAL PHRASE:** The dog is hiding under the porch.
> **VERB PHRASE:** The chef wanted to cook a different dish.
> **NOUN PHRASE:** The big, red barn rests beside the vacant chicken house.

An **APPOSITIVE PHRASE** is a particular type of noun phrase that renames the word or group of words that precedes it. Appositive phrases usually follow the noun they describe and are set apart by commas.

> Appositive phrase: My dad, a clock maker, loved antiques.

VERBAL PHRASES begin with a word that would normally act as a verb but is instead filling another role within the sentence. These phrases can act as nouns, adjectives, or adverbs.

> **NOUN:** To become a doctor had always been her goal.
> **ADJECTIVE:** Enjoying the stars that filled the sky, Ben lingered outside for quite a while.

EXAMPLE

11. Identify the type of phrase underlined in the following sentence:

<u>Dodging traffic</u>, Rachel drove to work on back roads.
- **A)** prepositional phrase
- **B)** noun phrase
- **C)** verb phrase
- **D)** verbal phrase

CLAUSES and TYPES of SENTENCES

CLAUSES contain both a subject and a predicate. They can be either independent or dependent. An **INDEPENDENT** (or main) **CLAUSE** can stand alone as its own sentence:

> The dog ate her homework.

Dependent (or subordinate) clauses cannot stand alone as their own sentences. They start with a subordinating conjunction, relative pronoun, or relative adjective, which will make them sound incomplete:

> <u>Because</u> the dog ate her homework

Table 7.8. Words That Begin Dependent Clauses

SUBORDINATING CONJUNCTIONS	RELATIVE PRONOUNS AND ADJECTIVES
after, before, once, since, until, when, whenever, while, as, because, in order that, so, so that, that, if, even if, provided that, unless, although, even though, though, whereas, where, wherever, than, whether	who, whoever, whom, whomever, whose, which, that, when, where, why, how

Sentences can be classified based on the number and type of clauses they contain. A **SIMPLE SENTENCE** will have only one independent clause and no dependent clauses. The sentence may contain phrases, complements, and modifiers, but it will comprise only one independent clause, one complete idea.

> The cat ran under the porch.

A **COMPOUND SENTENCE** has two or more independent clauses and no dependent clauses.

Language Skills 145

> The cat ran under the porch, and the dog ran after him.

A **COMPLEX SENTENCE** has only one independent clause and one or more dependent clauses.

> The cat, who is scared of the dog, ran under the porch.

A **COMPOUND-COMPLEX SENTENCE** has two or more independent clauses and one or more dependent clauses.

> The cat, who is scared of the dog, ran under the porch, and the dog ran after him.

Table 7.9. Sentence Structure and Clauses

SENTENCE STRUCTURE	INDEPENDENT CLAUSES	DEPENDENT CLAUSES
Simple	1	0
Compound	2 +	0
Complex	1	1 +
Compound-complex	2 +	1 +

EXAMPLE

12. Which of the following is a compound sentence?
    A) The turtle swam slowly around the pond.
    B) Alligators generally lie still, but they can move with lightning speed.
    C) Mice are most likely to come out at night after other animals have gone to sleep.
    D) Squirrels, to prepare for winter, gather and hide seeds and nuts underground.

Punctuation

Terminal punctuation marks are used to end sentences. The **PERIOD** (.) ends declarative (statement) and imperative (command) sentences. The **QUESTION MARK** (?) terminates interrogative sentences (questions). Lastly, **EXCLAMATION POINTS** end exclamatory sentences, in which the writer or speaker is exhibiting intense emotion or energy.

> Sarah and I are attending a concert.
> How many people are attending the concert?
> What a great show that was!

The colon and the semicolon, though often confused, each have a unique set of rules for their use. While both punctuation marks are used to join clauses, the construction of the clauses and the relationship between them is different. The **SEMICOLON** (;) is used to join two independent clauses (IC; IC) that are closely related.

> I need to buy a new car soon; my old car broke down last month.

The **COLON** (:) is used to introduce a list, definition, or clarification. The clause preceding the colon has to be independent, but what follows the colon can be an independent clause, a dependent clause, or a phrase.

> The buffet offers three choices: ham, turkey, or roast beef.
> He decided to drive instead of taking the train: he didn't think the train would arrive in time.

COMMAS show pauses in the text or set information apart from the main text. There are lots of rules for comma usage, so only the most common are summarized below.

1. Commas separate two independent clauses along with a coordinating conjunction.
   George ordered the steak, <u>but</u> Bruce preferred the ham.
2. Commas separate coordinate adjectives.
   She made herself a big bowl of <u>cold, delicious</u> ice cream.
3. Commas separate items in a series.
   The list of groceries included <u>cream, coffee, donuts, and tea</u>.
4. Commas separate introductory words and phrases from the rest of the sentence.
   <u>For example</u>, we have thirty students who demand a change.
5. Commas set off non-essential information and appositives.
   Estelle, <u>our newly elected chairperson</u>, will be in attendance.
6. Commas set off the day and month of a date within a text.
   I was born on February <u>16, 1988</u>.
7. Commas set up numbers in a text of more than four digits.
   We expect <u>25,000</u> visitors to the new museum.
8. Commas set off the names of cities from their states, territories, or provinces.
   She lives in <u>Houston, Texas</u>.

QUOTATION MARKS have a number of different purposes. They enclose titles of short, or relatively short, literary works such as short stories, chapters, and poems. (The titles of longer works, like novels and anthologies, are italicized.) Additionally, quotation marks are used to enclose direct quotations within the text of a document where the quotation is integrated into the text. Writers also use quotation marks to set off dialogue.

Language Skills 147

> We will be reading the poem "Bright Star" in class today.
> The poem opens with the line "Bright star, would I were steadfast as thou art."

APOSTROPHES, sometimes referred to as single quotation marks, have several different purposes.

1. They show possession.
   boy's watch, Ronald and Maria's house
2. They replace missing letters, numerals, and signs.
   do not = don't, 1989 = '89
3. They form plurals of letters, numerals, and signs.
   A's, 10's

Less commonly used punctuation marks include:

- **EN DASH (–)**: indicates a range
- **EM DASH (—)**: shows an abrupt break in a sentence and emphasizes the words within the em dashes
- **PARENTHESES ( )**: enclose nonessential information
- **BRACKETS [ ]**: enclose added words to a quotation and add insignificant information within parentheses
- **SLASH (/)**: separates lines of poetry within a text or indicates interchangeable terminology
- **ELLIPSES (…)**: indicates that information has been removed from a quotation or creates a reflective pause

EXAMPLES

13. Which sentence includes an improperly placed comma?
    A) Ella, Cassie, and Cameron drove to South Carolina together.
    B) Trying to impress his friends, Carl ended up totaling his car.
    C) Ice cream is my favorite food, it is so cold and creamy.
    D) Mowing the lawn, Navid discovered a family of baby rabbits.

14. The following sentence contains an error. How should it be rewritten?
    Oak trees—with proper care—can grow taller than thirty feet; providing shade for people, shelter for animals, and perches for birds.
    A) replace the em dashes with commas
    B) remove the comma after *people*
    C) insert an apostrophe at the end of *animals*
    D) replace the semicolon with a comma

Capitalization

CAPITALIZATION is writing the first letter of a word in uppercase and the remaining letters in lowercase. Capitalization is used in three main contexts. The first, and most common, is in the first word after a period or the first word of a text. For example, the first word in each sentence of this paragraph is capitalized.

The second most common usage of capitalization is for proper nouns or adjectives derived from proper nouns. For instance, **F**rance—as the name of a country—is capitalized. Similarly, **F**rench, the adjective derived from the proper noun *France*, is also capitalized. There is an exception to this rule: when the adjective has taken on a meaning independent of the original proper noun. For example, the term *french fries* is not capitalized.

The third usage of capitalization is in a title or honorific that appears before a name: "**P**resident George Washington never lived in the capital." If, however, that same title is used *instead of* the name, or if the name and title are separated by a comma, it remains lowercase. For example, "The first **p**resident, George Washington, never lived in the capital" or "The **p**resident did not originally live in the capital."

EXAMPLE

15. Which sentence CORRECTLY uses capitalization?
    A) Robert and Kelly raced across the River in their small boats.
    B) ducks flying in a V-formation cross the Midwest in the fall.
    C) The chairwoman of the board, Keisha Johnson, will lead today's meeting.
    D) The Senators from Virginia and Louisiana strongly favor the bill.

Common Language Errors
SUBJECT-VERB AGREEMENT

Verbs must agree in number with their subjects. Common rules for subject/verb agreement are given below.

1. Single subjects agree with single verbs; plural subjects agree with plural verbs.
   The <u>girl walks</u> her dog.
   The <u>girls walk</u> their dogs.

2. Ignore words between the subject and the verb: agreement must exist between the subject and verb.
   The new <u>library</u> ~~with its many books and rooms~~ <u>fills</u> a long-felt need.

Language Skills 149

3. Compound subjects joined by *and* typically take a plural verb unless considered one item.
   <u>Correctness and precision are required</u> for all good writing.
   <u>Macaroni and cheese makes</u> a great snack for children.

4. The linking verbs agree with the subject and not the subject complement (predicate nominative).
   My <u>favorite</u> is strawberries and apples.
   My <u>favorites are</u> strawberries and apples.

5. When a relative pronoun (*who, whom, which, that*) is used as the subject of the clause, the verb will agree with the antecedent of the relative pronoun.
   This is the <u>student who is receiving</u> an award.
   These are the <u>students who are receiving</u> awards.

6. All single, indefinite pronouns agree with single verbs.
   <u>Neither</u> of the students <u>is</u> happy about the play.
   <u>Each</u> of the many cars <u>is</u> on the grass.
   Every <u>one</u> of the administrators <u>speaks</u> highly of Trevor.

EXAMPLE

16. Which sentence in the following list is CORRECT in its subject and verb agreement?
    A) My sister and my best friend lives in Chicago.
    B) My parents or my brother is going to pick me up from the airport.
    C) Neither of the students refuse to take the exam.
    D) The team were playing a great game until the rain started.

PRONOUN-ANTECEDENT AGREEMENT

Similarly, pronouns must agree with their antecedents (the words they replaced) in number; however, some pronouns also require gender agreement (*him, her*). **PRONOUN/ANTECEDENT AGREEMENT** rules can be found below:

1. Antecedents joined by *and* typically require a plural pronoun.
   The <u>children and their dogs</u> enjoyed <u>their</u> day at the beach.
   If the two nouns refer to the same person, a singular pronoun is preferable.
   My <u>best friend and confidant</u> still lives in <u>her</u> log cabin.

2. For compound antecedents joined by *or*, the pronoun agrees with the nearer or nearest antecedent.
   Either the resident mice <u>or the manager's cat</u> gets <u>itself</u> a meal of good leftovers.

3. When indefinite pronouns function in a sentence, the pronoun must agree with the number of the indefinite pronoun.

<u>Neither</u> student finished <u>his or her</u> assignment.
<u>Both</u> students finished <u>their</u> assignments.

4. When collective nouns function as antecedents, the pronoun choice will be singular or plural depending on the function of the collective.
The <u>audience</u> was cheering as <u>it</u> rose to <u>its</u> feet in unison.
Our <u>family</u> are spending <u>their</u> vacations in Maine, Hawaii, and Rome.

5. When *each* and *every* precede the antecedent, the pronoun agreement will be singular.
<u>Each and every man, woman, and child</u> brings unique qualities to <u>his or her</u> family.
<u>Every creative writer, technical writer, and research writer</u> is attending <u>his or her</u> assigned lecture.

How would you complete the following sentence? "Every boy and girl should check _____ homework before turning it in." Many people would use the pronoun *their*. But since the antecedent is "every boy and girl," technically, the correct answer would be *his or her*. Using *they* or *their* in similar situations is increasingly accepted in formal speech, however. It is unlikely that you will see questions like this appear on the TSI, but if you do, it is safest to use the technically correct response.

EXAMPLE

17. Which sentence in the following list is CORRECT in its pronoun and antecedent agreement?
- **A)** The grandchildren and their cousins enjoyed their day at the park.
- **B)** Most of the grass has lost their deep color.
- **C)** The jury was relieved as their commitment came to a close.
- **D)** Every boy and girl must learn to behave themselves in school.

18. Which sentence in the following list is CORRECT in its pronoun and antecedent agreement?
- **A)** Either my brother or my dad will bring their van to pick us up.
- **B)** The university is having their tenth fundraiser tonight.
- **C)** Alyssa and Jacqueline bought herself a big lunch today.
- **D)** Each dog, cat, and rabbit has its own bowl and blanket.

VERB-TENSE AGREEMENT

In any passage, verb tense should be consistent and make sense in context of other verbs, adverbs, and general meaning. Verb tense questions appear frequently on the TSI, so pay attention to the context of the entire passage.

> **INCORRECT**: Deborah <u>was speaking</u> with her colleague when her boss <u>will appear</u>, demanding a meeting.

In this sentence, the subject, *Deborah*, is acting in an ongoing event in the past, so the verb describing this action, *speaking*, is conjugated in the continuous past tense. In the context of the sentence, the appearance of her boss is a completed event that happens during the conversation. The verb describing the boss' appearance should be conjugated in the simple past tense. The corrected sentence reads as follows:

> **CORRECT**: Deborah <u>was speaking</u> with her colleague when her boss <u>appeared</u>, demanding a meeting.

One clue to the correct conjugation of the verb *appeared* is the adverb *when*, which implies that a completed event occurred to interrupt the ongoing event (in this case, Deborah's talk with her colleague).

Pay attention to how verbs are conjugated in the beginning of a sentence or passage, and look for clues to spot any errors in verb tense agreement.

EXAMPLE

19. The following sentence contains an error. How should it be rewritten?
    Veronica attended cooking classes, and she goes to yoga classes too.
    A) Veronica attends cooking classes, and she went to yoga classes too.
    B) Veronica attended cooking classes, and she went to yoga classes too.
    C) Veronica attended cooking classes; she goes to yoga classes too.
    D) Veronica attended cooking classes. She goes to yoga classes too.

PARALLELISM

Errors in **PARALLELISM** prevent a writer from creating a smooth flow, or coherence, from word to word and sentence to sentence. Writers should create parallel structure in words, phrases, and clauses wherever two or more similar and equally important ideas exist next to each other in a sentence. Errors in parallel structure frequently appear in sentences with verb phrases, prepositional phrases, and correlative conjunctions like *either...or, neither...nor,* and *not only...but also.*

> **INCORRECT**: Adia could <u>program</u> computers, <u>repair</u> cars, and <u>knew how to make</u> croissants.
> **CORRECT**: Adia could <u>program</u> computers, <u>repair</u> cars, and <u>bake</u> croissants.

In the corrected sentence, the verbs are aligned in parallel structure. Furthermore, the first sentence contains a verb error. By omitting "program computers, repair cars," the sentence reads "Adia could...knew how to make croissants" Rewriting the sentence in parallel structure corrects the verb error.

In sentences with multiple prepositional phrases in a parallel series, the preposition must be repeated unless the same preposition begins each phrase.

> **INCORRECT:** You can park your car in the garage, the carport, or on the street.
> **CORRECT:** You can park your car in the garage, in the carport, or on the street.

EXAMPLE

20. The following sentence contains an error. How should it be rewritten?

    Shelly achieved more at nursing school because she was going to bed earlier, eating healthy food, and she started to stay home and study more.

    A) Shelly achieved more at nursing school. She was going to bed earlier, eating healthy food, and she started to stay home and study more.

    B) Shelly achieved more at nursing school because she was going to bed earlier, eating healthy food, and studying more.

    C) Shelly achieved more at nursing school; she was going to bed earlier, eating healthy food, and she started to stay home and study more.

    D) Shelly achieved more at nursing school; she was going to bed earlier, and she started to eat healthy food and studying more.

SENTENCE CONSTRUCTION ERRORS

SENTENCE ERRORS fall into three categories: fragments, comma splices (comma fault), and fused sentences (run-on). A **FRAGMENT** occurs when a group of words is not a complete sentence but is punctuated like one. The fragment might be a phrase or a dependent clause. To fix a fragment, an independent clause needs to be created.

> **FRAGMENT (PHRASE):** The girl in my class who asks a lot of questions.
> **CORRECT:** The girl in my class who asks a lot of questions sits in the back row.
> **FRAGMENT (DEPENDENT CLAUSE):** Because of the big storm we had last weekend.
> **CORRECT:** Because of the big storm we had last weekend, the park will be closed.

A **COMMA SPLICE** (comma fault) occurs when two independent clauses are joined together in a paragraph with only a comma to "splice" them together. **FUSED** (run-on) sentences occur when two independent clauses are joined with no punctuation whatsoever. To fix a comma splice or fused sentence, add the correct punctuation and/or conjunction.

> **COMMA SPLICE:** My family eats turkey at <u>Thanksgiving, we</u> eat ham at Christmas.
> **CORRECT:** My family eats turkey at <u>Thanksgiving, and we</u> eat ham at Christmas.
> **CORRECT:** My family eats turkey at <u>Thanksgiving. We</u> eat ham at Christmas.
> **CORRECT:** My family eats turkey at <u>Thanksgiving; we</u> eat ham at Christmas.
> **FUSED SENTENCE:** I bought a chocolate pie from the <u>bakery it</u> was delicious.
> **CORRECT:** I bought a chocolate pie from the <u>bakery. It</u> was delicious.
> **CORRECT:** I bought a chocolate pie from the <u>bakery, and it</u> was delicious.
> **CORRECT:** I bought a chocolate pie from the <u>bakery; it</u> was delicious.

EXAMPLE

21. Which of the following is CORRECTLY punctuated?
- **A)** Since she went to the store.
- **B)** The football game ended in a tie, the underdog caught up in the fourth quarter.
- **C)** The mall is closing early today so we'll have to go shopping tomorrow.
- **D)** When the players dropped their gloves, a fight broke out on the ice hockey rink floor.

EASILY CONFUSED WORDS

A, AN: *a* precedes words beginning with consonants or consonant sounds; *an* precedes words beginning with vowels or vowel sounds.

AFFECT, EFFECT: *affect* is most often a verb; *effect* is usually a noun. (*The experience affected me significantly* OR *The experience had a significant effect on me.*)

AMONG, AMONGST, BETWEEN: *among* is used for a group of more than two people or items; *amongst* is an uncommon, archaic term; *between* distinguishes two people or items.

AMOUNT, NUMBER: *amount* is used for noncountable sums; *number* is used with countable nouns.

CITE, SITE: the verb *cite* credits an author of a quotation, paraphrase, or summary; the noun *site* is a location.

EVERY DAY, EVERYDAY: *every day* is an indefinite adjective modifying a noun; *everyday* is a one-word adjective implying frequent occurrence. (*Our visit to the Minnesota State Fair is an everyday activity during August.*)

FEWER, LESS: *fewer* is used with a countable noun; *less* is used with a noncountable noun. (*Fewer parents are experiencing stress since the new teacher was hired; parents are experiencing less stress since the new teacher was hired.*)

GOOD, WELL: good is always the adjective; *well* is always the adverb except in cases of health. (*He writes well. She felt well after the surgery.*)

IMPLIED, INFERRED: *implied* is something a speaker does; *inferred* is something the listener does after assessing the speaker's message. (*The speaker implied something mysterious, but I inferred the wrong thing.*)

IRREGARDLESS, REGARDLESS: *irregardless* is nonstandard usage and should be avoided; *regardless* is the proper usage of the transitional statement.

ITS, IT'S: *its* is a possessive pronoun; *it's* is a contraction for *it is*.

PRINCIPAL, PRINCIPLE: as a noun, *principal* is an authority figure, often the head of a school; as an adjective, *principal* means *main*; the noun *principle* means idea or belief. (*The principal of the school spoke on the principal meaning of the main principles of the school.*)

QUOTE, QUOTATION: *quote* is a verb; *quotation* is a noun.

SHOULD OF, SHOULD HAVE: *should of* is improper usage—*of* is not a helping verb and therefore cannot complete the verb phrase; *should have* is the proper usage. (*He should have driven.*)

THAN, THEN: *than* sets up a comparison; *then* indicates a reference to a point in time. (*When I said that I liked the hat better than the gloves, my sister laughed; then she bought both for me.*)

THEIR, THERE, THEY'RE: *their* is the possessive case of the pronoun *they*. *There* is the demonstrative pronoun indicating location or place. *They're* is a contraction of the words *they are*.

TO LIE (TO RECLINE), TO LAY (TO PLACE): *to lie* is the intransitive verb meaning *to recline*; *to lay* is the transitive verb meaning *to place something*. (*I lie out in the sun; I lay my towel on the beach.*)

WHO, WHOM: *who* is the subject relative pronoun. (*My son, who is a good student, studies hard.*) Here, the son is carrying out the action of studying, so the pronoun is a subject pronoun (*who*). *Whom* is the object relative pronoun. (*My son, whom the other students admire, studies hard.*) Here, *son* is the object of the other students' admiration, so the pronoun standing in for him, *whom*, is an object pronoun.

YOUR, YOU'RE: *your* is the possessive case of the pronoun *you*. *You're* is a contraction of the words *you are*.

EXAMPLE

22. Which of the following sentences contains an error?
    A) I invited fewer people to my birthday party this year.
    B) The students asked the principle to postpone the meeting.
    C) My sister baked cookies then asked me to help clean the kitchen.
    D) She paints well even though she has no formal training.

Answer Key

1. **B) is correct.** Nouns are people, places, things, or ideas; they usually act as the subject or object in a sentence.

2. **D) is correct.** The reflexive pronoun *ourselves* refers back to the subject of the sentence. Because it is in the first person plural, the subject should also be in the first person plural (*we*).

3. **A) is correct.** The phrase *by this time tomorrow* describes as action that will take place and be completed in the future, so the future perfect tense (*will have arrived*) should be used.

4. **C) is correct.** *Package* is the direct object of the verb *brought*.

5. **B) is correct.** The speaker is comparing today's run to the norm, not to any additional instances, so the comparative is acceptable here. Furthermore, the word *than* appears, a clue that the comparative is appropriate. *Less* is the irregular comparative form of *little*.

6. **D) is correct.** *Carelessly* is an adverb modifying *sped* and explaining *how* the driving occurred. The subject was not mindful as he drove; he raced through a yellow light when he should have exercised caution.

7. **A) is correct.** This sentence includes two independent clauses: "He liked to cook" and "baking was his specialty." They can be connected with a comma and coordinating conjunction (the conjunction *and* is appropriate here). The sentence could also be written with a semicolon and no conjunction.

8. **A) is correct.** "While they read the paper" is a dependent clause; the subordinating conjunction *while* connects it to the independent clause "Anne and Peter drank their coffee languidly."

9. **B) is correct.** "Through the tunnel" is a prepositional phrase explaining the relationship between the subjects and the tunnel using the preposition *through* and the object *the tunnel*.

10. **D) is correct.** *Yay* is an expression of emotion and has no other grammatical purpose in the sentence.

11. **D) is correct.** The phrase is a verbal phrase modifying the noun *Rachel*. It begins with the word *dodging*, derived from the verb to *dodge*.

12. **B) is correct.** "Alligators...still" and "they...speed" are two independent clauses connected by a comma and the coordinating conjunction *but*.

13. **C) is correct.** "Ice cream...food" and "it...creamy" are two independent clauses. The writer should include a coordinating conjunction like *for* or separate the clauses with a semicolon.

14. **D) is correct.** "Providing shade..." is not an independent clause; therefore it cannot be preceded by a semicolon.

15. **C) is correct.** *Keisha Johnson*, as a proper noun, should be capitalized, but "chairwoman of the board" should not be because it is separated from the name by a comma.

16. **B) is correct.** The verb agrees with the closest subject—in this case, the singular *brother*.

17. **A) is correct.** The plural antecedents *grandchildren* and *cousins* match the plural possessive pronoun *their*.

18. **D) is correct.** When *each* precedes the antecedent, the pronoun agreement is singular. The pronoun *its* therefore agrees with the antecedents *Each dog, cat, and rabbit*.

19. **B) is correct.** In this sentence, the verbs *attended* and *went* are both correctly conjugated in the simple past tense.

20. **B) is correct.** In this sentence, three related clauses are written in parallel structure using the participles *going*, *eating*, and *studying*.

21. **D) is correct.** This is a complete sentence that is punctuated properly with a comma between the dependent and independent clauses.

22. **B) is correct.** A principle is a belief; a principal is the head of a school.

CHAPTER EIGHT
Writing

Writing a Thesis Statement

A **THESIS STATEMENT** articulates the main argument of the essay. No essay is complete without it: the structure and organization of the essay revolves around the thesis statement. The thesis statement is simply the writer's main idea or argument. It usually appears at the end of the introduction.

In a good thesis statement, the author states his or her idea or argument and why it is correct or true.

EXAMPLE

Take a position on the following topic in your essay. You can choose to write about either of the two viewpoints discussed in the prompt, or you may argue for a third point of view.

Many scientists argue that recent unusual weather patterns, such as powerful hurricanes and droughts, are due to climate change triggered by human activity. They argue that automobiles, oil and gas production, and manufacturing generate carbon emissions that artificially heat the atmosphere, resulting in extreme weather patterns. Others disagree. Some researchers and media pundits argue that climate change is natural, and that extreme weather has always been a feature of Earth's atmosphere.

Around the world more people than ever before are driving cars, and industrial production is at an all-time high: it is obvious that human activity is affecting the atmosphere and causing extreme weather events.

   I believe that temperatures and storms are more extreme than ever because of the environmental impact of human activity; not only do scientists have overwhelming evidence that climate change is unnatural, but I can also personally remember when there were fewer storms and variations in temperature.

> Society needs cars and manufacturing, but governments should restrict harmful emissions released into the atmosphere so we can slow down climate change and save lives.

Structuring the Essay

On the TSI, a strong essay will have an introduction, a body, and a conclusion. While there are many ways to organize an essay, on this exam it is most important that the essay is clearly structured. There is no need to get too complicated: this simple structure will do.

INTRODUCTIONS

Some writers struggle with the introduction, but it is actually an opportunity to present your idea or argument. On the TSI, the introduction can be one paragraph that ends with the thesis statement. In the rest of the paragraph, the writer provides some context for his or her argument. This context might include counterarguments, a preview of specific examples to be discussed later on, acknowledgement of the complexities of the issue, or even a reference to personal experience. The writer can reexamine some of these issues in the conclusion.

DID YOU KNOW?
If you're not sure what to include in your introduction, start your essay with just the thesis statement. You can go back and complete the introduction once the rest of the essay is finished.

EXAMPLE

In the example below, the writer has written an introduction that includes context for her argument: background information, a counterargument, and personal experience. As a result, the reader has a better idea of how complex the issue is and why the writer feels the way she does. The thesis statement appears at the end of the paragraph; as a result of the introduction as a whole, the thesis statement has more impact.

A century ago, there were barely any cars on the road. Oil had just been discovered in a few parts of the world. Industrial production existed but had not yet exploded with the introduction of the assembly line. Refineries and factories were not yet churning out the chemical emissions they are today. Certainly, hurricanes and droughts occurred, but the populations and infrastructure affected were far smaller. Now, scientists have evidence that human activity—like pollution from industry and cars—is affecting the atmosphere and making weather more extreme. In 2017, millions of people were affected by hurricanes and wildfires. It is true that some researchers disagree that human activity has caused these and other extreme weather events. But why take the risk? If we can limit destruction now and in the future, we should. Extreme weather events are a danger to people all around the world. Society needs cars and manufacturing, but governments should restrict harmful emissions released into the atmosphere so we can slow down climate change and save lives.

THE BODY PARAGRAPHS

Most writers find the body of the essay the easiest part to write. The body of the essay is simply several paragraphs, each beginning with a topic sentence. Each paragraph usually addresses an example that supports the argument made in the thesis statement or, in the case of an expository essay, explains the writer's reasoning. On the TSI, you may use specific examples or personal anecdotes, present problems and solutions, or compare and contrast ideas. You do not need to refer to any outside literature or documentation.

To strengthen the body of the essay, writers will maintain consistency in paragraphs, always beginning with a topic sentence, which introduces the main idea of each paragraph. Each paragraph deals with its own main topic, but writers should use transition words and phrases to link paragraphs with each other. A good essay maintains readability and flow.

EXAMPLE

This example body paragraph is related to the introduction provided above. It provides reasoning and historical evidence for the author's argument that human activity is impacting the earth and causing climate change.

Human industrial activity has been growing exponentially, putting more pollution into the atmosphere than ever. Over the past forty years, large countries like China and India have become industrialized and manufacture many of the world's products. As their populations become more prosperous, demand for automobiles also rises, putting more cars on the road—and exhaust in the air. While industrial development has benefited Asia and other areas, carbon emissions that cause climate change have multiplied. Meanwhile, previously industrialized countries in Europe and North America continue to produce carbon emissions. In the nineteenth century, only a few countries had industrial sectors; today, global industry strains the environment like never before. The past 150 years have seen unprecedented industrial growth. Even if the climate changes naturally over time, it cannot be denied that recent human activity has suddenly generated enormous amounts of carbon emissions that have impacted the atmosphere. Scientists say that the earth is warming as a result.

CONCLUSIONS

The conclusion does not need to be long. Its purpose is to wrap up the essay, reminding the reader why the topic and the writer's argument is important. It is an opportunity for the writer to reexamine the thesis statement and ideas in the introduction. It is a time to reinforce the argument, not just to repeat the introduction.

> **EXAMPLE**
>
> *This example is taken from the same essay as the introduction and body paragraph above. It reinforces the writer's argument without simply repeating what she said in the introduction. The writer does address the topics she spoke about in the introduction (climate change and protecting people from extreme weather) but she does not simply rewrite the thesis: she calls for action.*
>
> No doubt, scientists, pundits, and politicians will continue to argue over the reasons for extreme weather. Meanwhile, Mother Nature will continue to wreak havoc on vulnerable areas regardless of what we think. Because we have proof that climate change is related to extreme weather and we know that extreme weather threatens people's lives, the time to act is now. We can take steps to mitigate pollution without lowering quality of life. Doing anything else is irresponsible—and for some, deadly.

Providing Supporting Evidence

As discussed above, a good essay should have specific evidence or examples that support the thesis statement. On the TSI, a specific example should be something related to the idea of the paragraph and the essay, not a new idea. A specific example can be from your general knowledge; you do not need to know about specific academic issues to do well on the essay. Remember, you are being tested on your reasoning and argumentative skills.

The following are some examples of general statements and specific statements that provide more detailed support:

GENERAL: Human industrial activity has been growing exponentially, putting more pollution into the atmosphere than ever.

SPECIFIC: Over the past forty years, large countries like China and India have become industrialized and manufacture many of the world's products. As their populations become more prosperous, demand for automobiles also rises, putting more cars on the road—and exhaust in the air.

SPECIFIC: Meanwhile, previously industrialized countries in Europe and North America continue to produce carbon emissions. In the nineteenth century, only a few countries had industrial sectors; today, global industry strains the environment like never before.

GENERAL: More people than ever are affected by extreme weather.

SPECIFIC: In 2017, several hurricanes affected the United States and the Caribbean. In Texas, Hurricane Harvey led to historic flooding in Houston and the Texas Coast. Millions of people were affected; thousands lost their homes, jobs, and livelihoods.

Specific: Hurricane Irma damaged the US Virgin Islands and neighboring Caribbean nations. Soon after, Hurricane Maria catastrophically devastated Puerto Rico. Months later, Puerto Ricans were still without power and basic necessities. It is still not clear how many have died due to the storm and related damage.

EXAMPLE

In the example below, the paragraph is structured with a topic sentence and specific supporting ideas. This paragraph supports the introduction in the example above.

More people than ever are affected by extreme weather. In 2017, several hurricanes affected the United States and the Caribbean. In Texas, Hurricane Harvey led to historic flooding in Houston and the Texas Coast. Millions of people were affected; thousands lost their homes, jobs, and livelihoods. Hurricane Irma damaged Florida, the US Virgin Islands, and neighboring Caribbean nations. Soon after, Hurricane Maria catastrophically devastated Puerto Rico. Months later, Puerto Ricans were still without power and basic necessities. It is still not clear how many have died due to the storm and related damage. In California, severe droughts led to exceptionally large wildfires that threatened Los Angeles and destroyed neighboring communities. Meanwhile, those same areas—Southern California, the Texas Coast, and Florida—continue to grow, putting more people at risk when the next hurricane or fire strikes.

Writing Well

Using transitions, complex sentences, and certain words can turn a good essay into a great one. Transitions, syntax, word choice, and tone all help clarify and amplify a writer's argument or point and improve the flow of an essay.

TRANSITIONS

An essay consists of several paragraphs. **Transitions** are words and phrases that help connect the paragraphs and ideas of the text. Most commonly, transitions would appear at the beginning of a paragraph, but writers should also use them throughout a text to connect ideas. Common transitions are words like *also, next, still, although, in addition to,* and *in other words*. A transition shows a relationship between ideas, so writers should pay close attention to the transition words and phrases they choose. Transitions may show connections or contrasts between words and ideas.

Table 8.1. Common Transitions

Transition Type	Examples
addition	additionally, also, as well, further, furthermore, in addition, moreover
cause and effect	as a result, because, consequently, due to, if/then, so, therefore, thus
concluding	briefly, finally, in conclusion, in summary, thus, to conclude
contrast	but, however, in contrast, on the other hand, nevertheless, on the contrary, yet
examples	in other words, for example, for instance
similarity	also, likewise, similarly
time	after, before, currently, later, recently, subsequently, since, then, while

SYNTAX

Syntax refers to how words and phrases are arranged in writing or speech. Writing varied sentences is essential to capturing and keeping a reader's interest. A good essay features different types of sentences: simple, complex, compound, and compound-complex. Sentences need not always begin with the subject; they might start with a transition word or phrase, for instance. Variety is key.

Still, writers should keep in mind that the point of an essay is to get an idea across to the reader, so it is most important that writing be clear. They should not sacrifice clarity for the sake of flowery, overly wordy language or confusing syntax.

WORD CHOICE and TONE

Like syntax, word choice makes an impression on readers. The TSI does not test on specific vocabulary or require writers to use specific words on the essay. However, the essay is a good opportunity to use strong vocabulary pertaining to the prompt or issue under discussion. Writers should be careful, though, that they understand the words they are using. Writers should also avoid vague, imprecise, or generalizing language like *good*, *bad*, *a lot*, *a little*, *very*, *normal*, and so on.

EDITING, REVISING, and PROOFREADING

On the TSI, the writer has a limited amount of time to complete the essay. If there is time for editing or proofreading, writers should hunt for grammar, spelling, or punctuation mistakes that could change the meaning of the text or make it difficult to understand. These include sentence fragments, run-on sentences, subject-verb disagreement, and pronoun-antecedent disagreement.

CHAPTER NINE
Practice Test

Mathematics

Work the problem, and then choose the most correct answer.

1. If $j = 4$, what is the value of $2(j - 4)^4 - j + \frac{1}{2}j$?
   A) 0
   B) −2
   C) 2
   D) 4

2. Simplify: $\sqrt[3]{64} + \sqrt[3]{729}$
   A) 13
   B) 17
   C) 31
   D) 35

3. If the surface area of a cylinder with radius of 4 feet is 48π square feet, what is its volume?
   A) 1π ft.³
   B) 16π ft.³
   C) 32π ft.³
   D) 64π ft.³

4. The average speed of cars on a highway (s) is inversely proportional to the number of cars on the road (n). If a car drives at 65 mph when there are 250 cars on the road, how fast will a car drive when there are 325 cars on the road?
   A) 50 mph
   B) 55 mph
   C) 60 mph
   D) 85 mph

5. Which of the following is a solution of the given equation?
   $4(m + 4)^2 - 4m^2 + 20 = 276$
   A) 3
   B) 6
   C) 12
   D) 24

6. New York had the fewest months with less than 3 inches of rain in every year except:

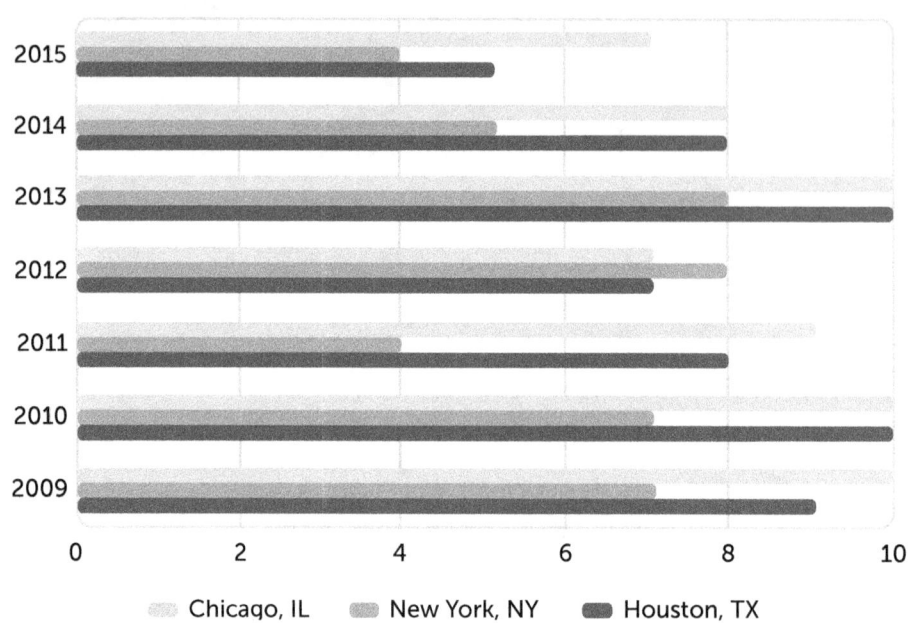

Number of Months with 3 or Fewer Than 3 Inches of Rain

- A) 2012
- B) 2013
- C) 2014
- D) 2015

7. Which of the following is a solution to the inequality $2x + y \leq -10$?
   - A) (0, 0)
   - B) (10, 2)
   - C) (10, 10)
   - D) (−10, −10)

8. If $\frac{4x - 5}{3} = \frac{\frac{1}{2}(2x - 6)}{5}$, what is the value of x?
   - A) $-\frac{2}{7}$
   - B) $-\frac{4}{17}$
   - C) $\frac{16}{17}$
   - D) $\frac{8}{7}$

9. Which of the following is the y-intercept of the given equation?
   $7y - 42x + 7 = 0$
   - A) $(0, \frac{1}{6})$
   - B) (6, 0)
   - C) (0, −1)
   - D) (−1, 0)

10. In a class of 20 students, how many conversations must be had so that every student talks to every other student in the class?
    - A) 190
    - B) 380
    - C) 760
    - D) 6840

11. What is the value of z in the following system?

    z − 2x = 14 | 2z − 6x = 18

    A) −7
    B) 3
    C) 5
    D) 24

12. Simplify: $\left(\dfrac{4x^{-3}y^4z}{8x^{-5}y^3z^{-2}}\right)^2$

    A) $\dfrac{x^4yz^3}{2}$
    B) $\dfrac{x^4y^2z^6}{2}$
    C) $\dfrac{x^4y^2z^6}{4}$
    D) $\dfrac{x^4yz^3}{4}$

13. The line f(x) is shown on the graph below. If g(x) = f(x − 2) + 3, which of the following points lies on g(x)?

    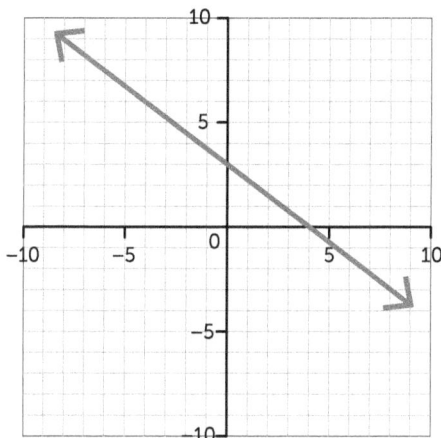

    A) (1,2)
    B) (2,3)
    C) (6,3)
    D) (7,2)

14. If △ABD ~ △DEF and the similarity ratio is 3:4, what is the measure of DE if AB = 12?

    A) 9
    B) 16
    C) 96
    D) 12

15. The line of best fit is calculated for a data set that tracks the number of miles that passenger cars traveled annually in the US from 1960 to 2010. In the model, x = 0 represents the year 1960, and y is the number of miles traveled in billions. If the line of best fit is y = 0.0293x + 0.563, approximately how many additional miles were traveled for every 5 years that passed?

    A) 0.0293 billion
    B) 0.1465 billion
    C) 0.563 billion
    D) 0.710 billion

16. The mean of 13 numbers is 30. The mean of 8 of these numbers is 42. What is the mean of the other 5 numbers?

    A) 5.5
    B) 10.8
    C) 16.4
    D) 21.2

17. Fifteen DVDs are to be arranged on a shelf. 4 of the DVDs are horror films, 6 are comedies, and 5 are science fiction. In how many ways can the DVDs be arranged if DVDs of the same genre must be placed together?

    A) 2,073,600
    B) 6,220,800
    C) 12,441,600
    D) 131,216,200

18. If the length of a rectangle is increased by 40% and its width is decreased by 40%, what is the effect on the rectangle's area?

    A) The area is the same.
    B) It increases by 16%.
    C) It increases by 20%.
    D) It decreases by 16%.

19. Which inequality is represented by the following graph?

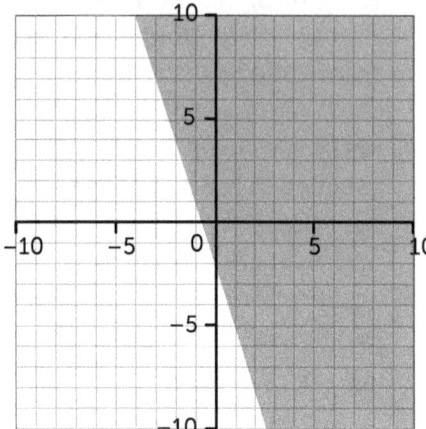

- **A)** $y \geq -3x - 2$
- **B)** $y \geq 3x - 2$
- **C)** $y > -3x - 2$
- **D)** $y \leq -3x - 2$

20. A cube is inscribed in a sphere such that each vertex on the cube touches the sphere. If the volume of the sphere is 972π cm^3, what is the approximate volume of the cube in cubic centimeters?

- **A)** 9
- **B)** 10.4
- **C)** 1125
- **D)** 1729

Reading

Read the passage, and then answer the questions that follow.

1. It's that time again—the annual Friendswood Village Summer Fair is here! Last year we had a record number of visitors, and we're expecting an even bigger turnout this year. The fair will be bringing back all our traditional food and games, including the famous raffle. This year, we'll have a carousel, petting zoo, and climbing wall (for teenagers and adults only, please). We're also excited to welcome Petey's BBQ and Happy Tummy's Frozen Treats, who are both new to the fair this year. Tickets are available online and at local retailers.

   According to the passage, which of the following will NOT be a new presence at the Fair this year?

   A) the raffle
   B) the petting zoo
   C) the carousel
   D) the climbing wall

2. In Greek mythology, two gods, Epimetheus and Prometheus, were given the work of creating living things. Epimetheus gave good powers to the different animals. To the lion he gave strength; to the bird, swiftness; to the fox, sagacity; and so on. Eventually, all of the good gifts had been bestowed, and there was nothing left for humans. As a result, Prometheus returned to heaven and brought down fire, which he gave to humans. With fire, human beings could protect themselves by making weapons. Over time, humans developed civilization and superiority.

   In sentence 4, the word "bestowed" most nearly means

   A) purchased
   B) forgotten
   C) accepted
   D) given

3. It has now been two decades since the introduction of thermonuclear fusion weapons into the military inventories of the great powers, and more than a decade since the United States, Great Britain, and the Soviet Union ceased to test nuclear weapons in the atmosphere. Today our understanding of the technology of thermonuclear weapons seems highly advanced, but our knowledge of the physical and biological consequences of nuclear war is continuously evolving.

   Which of the following best describes the topic of the passage?

   A) the impact of thermonuclear weapons on the military
   B) the technology of thermonuclear weapons
   C) atmospheric testing of nuclear weapons
   D) the physical and biological consequences of nuclear war

4. Alexander Hamilton and James Madison called for the Constitutional Convention to write a constitution as the foundation of a stronger federal government. Madison and other Federalists like John Adams believed in separation of powers, republicanism, and a strong federal government. Despite the separation of powers that would be provided for in the US Constitution, anti-Federalists like Thomas Jefferson called for even more limitations on the power of the federal government.

Details in the passage suggest that which of the following would most likely NOT support a strong federal government?

- **A)** Alexander Hamilton
- **B)** James Madison
- **C)** John Adams
- **D)** Thomas Jefferson

5. I say moreover that you make a great, a very great mistake, if you think that psychology, being the science of the mind's laws, is something from which you can deduce definite programs and schemes and methods of instruction for immediate schoolroom use. Psychology is a science, and teaching is an art; and sciences never generate arts directly out of themselves. An intermediary inventive mind must make the application, by using its originality.

What is the main purpose of this passage?

- **A)** to explain that psychology is a science.
- **B)** to emphasize that the science of psychology cannot determine educational programs and methods.
- **C)** to describe the artistic nature of educational practices, programming, and step-by-step planning.
- **D)** to compare the values of art to those of science.

6. In the eleven years that separated the Declaration of the Independence of the United States from the completion of that act in the ordination of our written Constitution, the great minds of America were bent upon the study of the principles of government that were essential to the preservation of the liberties which had been won at great cost and with heroic labors and sacrifices. Their studies were conducted in view of the imperfections that experience had developed in the government of the Confederation, and they were, therefore, practical and thorough.

The passage implies that the writers of the Constitution

- **A)** studied principles of government in relation to the government of the Confederation; their goal was to write a Constitution that would secure liberty in America.
- **B)** worked to make sure that Americans would never lose the freedom that they fought to achieve.
- **C)** were both thorough and practical as they wrote the Constitution.
- **D)** studied the government of the Confederation and worked very hard to take into account the imperfections of this government.

7. For an adult person to be unable to swim points to something like criminal negligence; every man, woman and child should learn. A person who cannot swim may not only become a danger to himself, but to someone, and perhaps to several, of his fellow beings. Children as early as the age of four may acquire the art; none are too young, none too old. – Frank Eugen Dalton, *Swimming Scientifically Taught*, 1912

What is the main purpose of this passage?

- **A)** to encourage the reader to learn to swim
- **B)** to explain how people who cannot swim are a danger to others
- **C)** to inform the reader that it's never too late to learn to swim
- **D)** to argue that people who cannot swim should be punished

The following passage applies to questions 8 and 9.

The greatest changes in sensory, motor, and perceptual development happen in the first two years of life. When babies are first born, most of their senses operate in a similar way to those of adults. For example, babies are able to hear before they are born; studies show that babies turn toward the sound of their mothers' voices just minutes after being born, indicating they recognize the mother's voice from their time in the womb.

The exception to this rule is vision. A baby's vision changes significantly in its first year of life; initially it has a range of vision of only 8 – 12 inches and no depth perception. As a result, infants rely primarily on hearing; vision does not become the dominant sense until around the age of 12 months. Babies also prefer faces to other objects. This preference, along with their limited vision range, means that their sight is initially focused on their caregiver.

8. Which of the following is an accurate summary of the passage?

- **A)** Babies have no depth perception until 12 months, which is why they focus only on their caregivers' faces.
- **B)** Babies can recognize their mothers' voices when born, so they initially rely primarily on their sense of hearing.
- **C)** Babies have senses similar to those of adults except for their sense of sight, which doesn't fully develop until 12 months.
- **D)** Babies' senses go through many changes in the first year of their lives.

9. According to the passage, which of the following senses do babies primarily rely on?

- **A)** vision
- **B)** hearing
- **C)** touch
- **D)** smell

The following passage applies to questions 10 and 11.

In its most basic form, geography is the study of space; more specifically, it studies the physical space of the earth and the ways in which it interacts with, shapes, and is shaped by its habitants. Geographers look at the world from a spatial perspective. This means that at the center of all geographic study is the question, where? For geographers, the where of any interaction, event, or development is a crucial element to understanding it.

This question of where can be asked in a variety of fields of study, so there are many sub-disciplines of geography. These can be organized into four main categories: 1) regional studies, which examine the characteristics of a particular place; 2) topical studies, which look at a single physical or human feature that impacts the whole world; 3) physical studies, which focus on the physical features of Earth; and 4) human studies, which examine the relationship between human activity and the environment.

10. According to the passage, a researcher studying the relationship between farming and river systems would be engaged in which of the following geographical sub-disciplines?

   A) regional studies
   B) topical studies
   C) physical studies
   D) human studies

11. Which of the following is a concise summary of the passage?

   A) The most important questions in geography are where an event or development took place.
   B) Geography, which is the study of the physical space on Earth, can be broken down into four sub-disciplines.
   C) Regional studies is the study of a single region or area.
   D) Geography can be broken down into four sub-disciplines: regional studies, topical studies, physical studies, and human studies.

The following passage applies to questions 12–15.

Skin coloration and markings have an important role to play in the world of snakes. Those intricate diamonds, stripes, and swirls help the animals hide from predators, but perhaps most importantly (for us humans, anyway), the markings can also indicate whether the snake is venomous. While it might seem counterintuitive for a venomous snake to stand out in bright red or blue, that fancy costume tells any nearby predator that approaching him would be a bad idea.

If you see a flashy-looking snake in the woods, though, those markings don't necessarily mean it's venomous: some snakes have found a way to ward off predators without the actual venom. The scarlet kingsnake, for example, has very similar markings to the venomous coral snake with whom it frequently shares a habitat. However, the kingsnake is actually nonvenomous; it's merely pretending to be dangerous to eat. A predatory hawk or eagle, usually hunting from high in the sky, can't tell the difference between the two species, and so the kingsnake gets passed over and lives another day.

12. The passage implies which of the following?
  A) The kingsnake is dangerous to humans.
  B) The coral snake and the kingsnake are both hunted by the same predators.
  C) It's safe to handle snakes in the woods because you can easily tell whether they're poisonous.
  D) The kingsnake changes its markings when hawks or eagles are close by.

13. Which statement is NOT a detail from the passage?
  A) Predators will avoid eating kingsnakes because their markings are similar to those on coral snakes.
  B) Kingsnakes and coral snakes live in the same habitats.
  C) The coral snake uses its coloration to hide from predators.
  D) The kingsnake is not venomous.

14. In sentence 2, the word "intricate" most nearly means
  A) complex
  B) colorful
  C) purposeful
  D) changeable

15. According to the passage, what is the difference between kingsnakes and coral snakes?
  A) Both kingsnakes and coral snakes are nonvenomous, but coral snakes have colorful markings.
  B) Both kingsnakes and coral snakes are venomous, but kingsnakes have colorful markings.
  C) Kingsnakes are nonvenomous while coral snakes are venomous.
  D) Coral snakes are nonvenomous while kingsnakes are venomous.

The following passage applies to questions 16–18.

We've been told for years that the recipe for weight loss is fewer calories in than calories out. In other words, eat less and exercise more, and your body will take care of the rest. As many of those who've tried to diet can attest, this edict doesn't always produce results. If you're one of those folks, you might have felt that you just weren't doing it right—that the failure was all your fault.

However, several new studies released this year have suggested that it might not be your fault at all. For example, a study of people who'd lost a high percentage of their body weight (>17%) in a short period of time found that they could not physically maintain their new weight. Scientists measured their resting metabolic rate and found that they'd need to consume only a few hundred calories a day to meet their metabolic needs. Basically, their bodies were in starvation mode and seemed to desperately hang on to each and every calorie. Eating even a single healthy, well-balanced meal a day would cause these subjects to start packing back on the pounds.

Other studies have shown that factors like intestinal bacteria, distribution of body fat, and hormone levels can affect the manner in which our bodies process calories. There's also the fact that it's actually quite difficult to measure the number of calories consumed during a particular meal and the number used while exercising.

16. Which of the following would be the best summary statement to conclude the passage?
- **A)** It turns out that conventional dieting wisdom doesn't capture the whole picture of how our bodies function.
- **B)** Still, counting calories and tracking exercise is a good idea if you want to lose weight.
- **C)** In conclusion, it's important to lose weight responsibly: losing too much weight at once can negatively impact the body.
- **D)** It's easy to see that diets don't work, so we should focus less on weight loss and more on overall health.

17. Which of the following type of arguments is used in the passage?
- **A)** emotional argument
- **B)** appeal to authority
- **C)** specific evidence
- **D)** rhetorical questioning

18. Which of the following would weaken the author's argument?
- **A)** a new diet pill from a pharmaceutical company that promises to help patients lose weight by changing intestinal bacteria
- **B)** the personal experience of a man who was able to lose a significant amount of weight by taking in fewer calories than he used
- **C)** a study showing that people in different geographic locations lose different amounts of weight when on the same diet
- **D)** a study showing that people often misreport their food intake when part of a scientific study on weight loss

The following passage applies to questions 19–24.

Popcorn is often associated with fun and festivities, both in and out of the home. It's eaten in theaters, usually after being salted and smothered in butter, and in homes, fresh from the microwave. But popcorn isn't just for fun—it's also a multimillion-dollar-a-year industry with a long and fascinating history.

While popcorn might seem like a modern invention, its history actually dates back thousands of years, making it one of the oldest snack foods enjoyed around the world. Popcorn is believed by food historians to be one of the earliest uses of cultivated corn. In 1948, Herbert Dick and Earle Smith discovered old popcorn dating back 4000 years in the New Mexico Bat Cave. For the Aztec Indians who called the caves home, popcorn (or *momochitl*) played an important role in society, both as a food staple and in ceremonies. The Aztecs cooked popcorn by heating sand in a fire; when it was heated, kernels were added and would pop when exposed to the heat of the sand.

The American love affair with popcorn began in 1912, when popcorn was first sold in theaters. The popcorn industry flourished during the Great Depression when it was advertised as a wholesome and economical food. Selling for five to ten cents a bag, it was a luxury that the downtrodden could afford. With the introduction of mobile popcorn machines at the World's Columbian Exposition, popcorn moved from the theater into fairs and parks. Popcorn continued to rule the snack food kingdom until the rise in popularity of home televisions during the 1950s.

The popcorn industry reacted to the decline in sales quickly by introducing pre-popped and unpopped popcorn for home consumption. However, it wasn't until microwave popcorn became commercially available in 1981 that at-home popcorn consumption began to grow exponentially. With the wide availability of microwaves in the United States, popcorn also began popping up in offices and hotel rooms. However, the home still remains the most popular popcorn eating spot: today, 70 percent of the 16 billion quarts of popcorn consumed annually in the United States are eaten at home.

19. The passage implies that
- **A)** People ate less popcorn in the 1950s than in previous decades because they went to the movies less.
- **B)** Without mobile popcorn machines, people would not have been able to eat popcorn during the Great Depression.
- **C)** People enjoyed popcorn during the Great Depression because it was a luxury food.
- **D)** During the 1800s, people began abandoning theaters to go to fairs and festivals.

20. In paragraph 2, the word "staple" most nearly means
- **A)** something produced only for special occasions
- **B)** something produced regularly in large quantities
- **C)** something produced by cooking
- **D)** something fastened together securely

21. What is the main purpose of this passage?
- **A)** to explain how microwaves affected the popcorn industry
- **B)** to show that popcorn is older than many people realize
- **C)** to illustrate the history of popcorn from ancient cultures to modern times
- **D)** to demonstrate the importance of popcorn in various cultures

22. Which factor does the author of the passage credit for the growth of the popcorn industry in the United States?
- **A)** the use of popcorn in ancient Aztec ceremonies
- **B)** the growth of the home television industry
- **C)** the marketing of popcorn during the Great Depression
- **D)** the nutritional value of popcorn

23. Which of the following is NOT a fact stated in the passage?
- **A)** Archaeologists have found popcorn dating back 4000 years.
- **B)** Popcorn was first sold in theaters in 1912.
- **C)** Consumption of popcorn dropped in 1981 with the growing popularity of home televisions.
- **D)** 70 percent of the popcorn consumed in the United States is eaten in homes.

24. Which of the following is the best summary of this passage?
- **A)** Popcorn is a popular snack food that dates back thousands of years. Its popularity in the United States has been tied to the growth of theaters and the availability of microwaves.
- **B)** Popcorn has been a popular snack food for thousands of years. Archaeologists have found evidence that many ancient cultures used popcorn as a food staple and in ceremonies.
- **C)** Popcorn was first introduced to America in 1912, and its popularity has grown exponentially since then. Today, over 16 billion quarts of popcorn are consumed in the United States annually.
- **D)** Popcorn is a versatile snack food that can be eaten with butter or other toppings. It can also be cooked in a number of different ways, including in microwaves.

Writing

Directions for questions 1–7: Read the following early draft of an essay and then choose the best answer to the question or the best completion of the statement.

(1) Becoming president of the United States is a privilege few people will ever get to experience. (2) Since its founding in 1776, <u>many years ago,</u> the country has seen only forty-four presidents in office. (3) Most of them have since left office and have gone on to lead lives of comfort and influence. (4) <u>However,</u> they may never again experience the power or the excitement of their former office, retired presidents continue to enjoy many benefits as a result of their service as president of the United States.

(5) Presidents receive a number of benefits upon retirement, many of which are afforded by the Former Presidents Act of 1958. (6) First and foremost, they receive an <u>annual pension payment. (7) The amount of the pension</u> has been reviewed and changed a number of times, most recently to reflect the salary of a high-level government executive (roughly $200,000 in the 2010s). (8) In addition to their pension, retired presidents and their families are also entitled to ongoing Secret Service protection, which lasts until the death of the president.

(9) In addition to the assurances of safety and stability, retired presidents continue to enjoy some of the influence <u>that accompanies their former office and a few have even gone on</u> to accomplish great work in their post-presidency years. (10) <u>Particularly notable are</u> the careers of William Howard Taft and Jimmy Carter. (11) In 1921, eight years after leaving office, William Howard Taft was appointed Chief Justice of the Supreme Court by President Warren G. Harding, an office he filled until just before his death; to this day, he is the only individual to ever fill both offices. (12) Jimmy Carter went on to become an enthusiastic and impactful campaigner for human rights. (13) He started the Carter Center in 1982 to advance his efforts and, in 2002, was granted the Nobel Peace Prize for his work.

1. Which of the following replacements for the underlined phrase in sentence 2 (reproduced below) most impactfully communicates the amount of time that has passed since 1776?

    Since its founding in 1776, <u>many years ago,</u> the country has seen only forty-four presidents in office.

    A) as it is now
    B) long before any of our grandparents were born,
    C) which no one alive can remember,
    D) almost 250 years ago,

Practice Test 179

2. In context, which of the following replacements for the underlined portion would best begin sentence 4 (reproduced below)?

   However, they may never again experience the power or the excitement of their former office, retired presidents continue to enjoy many benefits as a result of their service as president of the United States.

   A) Therefore,
   B) Consequently,
   C) Though
   D) Still,

3. Which of the following would NOT be an acceptable way to revise and combine sentences 6 and 7 (reproduced below) at the underlined point?

   First and foremost, they receive an <u>annual pension payment. The amount of the pension</u> has been reviewed and changed a number of times, most recently to reflect the salary of a high-level government executive (roughly $200,000 in the 2010s).

   A) as it is now
   B) annual pension payment, the amount of which
   C) annual pension payment; the amount of the pension
   D) annual pension payment, the amount of the pension

4. Which of the following would provide the most logical conclusion to the second paragraph?

   A) Interestingly, Richard Nixon was the only president ever to relinquish his right to ongoing Secret Service security.
   B) However, spouses who remarry after the president has left office become ineligible for Secret Service security.
   C) The Secret Service is a special security task force that is responsible for protecting the president, the vice president, and their families.
   D) These measures ensure that retired presidents, as thanks for their years of demanding service, continue to live lives of safety and security.

5. Which of the following is the best version of the underlined portion of sentence 9 (reproduced below)?

   In addition to the assurances of safety and stability, retired presidents continue to enjoy some of the influence <u>that accompanies their former office and a few have even gone on</u> to accomplish great work in their post-presidency years.

   A) as it is now
   B) that accompanies their former office; however, a few have even gone on
   C) that accompanies their former office; a few have even gone on
   D) that accompanies their office—a few have even gone on

6. Which of the following would NOT be an acceptable replacement for the underlined portion of sentence 10 (reproduced below)?

<u>Particularly notable are</u> the careers of William Howard Taft and Jimmy Carter.

- **A)** Exceptionally outstanding are
- **B)** Of particular interest are
- **C)** Especially noteworthy are
- **D)** Of particular interest were

7. Which of the following would be the most effective introductory phrase for sentence 12 (reproduced below)?

Jimmy Carter went on to become an enthusiastic and impactful campaigner for human rights.

- **A)** Eventually,
- **B)** After his own presidency,
- **C)** When he was not in office,
- **D)** However,

Directions for questions 8 – 15: Select the best version of the underlined part of the sentence. If you think the original sentence is best, choose the first answer.

8. The famously high death toll at the end of the Civil War was not exclusively due to battle losses; <u>in addition,</u> large numbers of soldiers and civilians fell ill and died as a result of living conditions during the war.

- **A)** in addition,
- **B)** therefore,
- **C)** however,
- **D)** on the other hand,

9. The public defense attorney was able to maintain her optimism despite <u>her dearth of courtroom wins, lack of free time she had, and growing list of clients she was helping.</u>

- **A)** her dearth of courtroom wins, lack of free time she had, and growing list of clients she was helping.
- **B)** her dearth of courtroom wins, lack of free time, and growing list of clients.
- **C)** her dearth of courtroom wins, the free time she lacked, and the list of clients she was growing.
- **D)** the losses she had experienced, the free time she lacked, and her growing client list.

Practice Test 181

10. <u>Being invented in France in the early nineteenth century,</u> the stethoscope underwent a number of reiterations before the modern form of the instrument was introduced in the 1850s.

  A) Being invented in France in the early nineteenth century,

  B) It was invented in France in the early nineteenth century,

  C) Though it was invented in France in the nineteenth century,

  D) Invented in France in the early nineteenth century,

11. In 1983, almost twenty years after his death, T. S. Eliot won two Tony Awards for his contributions to the well-loved musical *Cats*, <u>it was based on a book of his poetry.</u>

  A) it was based on a book of his poetry.

  B) which was based on a book of his poetry.

  C) being based on a book of his poetry.

  D) having been based on a book of his poetry.

12. Because the distance between stars in the galaxy is far greater than the distance between planets, interstellar travel <u>is expected to be an even bigger challenge than</u> interplanetary exploration.

  A) is expected to be an even bigger challenge than

  B) will be expected to be an even bigger challenge than

  C) is expected to be an even bigger challenge then

  D) is expecting to be an even bigger challenge than

13. The <u>painters who are often confused for each other</u> Claude Monet and Édouard Manet actually did have a couple things in common: they were born only six years apart in Paris, France, and both contributed important early Impressionist works to the artistic canon.

  A) painters who are often confused for each other

  B) common confused painters

  C) painters who are confusing because of their similar names

  D) commonly confused painters

14. The field of child development is concerned with <u>the emotional, the psychological, and biological developments</u> of infants and children.

  A) the emotional, the psychological, and biological developments

  B) the emotional, psychological, and biological developments

  C) the emotional developments, the psychological, and the biological developments

  D) emotional, psychological, and the biological developments

15. Though it is often thought of as an extreme sport, spelunking involves much more than adrenaline: enthusiasts dive into unexplored caves <u>to study structures of, take photographs, and create maps of</u> the untouched systems.

- **A)** to study structures of, take photographs, and create maps of
- **B)** to study structures of, to take photographs, and create maps of
- **C)** to study structures of, taking photographs of, and creating maps of
- **D)** to study structures, take photographs, and create maps of

Directions for questions 16 – 20: Think about how you would rewrite the sentence according to the directions given, and then choose the best answer. Keep in mind that your revision should not change the meaning of the original sentence.

16. The city of Trieste in northern Italy was the fourth-largest city of the Austro-Hungarian Empire and a cultural crossroads where people of Latin, Slavic, and Germanic backgrounds historically mixed.

Rewrite, beginning with

<u>The fourth-largest city of the Austro-Hungarian Empire, the city of Trieste in northern Italy</u>

...

The next words will be

- **A)** was a cultural crossroads where people
- **B)** and a cultural crossroads where people
- **C)** historically mixed a cultural crossroads
- **D)** where a cultural crossroads of people was

17. Significant groups of Christians and Muslims live in the small African country of Togo, but those with indigenous beliefs make up the largest religious community.

Rewrite, beginning with

<u>Even though significant groups of Christians and Muslims live in the small African country of Togo,</u>

...

The next words will be

- **A)** they make up the largest religious community
- **B)** however those with indigenous beliefs make up the largest
- **C)** the largest religious community makes up indigenous beliefs
- **D)** the largest religious community is made up of those with indigenous

Practice Test 183

18. Thanks to its flexible hind paws, the squirrel can climb down trees headfirst, a trait unique to the species.

Rewrite, beginning with

Squirrels' unique ability to climb down trees headfirst

...

The next words will be

- **A)** thanks to its flexible hind paws.
- **B)** is thanks to their flexible hind paws.
- **C)** is a trait unique to the species.
- **D)** is thanks to its flexible hind paws.

19. The tusk of the narwhal, previously thought to be a defensive tool for the animal, is now known to be a sensory organ.

Rewrite, beginning with

Narwhal tusks are sensory organs

...

The next words will be

- **A)** but had previously been used for defensive purposes.
- **B)** but had previously been believed to be defensive tools.
- **C)** previously known to be a defensive tool for the animal.
- **D)** previously they had been believed to be defensive tools.

20. To change a tire, be sure you are in a safe location, turn your hazard lights on, and apply the parking brake before beginning work.

Rewrite, beginning with

It is important to find a safe location, turn the hazard lights on,

...

Your new sentence will include

- **A)** after applying the parking brake
- **B)** before applying the parking brake
- **C)** before changing a tire
- **D)** after changing a tire

The Essay

On this essay, you must effectively express and develop your ideas in writing. Read a short passage; an assignment question follows about an important issue. Develop your own point of view on the issue in an essay. Be sure to support your argument with examples and reasoning. Your perspective on the issue will not influence your score.

PASSAGE

O judgment! Thou art fled to brutish beasts, and men have lost their reason.
    From William Shakespeare, *Julius Caesar*

Don't judge a book by its cover.
    From George Eliot, *The Mill on the Floss*

ASSIGNMENT: Can we be too quick to judge the actions of another person?

Answer Key
MATHEMATICS

1. **B)** Plug 4 in for j and simplify.
   $2(j - 4)^4 - j + \frac{1}{2}j$
   $2(4 - 4)^4 - 4 + \frac{1}{2}(4) = \mathbf{-2}$

2. **A)** Simplify each root and add.
   $\sqrt[3]{64} = 4$
   $\sqrt[3]{729} = 9$
   $4 + 9 = \mathbf{13}$

3. **C)** Find the height of the cylinder using the equation for surface area.
   $SA = 2\pi rh + 2\pi r^2$
   $48\pi = 2\pi(4)h + 2\pi(4)^2$
   $h = 2$
   Find the volume using the volume equation.
   $V = \pi r^2 h$
   $V = \pi(4)^2(2) = \mathbf{32\pi \text{ ft.}^3}$

4. **A)** Use the formula for inversely proportional relationships to find k and then solve for s.
   $sn = k$
   $(65)(250) = k$
   $k = 16{,}250$
   $s(325) = 16{,}250$
   $\mathbf{s = 50}$

5. **B)** Plug each value into the equation.
   $4(3 + 4)^2 - 4(3)^2 + 20 = 180 \neq 276$
   $4(6 + 4)^2 - 4(6)^2 + 20 = \mathbf{276}$
   $4(12 + 4)^2 - 4(12)^2 + 20 = 468 \neq 276$
   $4(24 + 4)^2 - 4(24)^2 + 20 = 852 \neq 276$

6. **A)** In 2012, New York had more months with less than 3 inches of rain than either Chicago or Houston.

7. **D)** Plug in each set of values and determine if the inequality is true.
   $2(0) + 0 \leq -10$ FALSE
   $2(10) + 2 \leq -10$ FALSE
   $2(10) + 10 \leq -10$ FALSE
   $2(-10) + (-10) \leq -10$ TRUE

8. **C)** Cross multiply and solve for x.
   $\frac{4x - 5}{3} = \frac{\frac{1}{2}(2x - 6)}{5}$
   $5(4x - 5) = \frac{3}{2}(2x - 6)$
   $20x - 25 = 3x - 9$
   $17x = 16$
   $x = \frac{16}{17}$

9. **C)** Plug 0 in for x and solve for y.
   $7y - 42x + 7 = 0$
   $7y - 42(0) + 7 = 0$
   $y = -1$
   The y-intercept is at $\mathbf{(0, -1)}$.

10. **A)** Use the combination formula to find the number of ways to choose 2 people out of a group of 20.
    $C(20, 2) = \frac{20!}{2!\, 18!} = \mathbf{190}$

11. **D)** Solve the system using substitution.
    $z - 2x = 14 \rightarrow z = 2x + 14$
    $2z - 6x = 18$
    $2(2x + 14) - 6x = 18$
    $4x + 28 - 6x = 18$
    $-2x = -10$
    $x = 5$

$z - 2(5) = 14$

$z = 24$

12. **C)** Use the rules of exponents to simplify the expression.

    $\left(\dfrac{4x^{-3}y^4z}{8x^{-5}y^3z^{-2}}\right)^2 = \left(\dfrac{x^2yz^3}{2}\right)^2 = \mathbf{\dfrac{x^4y^2z^6}{4}}$

13. **C)** The function $g(x) = f(x - 2) + 3$ is a translation of $\langle 2,3 \rangle$ from $f(x)$. Test each possible point by undoing the transformation and checking if the point lies on $f(x)$.

    $(1,2) \rightarrow (-1,-1)$: This point is not on $f(x)$.

    $(2,3) \rightarrow (0,0)$: This point is not on $f(x)$.

    $(6,3) \rightarrow (4,0)$: **This point is on f(x).**

    $(7,2) \rightarrow (5,-1)$: This point is not on $f(x)$.

14. **B)** Set up a proportion and solve.

    $\dfrac{AB}{DE} = \dfrac{3}{4}$

    $\dfrac{12}{DE} = \dfrac{3}{4}$

    $3(DE) = 48$

    DE = 16

15. **B)** The slope 0.0293 gives the increase in passenger car miles (in billions) for each year that passes. Muliply this value by 5 to find the increase that occurs over 5 years: $5(0.0293) =$ **0.1465 billion miles**.

16. **B)** Find the sum of the 13 numbers whose mean is 30.

    $13 \times 30 = 390$

    Find the sum of the 8 numbers whose mean is 42.

    $8 \times 42 = 336$

    Find the sum and mean of the remaining 5 numbers.

    $390 - 336 = 54$

    $\dfrac{54}{5} =$ **10.8**

17. **C)** Use the fundamental counting principle to determine how many ways the DVDs can be arranged within each category and how many ways the 3 categories can be arranged.

    ways to arrange horror = 4! = 24

    ways to arrange comedies = 6! = 720

    ways to arrange science fiction = 5! = 120

    ways to arrange categories = 3! = 6

    $(24)(720)(120)(6) =$ **12,441,600**

18. **D)** Use the formula for the area of a rectangle to find the increase in its size.

    $A = lw$

    $A = (1.4l)(0.6w)$

    $A = 0.84lw$

    The new area will be 84% of the original area, a decrease of **16%**.

19. Eliminate answer choices that don't match the graph.

    A) Correct.

    B) The graph has a negative slope while this inequality has a positive slope.

    C) The line on the graph is solid, so the inequality should include the "or equal to" symbol.

    D) The shading is above the line, meaning the inequality should be "y is greater than."

20. **C)** Use the formula for the volume of a sphere to find its radius.

    $V = \dfrac{4}{3}\pi r^3$

    $972\pi = \dfrac{4}{3}\pi r^3$

    $r = 9$

Use the super Pythagorean theorem to find the side of the cube.

$d^2 = a^2 + b^2 + c^2$

$18^2 = 3s^2$

$s \approx 10.4$

Use the length of the side to find the volume of the cube.

$V = s^3$

$V \approx (10.4)^3$

$V \approx 1{,}125$

READING

1. **A)** The raffle is the only feature described as an event the organizers will be "bringing back[.]"

2. **D)** The word given best describes the idea that the gifts have been handed out: "to the lion [Epimetheus] gave strength; to the bird, swiftness; to the fox, sagacity; and so on."

3. **D)** The passage gives a short history of thermonuclear weapons and then introduces its main topic—the physical and biological consequences of nuclear war.

4. **D)** In the passage, Thomas Jefferson is defined as an anti-Federalist, in contrast with Federalists who believed in a strong federal government.

5. **B)** The text states that educational programs and plans cannot be deduced from the laws of the mind.

6. **A)** The suggested idea is how thorough and practical the writers were as they studied the principles of government and analyzed their experience with government of the Confederation.

7. **A)** The author argues that "every man, woman and child should learn" to swim, and then explains to the reader why he or she should be able to swim.

8. **C)** The passage states that babies' senses are much like those of their adult counterparts with the exception of their vision, which develops later.

9. **B)** The passage states that "infants rely primarily on hearing."

10. **D)** The passage describes human studies as the study of "the relationship between human activity and the environment," which would include farmers interacting with river systems.

11. **B)** Only this choice summarizes the two main points of the passage: the definition of geography and the breakdown of its sub-disciplines.

12. **B)** The final paragraph of the passage states that the two species "frequently [share] a habitat" and that "[a] predatory hawk or eagle, usually hunting from high in the sky, can't tell the difference between the two species, and so the kingsnake gets passed over and lives another day."

13. **C)** The first paragraph states that "[w]hile it might seem counterintuitive for a venomous snake to stand out in bright red or blue, that fancy costume tells any nearby predator that approaching him would be a bad idea." The coral snake's markings do not allow it to hide from predators but rather to "ward [them] off[.]"

14. **A)** The passage states that "intricate diamonds, stripes, and swirls help the animals hide from predators[,]" implying that these markings are complex enough to

allow the animals to blend in with their surroundings.

15. **C)** The second paragraph states that "[t]he scarlet kingsnake, for example, has very similar markings to the venomous coral snake with whom it frequently shares a habitat. However, the kingsnake is actually nonvenomous[.]"

16. **A)** The bulk of the passage is dedicated to showing that conventional wisdom about "fewer calories in than calories out" isn't true for many people and is more complicated than previously believed.

17) **C)** The author cites several scientific studies to support the argument.

18. **D)** People misreporting the amount of food they ate would introduce error into studies on weight loss and might make the studies the author cites unreliable.

19. **A)** The author states that "popcorn continued to rule the snack food kingdom until the rise in popularity of home televisions during the 1950s" when the industry saw a "decline in sales" as a result of the changing pastimes of the American people.

20. **B)** The author states, "For the Aztec Indians who called the caves home, popcorn (or *momochitl*) played an important role in society, both as a food staple and in ceremonies." This implies that the Aztec people popped popcorn both for special occasions ("in ceremonies") and for regular consumption ("as a food staple").

21. **C)** In the opening paragraph the author writes, "But popcorn isn't just for fun—it's also a multimillion-dollar-a-year industry with a long and fascinating history." The author then goes on to illustrate the history of popcorn from the ancient Aztecs, to early twentieth century America, to the present day.

22. **C)** The author writes, "The popcorn industry flourished during the Great Depression when it was advertised as a wholesome and economical food."

23. **C)** The author writes, "However, it wasn't until microwave popcorn became commercially available in 1981 that at-home popcorn consumption began to grow exponentially. With the wide availability of microwaves in the United States, popcorn also began popping up in offices and hotel rooms."

24. **A)** This statement summarizes the entire passage, including the brief history of popcorn in ancient cultures and the growth in the popularity of popcorn in America.

WRITING

1. **D)** This choice provides specific information, making it impactful and memorable.

2. **C)** *Though* signifies an important contradiction between the two clauses in this sentence.

3. **D)** This choice creates two complete sentences but joins them incorrectly with a comma, creating a comma splice.

4. **D)** This choice is appropriately specific and provides a brief summary of the information mentioned in the paragraph.

5. **C)** This choice correctly joins two related complete sentences with a semicolon.

6. **D)** *Were* is a plural verb that agrees with the plural subject *careers*; however, *of particular interest* suggests relevance to the author's point, which should be referred to in present tense.

7. **B)** *After his own presidency* provides an appropriate amount of detail to describe when the action took place—immediately following his retirement.

8. **A)** *In addition* is the appropriate introductory phrase to signify the additive relationship between the two clauses.

9. **B)** In this iteration, all items in the list are nouns (*dearth*, *lack*, and *list*), followed by prepositions (*of*) and objects of the prepositions (*wins*, *time*, and *clients*).

10. **D)** *Invented*, the past participle of *invent*, appropriately introduces this participial phrase that provides more information about the subject of the sentence (*stethoscope*).

11. **B)** *Which* is used correctly here to introduce an additional, nonrestrictive clause about an element of the sentence (the musical).

12. **A)** *Is* is a present-tense verb, used correctly to refer to current mind-sets; *than* is used correctly to show comparison.

13. **D)** *Commonly* is an adverb describing *confused*, which is an adjective describing *painters*.

14. **B)** The three phrases share a structure; they are parallel adjectives.

15. **D)** The three phrases have a similar (*parallel*) structure (verb + direct object).

16. **A)** The sentence should be rewritten "The fourth-largest city of the Austro-Hungarian Empire, the city of Trieste in northern Italy was a cultural crossroads where people of Latin, Slavic, and Germanic backgrounds historically mixed." Choice A correctly places the verb (*was*) after the subject (*the city of Trieste in northern Italy*, or, more precisely, *the city*).

17. **D)** Choice D begins a main clause that describes the largest community as that with indigenous beliefs, the true

statement of the sentence. The sentence should be rewritten "Even though significant groups of Christians and Muslims live in the small African country of Togo, the largest religious community is made up of those with indigenous beliefs."

18. **B)** The sentence should be rewritten "Squirrels' unique ability to climb down trees headfirst is thanks to their flexible hind paws." The verb *is* immediately follows and introduces the second idea of the sentence: the flexible hind paws of the squirrel.

19. **B)** The new sentence should read "Narwhal tusks are sensory organs but had previously been believed to be defensive tools."

20. **C)** The new sentence should read "It is important to find a safe location, turn the hazard lights on, and apply the parking brake before changing a tire." All three steps—finding a safe location, turning on the hazard lights, and applying the parking brake—must happen before the tire-changing process can begin. The preposition *before* signals all those steps have occurred.

SAMPLE ESSAY — SCORE OF 8

All people make mistakes, and it is easy to judge them from the outside. However, sometimes people behave in harmful ways as a result of unseen hardships. People should refrain from judgment until they have the full story. Still, an unusual challenge does not absolve someone from all responsibilities. Even those at a disadvantage are accountable for their responsibilities, but they may be forgiven for certain harms as long as they take steps to rectify them.

For instance, my parents do not get along with their neighbor because he has a messy yard, which brings down their property value. He also has a dog which he lets wander on the streets. My parents' dog, on the other hand, must stay in the house and is only allowed to run freely behind the fence in the yard or at a dog park. However, everyone in the area has approximately the same income. Furthermore, the neighbor is seemingly in good physical health and works normal hours. There seems to be no reason that he cannot spend a little time each week on yard work and keep his dogs in his yard like everyone else. However, he does have one unique characteristic: allergies.

The neighbor's health situation presents a dilemma. While he is responsible for cleaning his yard, he struggles with yardwork because his allergies prevent him from spending too much time among shrubs, bushes, and trees. In addition, it is hard for him to keep his dog in his house for long periods of time, as pet dander makes his allergies worse, but the more time the dog spends in the yard, the messier the yard gets. And on top of all that, he lives alone, with no one to help with chores. Meanwhile, both of my parents enjoy outdoor activity, have no allergies, and can tackle yardwork together quite easily. They are able to keep their dog inside without any health concerns and can take turns walking him. Taking these differences into account, it becomes clearer why the neighbor's yard is in disarray and why his dog is often out. These issues may be less about his character than his circumstances.

Still, the neighbor has a responsibility to those around him. First, he should not have a dog if he cannot properly care for it or keep it in his home. Not only is a dog roaming the streets a nuisance to other neighbors, but it is unsafe for the dog, which could be hit by a car or injured in some other way. Next, he should find a way to properly care for his yard. Perhaps he could pursue medical treatment for his allergies, hire workers to assist periodically, or even ask a friend, family member, or neighbor for assistance if his budget is tight. Even if he is struggling to care for his yard, as a homeowner he is responsible for it.

In this case, the neighbor could be forgiven if he took steps to fix the situation, because he is clearly at a disadvantage when it comes to yardwork and pet care due to his allergies, which are not his fault. However, if he does not take responsibility and make amends, his disadvantages do not matter, and he should not be forgiven. At that point, he could be judged as a poor neighbor or as a person of poor character because he has chosen to remain a nuisance in the neighborhood despite other options.

Answer Explanation

This essay received an 8 because it demonstrates outstanding critical thinking, developing a nuanced argument even while answering the question (Even those at a disadvantage are accountable for their responsibilities, but they may be forgiven for certain harms as long as they take steps to rectify them). The writer supports the argument with one anecdotal example, but the level of detail in the scenario is sufficient to illustrate the author's argument that some disadvantages may be hidden and so one should not be quick to judge: There seems to be no reason that he cannot spend a little time each week on yard work... However, he does have one unique characteristic: allergies. The author offers possible solutions to the harms the neighbor brings on the neighborhood, which would allow him to be forgiven ("he could pursue medical treatment...hire workers to assist...or even ask a friend, family member, or neighbor for assistance" in cleaning the yard). The writing and organization is clear and coherent; the thesis is presented in the introduction, and the anecdotal scenario is fully developed. The writer uses varied sentence structure, strong vocabulary, and transition words. There are few, if any, mechanical errors.

Follow the link below to take your second TSI practice test and to access other online study resources:

www.acceptedinc.com/tsi-online-resources